£2.50

112.95

KEEP AS FAST ADD.
SHELVE ON RETURN.

VOGUE

DOLLS & TOYS

Writer: *Susanna Pfeffer*
Illustrator: *Phoebe Adams Gaughan*
Editor: *Helen Moore*
Coordinator for Butterick: *Patricia Perry*
Butterick staff: *Janet DuBane, Carol Sharma, Ron Ferguson, Josephine Gillies*
Coordinator for Harper & Row: *Carol Cohen*
Harper & Row production staff: *Leta Evanthes, Lydia Link*

VOGUE DOLLS & TOYS. Copyright © 1986 by Butterick Company, Inc. All rights reserved. Printed in the United States of America. No part of this book may be used or reproduced in any manner whatsoever without written permission except in the case of brief quotations embodied in critical articles and reviews. For information address Harper & Row, Publishers, Inc., 10 East 53rd Street, New York, N.Y. 10022. Published simultaneously in Canada by Fitzhenry & Whiteside Limited, Toronto.

FIRST EDITION

Designed by Jos. Trautwein/Bentwood Studio

Library of Congress Cataloging-in-Publication Data
Vogue dolls & toys.

Includes index.
1. Dollmaking.   2. Soft toy making.   3. Sewing.
TT175.V64   1986   745.592   86-342
ISBN 0-06-181131-9 (U.S.A. and Canada)
ISBN 0-06-337045-X (outside U.S.A. and Canada)

87 88 89 90   FG   10 9 8 7 6 5 4 3 2 1

VOGUE

DOLLS & TOYS

HARPER & ROW, PUBLISHERS, NEW YORK

Cambridge, Philadelphia, San Francisco, London
Mexico City, São Paulo, Singapore, Sydney

Other books from Vogue:

VOGUE SEWING
VOGUE CHRISTMAS
VOGUE EASY SEWING
VOGUE FITTING
VOGUE SEWING FOR THE HOME

Contents

How to Use This Book

• *Welcome to the realm of* Vogue Dolls & Toys! *The first section,* Craft Techniques, *is a collection of all the basics needed to create the dolls and toys pictured later on. To make it easy for you to use this section, we've arranged all the craft techniques in alphabetical order. Use it when you work on future projects, too!*

The second section of the book, Dolls & Toys, *is devoted to the more than a dozen appealing dolls and toys specially chosen for this book. The instructions for each of these projects include a list of all the materials needed, plus complete directions for cutting, assembling and finishing.*

Throughout this book you will find cross

references to various methods and procedures provided in the Craft Techniques section. A reference following a sewing term is written in SMALL CAPITAL LETTERS "Make one row of gathering stitches (see GATHERING)." This is your signal to refer directly to that topic, in this case Gathering, in the Craft Techniques section. As you learned earlier, the techniques are arranged in alphabetical order to make it easy to locate this helpful information. Sometimes, when a Craft Techniques section is long, you are directed to a specific subsection such as "Easestitch (see under MACHINE STITCHING)." In this case, you look up Machine stitching in the M's, locate the subsection on Easestitch, and you're all set to sew. •

PATTERNS

Patterns for all doll and toy projects are gathered in one section following the last project. As many pieces as possible are shown actual size and do not appear on a grid. When patterns are too large to fit on the page, they've been reduced and placed on a grid. On this grid each square equals 1 inch to simplify enlarging. Where a pattern appears in grey on the same page it is to be sized using the same grid as those printed in black. There are no seamlines printed on the patterns; however, seam allowances are included on all pieces. The project instructions specify how wide the seam allowances are. Construction markings, such as symbols and placement lines, are given on the patterns; more about these later.

To use actual-size patterns, trace them directly onto tracing paper, including any markings, and cut your fabric as directed in the project instructions. How-to's for enlarging reduced patterns are given on p. 26.

For some simple shapes, such as circles, squares or rectangles, no patterns are needed. The project instructions tell you the exact size and shape to cut.

CUTTING

Fabric requirements are generous enough to accommodate all the pattern pieces needed for any given project. However, since there are no cutting layouts, you should lay out all your pattern pieces first, before cutting, to make them fit on the amount of fabric specified. Whenever a pattern piece has a grainline marking, be sure to place that piece on the lengthwise or crosswise grain of the fabric. Pieces with a foldline arrow must be placed on a fold of the fabric; be careful not to cut on the fold. Where there are no grainlines marked, place the pieces wherever they fit most economically.

If your pattern pieces have notches, you may cut them with the points facing out, or mark them as described below, but don't cut them in, since seam allowances are too narrow. To cut two pieces from the same pattern piece, fold the fabric right sides together and cut both pieces at the same time, unless you're cutting pile fabric (see p. 28). To cut a single piece, place the pattern piece right side up on the right side of the fabric, then cut. If your fabric is directional, that is, if it has nap or pile, shading or a one-way design, be sure to place all pattern pieces so their top edges face in the same direction.

MARKING

Leave the pattern pieces pinned to the fabric until after you have transferred any markings. These include symbols such as ●'s and ▲'s, placement lines, button and buttonhole markings and designs for embroidery or appliqué. If you didn't cut notches with the points out, mark these as well. See TRANSFERRING MARKINGS for specific methods. Always mark on the wrong side; when necessary, markings can be transferred to the right side later on. If your fabric appears to be identical on both sides, designate one side as the wrong side before you cut out the patterns; then mark the wrong side of each piece as you cut it out, with chalk or a bit of tape on the seam allowance.

SPECIAL CONSIDERATIONS

It's a good idea to preshrink any fabric intended for a doll or toy. When the fabric is washable, you can preshrink it by soaking it briefly and then drying, followed by pressing. Preshrink any washable trims at the same time.

The dolls and toys in this book are suitable for a wide range of ages from toddler to teen. If you are planning to make a project for a very young child, remember that little ones are experts at dismantling seemingly indestructible toys, not to mention their tendency to taste everything. Therefore, you should be extra careful in stitching seams, closing openings and attaching trims and buttons. Use only nontoxic materials. On toys for tots, it's probably better to sew, rather than glue, any trims in place. For safety's sake, consider substituting embroidered facial features for buttons or trims whenever possible.

Craft
Techniques

Adhesives

• *There are three basic types of adhesives: glue, tape and fusible web. Wherever an adhesive is required for a project in this book, the instructions specify what type to use. Tapes are generally used when you want to create a temporary bond, such as holding yarn hair in place for stitching. Glues and webs, on the other hand, are considered more permanent, since they are often used alone without any further stitching. It's important to choose an adhesive that will continue to stick after washing or dry cleaning. To be sure, read manufacturers' labels or test washability on scraps of the fabric and trims that you plan to use.* •

GLUES

White Glue White craft glue, such as Elmer's Glue-All® or Sobo®, is an all-purpose permanent glue that works well on most medium- to heavyweight fabrics, as well as on paper, leather, suede and similar materials. It dries clear in about 30 minutes and creates a strong bond. For best results, spread white glue evenly and thinly, to avoid lumps when dry. To be sure the glue won't soak through and stain your fabric, test it first on a scrap. You can wash off white glue with water before it dries.

Tacky White Glue Tacky white glue, such as Aleene's, is another all-purpose, permanent glue; it doesn't soak into fabrics. You can use tacky white glue for felt, leather and suede, ribbons and any lightweight, loosely woven or nonwoven fabrics and trims.

Glue Stick For quick glue jobs that don't require great holding power, you can use a glue stick. Try it for holding trims or appliqués in place before stitching, but apply the glue away from the path of your needle.

TAPES

Basting Tape A tape that is sticky on both sides, basting tape comes in ⅛" (3mm) and ¼" (6mm) widths. It's useful for holding trims such as ribbon, braid and wide rickrack in place for stitching. You can also use it instead of basting when inserting zippers and sewing hems. To avoid gumming up your sewing-machine needle, place the tape away from the stitching line.

Basting tape can be used on most fabrics except for pile fabrics (removing the tape pulls out the pile) and sheers. If in doubt, simply test first. There is a new type of basting tape on the market that washes out when the project is laundered.

Transparent Tape These tapes, which come in a dispenser roll, can be single-sided or double-sided. They are intended for temporary use only. Single-sided tape comes in handy for such craft techniques as making yarn hair for dolls. It's also good for holding synthetic leather and suede pieces in place for cutting and stitching (see under FABRICS). As with bast-

ing tape, avoid stitching through these tapes if possible. If you must stitch through the tape, and your machine needle sticks or skips stitches, clean the needle with rubbing alcohol to remove any glue residue.

FUSIBLE WEB

Available in sheets, by the yard and in strips of different widths, fusible web has simplified sewing and crafting. Using web, you can bond fabrics together as well as apply trims and appliqués. Most fusible webs require heat, steam and pressure to create a permanent bond; always check the manufacturer's instructions to be sure. Therefore, use webs only on smooth, flat-surfaced fabrics that can withstand the heat and pressure of a steam iron. Once applied, fusible web is invisible and permanent, as well as washable and dry-cleanable.

Appliqué

• *The term* appliqué *applies both to the technique of attaching a fabric shape to a background fabric and to the shaped piece itself. Appliqués may be sewn in place by hand or machine, or fused. In this book, all appliqués are machine-stitched for durability.* •

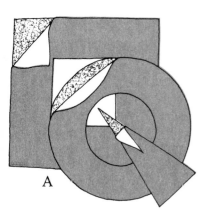

A

MACHINE-STITCHED

Cutting Using the pattern provided, cut out the appliqué shape(s) without seam allowances. At the same time, cut a piece of fusible web (see under ADHESIVES) the same shape and size as the appliqué or a bit smaller to avoid getting the web on your iron, to help hold the appliqué in place securely as you stitch. With the fusible web between the appliqué and the background fabric, position the appliqué along the marked placement lines. Then, following the manufacturer's instructions, fuse in place (A).

Stitching Set your machine for a narrow- to medium-width zigzag stitch, closely spaced (short stitch length). Together these settings produce a smooth, even, satin-stitch effect. Generally speaking, the smaller and more curved the shapes, the narrower the zigzag stitch should be. Test your settings first on scraps to be sure you're getting the desired stitch.

To help control your stitching, hold the fabric taut with your left hand behind the needle. Use your right hand to guide the appliqué under the needle. Start stitching with the appliqué to the left of the needle (B). When the needle swings to the right, it should enter the background fabric just outside the edge of the appliqué shape; the stitching should cover the edges almost completely. Hold the needle thread at the back of the needle as you take the first few stitches. Then stitch slowly all around the appliqué, keeping the needle in the position just described. When you come back to the beginning, overlap the stitching very slightly; then remove from

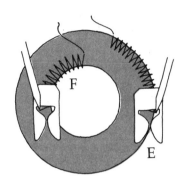

the machine, leaving long ends. Pull all thread ends to the wrong side, tie together and trim.

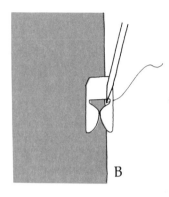

B

As an alternative, you can stitch appliqués using a straight stitch close to the edges instead of zig-zag-stitching.

Corners To stitch an *outside* corner, stitch to the very corner of the appliqué, stopping with the needle in the fabric to the right and aligned with the appliqué. Pivot the fabric and continue along the appliqué to the next corner (C). To stitch an *inside* corner, stitch past the corner, onto the appliqué for a distance equal to the width of the zigzag stitch; stop with the needle to the left and in the fabric. Pivot and continue stitching (D).

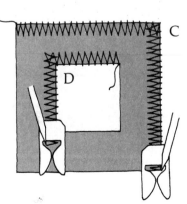

Curves On an *outside* curve, when the needle swings to the right, pivot the fabric slightly to keep the needle from going too far off to the right (E). On an *inside* curve, pivot as needed when the needle swings to the left, to keep the needle from going too far away from the curve (F).

Points Stitch until the needle is in the left-hand position and just off the left-hand edge near the point. Pivot the fabric slightly to center the point under the presser foot. Then begin decreasing the stitch width and continue stitching, with the needle entering the background fabric on each side of the point. Stitch slowly, decreasing stitch width until almost zero at the point (G). Pivot, then stitch back over the first stitching, increasing the stitch width gradually as you stitch until it is the original width. Then continue along next edge.

NONSTITCHED

Appliqués of felt or other nonraveling fabrics can be fused or glued in place (see under ADHESIVES). Or you can create your own iron-on appliqués with a special product that transfers fusible web to the back of your own fabric. Some trade names are Release Paper® by Applications, Transfuse® by Stacy and Norlon Pressing Sheet® by EZ International.

G

Bias Tape

• *Packaged bias tape is available in a wide range of colors. It comes in single-fold, with the edges turned to meet in the middle; and double-fold, folded once more to make double layers, with one layer slightly narrower than the other. Bias tape is available in widths from ¼" (6mm) to ⅞" (22mm). It is a versatile sewing notion that can be used as a band trim, a binding or a facing.* •

PRESHAPING

Cut bias tape about 1" (25mm) longer than the area where it is to be used, to allow for finishing. If it is to be applied to a curve, shape it to correspond to that curve by positioning the tape on the pattern piece and gently steampressing it into the desired shape (A).

BINDING

Use double-fold bias tape, preshaping the tape to fit any curves on the project. With the narrower side of the tape on the right side of the raw edge to be bound, encase the edge, then pin the tape in place. If the ends are to meet, cut them on the straight grain, allowing ½" (13mm) at each end for

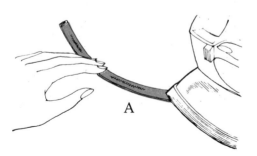

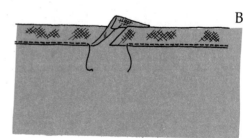

lapping. Turn one end under ½" (13mm) and lap it over the raw end. Stitch the binding in place close to the folded edge, catching in all layers (B). Slipstitch (see under HAND SEWING) the overlapped edges. At a finished edge, trim the binding to ½" (13mm) beyond the edge, then turn the end under so it is even with the finished edge. Stitch the binding in place, stitching across the folded ends at the finished edge (C).

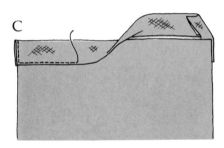

C

BANDS

Use single-fold or double-fold bias tape as your pattern directs, pre-shaping the tape to fit any curves on the project. Cut bias tape to fit the area where it will be applied, adding extra only if the ends are to be lapped or finished. Pin along the marked placement lines, or use narrow basting tape or glue stick

(see ADHESIVES) to hold the tape in place. Stitch in place close to both long edges (D). If the ends are to be caught in a seam, no further stitching is needed. If necessary, finish ends by lapping or turning under as described above for Binding.

FACING

Use single-fold bias tape, pre-shaping the tape to fit any curves on the project and allowing ½" (13mm) to turn under the ends. Open out one fold. With right sides together, pin the tape to the edge to be faced, matching the crease line of the tape to the seamline of the project; be careful not to stretch the tape. Turn each end of the tape under ¼" (6mm) so the ends will be finished when the facing is turned to the inside. The ends should meet but not overlap. Stitch along the crease line of the tape, then trim the seam allowance even with the edge of the tape, if necessary, and clip or notch the seam allowances (E).

Turn the bias tape to the inside and press. Edgestitch (see under MACHINE STITCHING) the lower folded edge in place (F); or slipstitch if preferred.

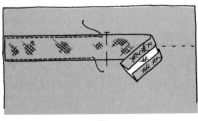

D

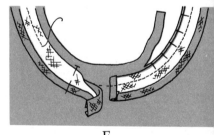

E

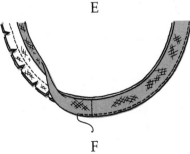

F

Casings

• *A casing is a closed tunnel of fabric through which elastic is drawn to control fullness, usually at a neckline, a waistline or the lower edges of sleeves or pants. Basically, there are two kinds of casings, folded and applied.* •

FOLDED

A folded casing is always found at a garment edge, since it's just an extension of the fabric folded to the wrong side and stitched in place.

First, machine-baste or fuse the pressed-open seam allowances to your project in the casing area, to prevent catching the elastic when you draw it through (A, B). Next,

turn the raw edge under ¼" (6mm) (or the amount your pattern specifies) and press. Then turn the fabric under along the foldline and press again (C).

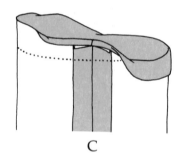

C

Beginning and ending near one seamline and leaving an opening, edgestitch (see under MACHINE STITCHING) the turned-under edge.

If desired, edgestitch the opposite edge of the casing as well to keep the elastic from twisting (D). Insert and secure elastic (see ELASTIC). Then edgestitch the opening closed, aligning the stitches with the stitching already done and stretching the elastic as you stitch (E).

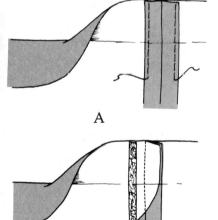

A

B

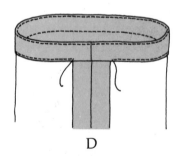

D

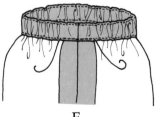

E

If you are making a casing along an edge where both ends are left open, follow the directions given, basting or fusing any seam allowances away from edges, then stitch from end to end (F). After inserting elastic, stitch across ends to secure.

APPLIED

An applied casing requires a separate strip of fabric. Single-fold or double-fold bias tape (see BIAS TAPE) makes a good applied casing. Choose a width slightly wider than your elastic. If using double-fold bias tape, press out the center fold before you begin sewing.

Away from the Edge Cut bias tape 1″ (25mm) longer than the area to which it will be applied. Pin the tape to your project, usually on the wrong side, along the placement markings. Turn the ends under ½″ (13mm) to meet but not overlap. Edgestitch both long edges, but leave the short ends open (G). Insert elastic through the opening, then slipstitch (see under HAND SEWING) the opening closed.

At the Edge Cut bias tape 1″ (25mm) longer than the edge to which it will be applied. Open out one fold of the bias tape. With right sides together, pin the tape to the edge, with the crease line of the tape along the seamline of the edge. Turn the ends to the wrong side ½″ (13mm) so they meet without overlapping (H).

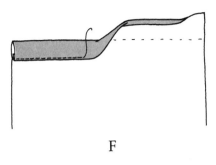

F

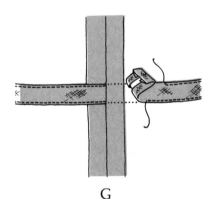

G

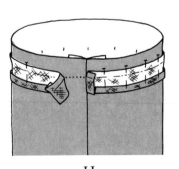

H

Stitch along the crease line of the tape. Then, if necessary, trim the seam allowance even with the edge of the tape (I).

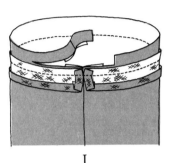

I

Turn the tape to the inside and press. Edgestitch the lower folded edge in place, leaving the ends open (J). Insert and secure elastic, then slipstitch the opening closed.

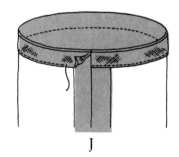

J

Corners and Curves

• *Dolls and toys tend to have lots of corners and curves. Handling them correctly ensures smooth seams and professional-looking results. All the special stitching, trimming and clipping techniques are included here.*•

CORNERS

Sharp corners are a sure sign of an accomplished sewer. You can achieve these easily by using the proper stitching and trimming techniques.

Stitching An inside corner is especially vulnerable to fraying; so, before joining pieces, reinforce (see under MACHINE STITCHING) each corner as your pattern directs. Then, when you join the pieces together, stitch over the previous stitching, using 12 to 15 stitches per inch (per 25mm) (A).

A

To stitch a sharp outside corner, use 10 to 12 stitches per inch (per 25mm) to within 1" (25mm) of the corner. Then switch to 12

to 15 stitches per inch (per 25mm). At the corner, take one or two stitches diagonally across the cor-

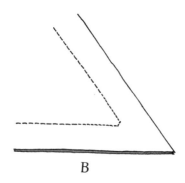

B

ner (B) before proceeding along the next side. When you are about 1" (25mm) away from the corner, switch back to the previous stitch length.

Clipping and Trimming On an *inside* corner, clip diagonally, close to, but not through, the stitching (C). On an *outside* corner, trim across the point close to the stitching; then trim and grade (see p. 21) the seam allowances diago-

nally along each side of the point, to eliminate bulk when the piece is turned (D).

C

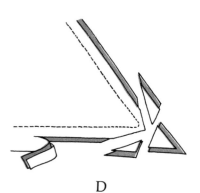

D

20

CURVES

Inside and outside curves both require care in cutting and stitching, especially in craft projects where seam allowances are narrow.

Stitching If your pattern directs, staystitch (see under MACHINE STITCHING) the curved edges. Then pin the pieces together, matching edges, notches and symbols exactly. Use a seam guide to help keep your stitching exactly on the seamline. For sharp curves, use a short stitch length (12 to 15 stitches per inch [per 25mm]) and stitch slowly for best control. If you want extra strength in a curved seam, stitch again over the previous stitching.

Trimming For seam allowances 3/8" (10mm) wide or less, trimming is necessary only if the fabric is bulky or if the piece is very small and must be turned, such as a doll's arm. Trim the seam allowances to 1/8" (3mm), holding the shears at an angle so that one seam allowance will be slightly narrower than the other; this is called grading, and will further reduce bulk (E).

Clipping and Notching On an *inside* curve, clip into the seam allowances every 1/2" to 1" (13mm to 25mm), depending on the sharpness of the curve. Cut close to the stitching, but not through it (F). On an *outside* curve, notch by cutting out small wedges in the seam allowances (G).

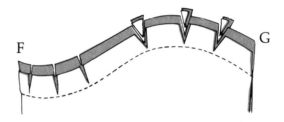

JOINING A CURVE TO A STRAIGHT EDGE

Several projects in this book call for joining a circular or an oval shape to a straight edge. Unless the instructions specify otherwise, first staystitch the straight edge. Then pin it to the curved edge, matching edges, notches and symbols. You may need to clip the straight edge up to, but not through, the staystitching, to help it fit around the curve (H); then stitch the seam.

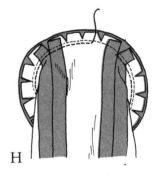

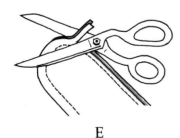

E

Elastic

• Elastic is used to control fullness and comes in many different widths. It may be inserted in a casing (see CASINGS*) or applied directly to a fabric section. Your project instructions specify the width to use and the length to cut. •*

INSERTED IN A CASING

You'll need a bodkin or safety pin and a straight pin. Attach one end of the elastic to the bodkin or safety pin and insert it through the opening in the casing. With the straight pin, fasten the other end of the elastic to the seam allowance at the opening, to keep it from getting lost in the casing. Push the bodkin through the casing, pulling the elastic with it. Work slowly and carefully to keep the elastic flat (A).

When the bodkin emerges from the opening, unfasten both ends of the elastic and, with care to keep it flat, lap the ends ½" (13mm). Pin the ends together evenly. Try the item on the toy or doll to be sure the elastic is the right length. If needed, adjust the length. Then stitch across the ends several times to secure them (B). Give the casing a sharp tug to work the joined ends into it, adjust the fullness, and close the opening (see CASINGS).

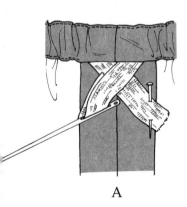

A

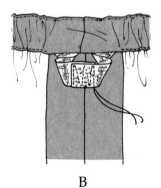

B

If the casing is open at both ends and will be seamed later on, pin the free end of the elastic to one end of the casing. When the elastic emerges at the other end, adjust so ends are even with casing, then baste across both ends of the casing and elastic to secure.

APPLIED DIRECTLY

If this method is specified, apply the elastic along the placement markings or at the distance from the edge specified by your project instructions.

Fold the elastic in half crosswise to find the center; mark with a pin. Mark the center of the placement line the same way. With all edges even, pin the ends of the elastic in place at the ends of the placement line; then pin at the center. Using a widely spaced zigzag stitch, stitch the elastic in place along the middle, stretching it enough to keep the fabric section flat and backstitching it (see under MACHINE STITCHING) at each end for security (C); remove pins. The ends of the elastic will usually be caught in a seam later on.

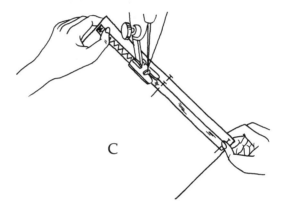

C

Embroidery

• Two of the most commonly used threads are embroidery floss and crewel yarn, both of which are used for projects in this book. If you wish to substitute other threads or yarns for those suggested, you may certainly do so, as long as the weight and texture of the thread are compatible with those of the fabric. •

THREADS

Embroidery Floss Six-strand embroidery floss can easily be separated into one or more strands, depending on how bold or delicate an effect is desired. Your instructions usually specify how many strands to use. The most familiar form of embroidery floss is the shiny cotton variety, but it also comes in a matte-finish cotton as well as in shiny crimped rayon. Each is suitable for most fabrics and craft projects.

Crewel Yarn Wool or acrylic crewel yarn consists of three lightly twisted plies or strands that can be separated easily. It is best used on medium- to heavyweight fabrics; it's also good on textured or pile fabrics because it shows up well. The instructions specify how many strands to use.

Other Threads Perle cotton is a twisted thread that comes in different thicknesses. The thinner ones can be used in place of embroidery floss. One-sixteenth-of-an-inch (2mm) satin ribbon and very fine braid are also suitable for decorative embroidery, except facial features, on all but the sheerest fabrics.

NEEDLES

Match your embroidery needle to the thread and fabric being used, and you'll have no trouble. Choose needles that pierce the fabric easily: a fine one for closely woven, lightweight fabrics; a heavier one for more coarsely woven, heavier fabrics. The eye of the needle should be just large enough for the thread; the point should be sharp or blunt according to the fineness or coarseness of the fabric weave. The needles described here all come in different sizes.

Crewel A good all-purpose needle, the crewel needle is long and sharp and has an elongated eye.

Tapestry The chief feature of a tapestry needle is its blunt point, which makes it ideal for working on coarse or open-weave fabrics as well as on needlepoint canvas. It has a long rounded eye to accommodate bulky threads and yarns.

Chenille Shorter than a tapestry needle and with a sharp point, the chenille needle has a large eye, making it a good choice for thick threads and yarns.

HOOPS

An embroidery hoop (actually a set of two hoops, one of which fits snugly into the other) keeps the fabric taut as you work and helps to ensure smooth, pucker-free stitches. Round or oval hoops are made of wood, plastic or metal.

They are available in many sizes, from tiny to very large. For your project, choose a size a little larger than the actual design area you are working on.

STITCHES

Backstitch To outline a design, you may use a backstitch. Work from right to left. Bring the needle up a little to the left of the end of the design line. Insert the needle at the end of the line and bring it up to the left of the point where it first came up, at a distance equal to the first stitch. Repeat, inserting needle where it first came up and bringing it up to the left of the last completed stitch; keep all stitches the same length (A).

A

Chain Stitch You can use the chain stitch to outline or fill in an area. Work in any direction. Bring the needle up at one end of the design line. Form a small loop with the thread in front of the needle; hold in place with your thumb. Insert the needle next to the spot where it first came up, then bring it up where you want the next stitch to begin, just behind the loop, holding the top of the loop under the needle as it emerges (B).

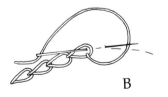

B

Couching Stitch A good outlining stitch, the couching stitch is often used for facial features. This stitch uses two lengths of thread. The one to be couched is placed along the design line. The second thread is used to take small stitches over the thread every ⅛" to ¼" (3mm to 6mm), depending on how curved the design line is (C).

Satin Stitch The most popular filling stitch, satin stitching is especially suitable for creating eyes, mouths and noses. Start at one end or edge of the area to be filled in. Bring the needle up and insert it at the opposite edge. Continue in this way, keeping stitches very close together to create a solid filling (D). You can keep all stitches at the same angle, or very gradually change the angle. To make a padded satin stitch, first fill in the area with stitches perpendicular to the desired finished stitches; then work at right angles over the first stitching (E).

Stem Stitch Work this outlining stitch from left to right. Bring the needle up at the left end of the design line. Insert it a short distance to the right, then bring it up where the previous stitch ended (F). For straight lines, keep the thread above the needle; for curved lines, keep the thread below the needle.

Straight Stitch Use straight stitch for long or short lines. Bring the needle up at one end of the line, then insert it at the other end, bringing it up again at one end of the next stitch (G).

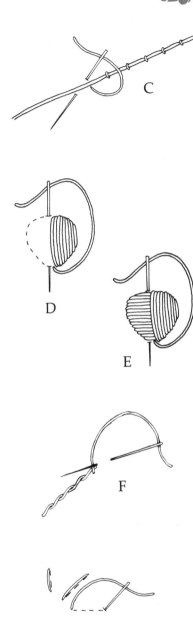

C

D

E

F

G

Enlarging Patterns

• *When a full-size pattern is too large to fit on a page, it is reduced and given on a grid. To enlarge the pattern to its full size, you may use either of the following methods.*•

COPYING ON A GRID

You'll need a large sheet of paper, plus pencil and ruler. Check the scale on the grid: 1 square = 1" (25mm). Count the number of squares on the grid in each direction. Now rule off the paper in the number and size of squares specified.

Next, copy the pattern square by square on your full-size grid. Copy all pattern markings, placement lines and design lines. When you have finished copying the pattern, cut out all the pieces and put them together to be sure they fit one another correctly *before* you cut them from fabric. If the pieces don't fit, you may have made a mistake in copying. Redraw any pieces that require fixing.

Instead of drawing your own grid, you can use graph paper or graph fabric. Graph paper is sold at art, drafting or office supply shops. It is ruled in various frac-tions of an inch (25mm). If each inch (25mm) is not already high-lighted with a heavier line, you can do it yourself with a ruler and pencil. Tape small sheets together as needed to create the size you need.

Graph cloth, such as Pellon® Tru-Grid®, can be found where sewing supplies are sold. It is a 22" × 36" (56cm × 91.5cm) sheet of nonwoven material similar to interfacing, ruled in 1" (25mm) squares.

PHOTOCOPY AND PHOTOSTAT

If you don't wish to make your own grid and copy the pattern, you can take the reduced pattern to a photocopy or photostat shop and have them enlarge it for you. This can be expensive, but it is convenient and accurate.

Fabrics

• *Choosing the right fabric for your craft project requires some thought and care, but it can also be fun. If you're making an animal toy, you'll probably want a fabric that resembles that particular creature's fur. If it's a doll you might choose a smooth, skin-toned fabric for the body; doll clothing can be made from a wide range of fabrics. Always check your pattern or project instructions first for fabric suggestions. Here are some additional points to consider.* •

IMPORTANT CONSIDERATIONS

Weave Closely woven fabrics that do not ravel easily work best for most craft projects, especially if the pieces are small and the seam allowances are narrow. Stable knit fabrics can also be used, but be sure that your project instructions recommend these specifically; otherwise, use wovens.

Weight You'll find that light- to medium-weight fabrics are easier to work with than heavyweight ones, especially where there are narrow seam allowances and small details.

Texture Many textured fabrics, such as fur, velvet, corduroy and suede lookalikes, work beautifully, as they add dimension and

authenticity to toy and doll projects. Just be sure that the fabric weight is suitable for the size of the project, and that its texture doesn't obscure important details.

Design The scale of the fabric design is very important, since you don't want to overpower a small project. As a rule, the smaller the project, the smaller the fabric design should be. If you wish to use a print or a plaid, choose a small-scale one, selecting trims in the same general size range.

SPECIAL FABRICS

Synthetic furs, suedes and leathers and other special fabrics all vary somewhat in handling, so it's very important to test stitching and pressing techniques on scraps first

to be sure you're getting the desired results.

Felt A nonwoven fabric, felt is made by compressing tiny fibers of wool or synthetics together to form a sheet of fabric. It's popular for craft projects because it comes in many colors, handles easily and doesn't ravel.

Felt has no grain, so you can cut pieces in any direction to save space. Be sure your scissors are very sharp; the smaller the pieces, the smaller scissors should be.

Use 8 to 10 stitches per inch (per 25mm) for stitching; smaller stitches make too many holes in the fabric, weakening the seams. Press seams on the wrong side, using steam and very light pressure. Try to avoid pressing on the right side, since you may create unwanted shine.

Long-Pile and Furlike Fabrics

Before cutting out a furlike fabric, mark the wrong side with an arrow to show the direction of the pile, since all pattern pieces must be laid out in the same direction (for animals, the pile should run from the head down). Instead of pinning, hold pattern pieces in place with tape, on the wrong side of the fabric. Cut only one layer at a time. If you need to cut more than one piece from the same pattern piece, first lay out the pattern with the printed or right side up and cut; then turn the pattern over and cut again. Repeat as needed.

You can use sharp scissors or shears, but you may find it easier and more accurate to use a single-edge razor blade, a mat knife or an X-acto® knife. If you do use scissors, be careful not to cut away the fur. To cut with a blade or knife, lift the fabric slightly with one hand and, with the blade in the other hand, make smooth downward cuts, applying even pressure. Instead of cutting notches in or out, mark with chalk or soft pencil.

Rather than pinning seams together, try holding them with paper clips or bobby pins, removing these as they approach the needle. Depending on the weight and thickness of the fur, you can use a size 14, 16 or 18 needle, either regular or all-purpose. Cotton-wrapped polyester or heavy-duty mercerized cotton thread usually works well; be sure to match the needle to the thread. Use 8 to 10 stitches per inch (per 25mm). You may need to lighten the pressure for the fabric to feed smoothly. Some very densely constructed, long-pile fabrics may require you to do quite a lot of machine ad-justment and experimentation before you get satisfactory stitching; be patient! After stitching, use a pin or a needle to free any pile caught in the stitching (A).

A

If seams are to be pressed open, do this with your fingers. Or, if your fabric will allow it, hold a steam iron over, but not on, the seam and then finger-press the seam, holding seam allowances flat and open with your fingers for a few seconds. Never press on the right side. Press open any seam that will intersect with another seam before joining. With sharp scissors, trim away as much of the pile as possible from the seam allowances, then trim the corners diagonally, to reduce bulk (B). Your project may also require trimming away pile from certain areas, for example, from an animal's face; do this with sharp scissors, as your instructions direct.

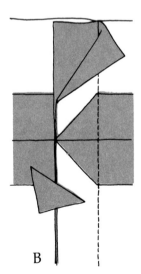

B

When joining furlike fabric to smooth fabric, follow these steps: first baste the fur to the other fabric, then trim away the pile from the seam allowance and pull out any remaining fur from the seam. With the smooth fabric up, stitch the seam in the direction of the fur pile.

Synthetic Leather and Suede

Many of the techniques used for cutting furlike fabrics can be used for leather and suede lookalikes. Follow the grainline on the backing, if any, or mark the direction of the nap, on the wrong side. Tape pattern pieces in place on the wrong side and cut a single layer only, as for furlike fabric. Use sharp scissors or shears to cut all but the thickest leather or suedes, making continuous and even cuts without closing the scissors all the way. If you prefer, you may cut with a blade or knife, as for furs. Mark on the wrong side with chalk or nonsmearing felt-tip pen.

For stitching, you may use a regular needle or a special leather or wedge-point needle, size 11 or 14, and any standard sewing thread. Adjust tension and pressure to less than normal, to help fabric feed smoothly through the machine. If necessary, insert strips of tissue paper between the presser foot and the fabric, or between the fabric and the feed dog, or in both places. Hold fabric pieces together for stitching with paper clips, hair clips or bobby pins, removing them as they approach the needle. Stitch, using 8 to 10 stitches per inch (per 25mm). Instead of backstitching at ends of seams, which could weaken the fabric, tie thread ends together, then trim.

Do not press synthetic leathers and suedes, since some can be damaged by a hot iron. Instead, finger-press (as explained earlier for LONG-PILE AND FURLIKE FABRICS in this section), glue or pound the seam allowances to flatten them.

Fasteners

• *Almost any device that holds two edges closed can be called a fastener. On craft projects, these are often small buttons and buttonholes, hooks and eyes and regular or no-sew snaps.* •

BUTTONS AND BUTTONHOLES

Mark button and buttonhole positions on the right side of your project. Your pattern or project instructions will specify the size and type of buttons to use. For security, use a double strand of cotton-wrapped polyester, heavy-duty or carpet thread, coating it with beeswax first, if desired.

Sew-through Buttons Take a few stitches at the button marking to fasten the thread. Place a toothpick or pin over the button to help create a shank, which allows the fabric to lie flat when buttoned. Sew over the toothpick to attach the button. Remove the toothpick, pull the button away from the fabric, then wind the thread around the stitches a few times to make the shank. To fasten the thread, backstitch (see under HAND SEWING) several times into the shank (A).

Shank Buttons Fasten thread as for sew-through button. Align the button shank with the direction of the buttonhole, either vertical or horizontal. Take several stitches through the shank and the fabric until button is secure, then fasten the thread by backstitching (B).

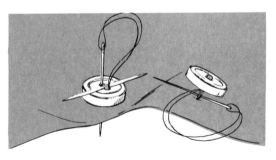

A

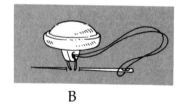

B

Machine-sewn Buttons If you have a zigzag sewing machine, you can use it to sew two-hole or four-hole buttons in place. The instruction manual that comes with your machine tells you how to do it.

Buttonholes Make a test buttonhole on your machine, using the same fabric and number of layers as your project, in order to determine the correct settings. Once these are established, you can make the buttonholes on your project. After stitching the buttonholes, cut them open—carefully!—using very sharp scissors or buttonhole scissors. To keep scissors from cutting too far, place a pin across each end of the buttonhole (C).

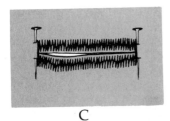

C

Thread Loops These may be used instead of buttonholes, especially for tiny buttons on doll clothes. Using double thread or single buttonhole twist, start by making 2 or 3 foundation stitches at the edge opposite the button, making sure that the loop you create will be large enough to accommodate your button with ease; secure the ends with backstitches. Then, with the same thread, work closely spaced blanket stitches over the entire length of the foundation stitches. To work blanket stitches, point the needle toward you and insert it under the foundation stitches and over the loop of thread coming from the needle (D); pull to close the loop. Repeat, placing stitches next to each other, until foundation stitches are covered.

D

HOOKS AND EYES

Small metal hooks and eyes are often used where opening edges meet on doll clothes. Sew them to the wrong side of the project, placing the hook 1/16" (2mm) from one edge, and the eye projecting slightly from the other edge. Sew around each hole; then sew around the end of the hook and the eye to secure them and keep them flat (E).

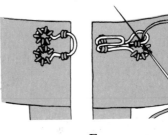

E

SNAP FASTENERS

Conventional sew-on snaps may be used in areas where there is no stress. They come in various sizes from 4, the largest, to 4/0, the smallest. No-sew snaps, in addition to being decorative, have great holding power, so they can be used in areas where there is strain.

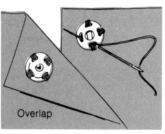

F

Sew-on Snaps First, sew the ball half of the snap to the underside of the overlapping edge, sewing through each hole and picking up only a few threads of the fabric; stitching should not show on the right side. To mark the position of the socket half, rub chalk on the ball, and close the edges to transfer the marking. Sew the socket half in place (F).

No-sew Snaps These fasteners must be attached with the help of tools, which may be of several different types. Sometimes the snaps are included; otherwise, they must be bought separately. Follow the manufacturer's instructions for using your particular tool.

EYELETS

Metal eyelets are attached by means of a plierlike tool. They are used to create holes through which cord or shoelaces can be drawn to fasten edges together. Follow the instructions that come with the eyelet tool.

Gathering

BY MACHINE

For machine gathering, seam allowances should be ⅜" (10mm) or wider, but if your fabric is closely woven and doesn't ravel easily, you can gather ¼" (6mm) seam allowances as well.

Set the stitch length at 6 to 8 stitches per inch (per 25mm) and loosen the tension slightly. Stitch on the seamline, leaving 4" to 5" (10cm to 12.5cm) thread ends at each end; do not backstitch. Stitch again ⅛" to ¼" (3mm to 6mm) away from first stitching, in the seam allowance (A). Two rows of stitches make it easier to control the gathers and create a nicer appearance than a single row.

bin threads until the gathers fit, adjusting the fullness equally and holding the edges together with pins. To hold the thread ends in place, wind them in a figure eight around the pins at each end (C).

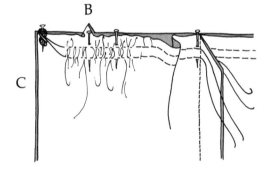

B

C

Stitch the pieces together with the gathered side up so you can control the folds (D); remove pins as you come to them. If gathers at an edge are to be pressed, press gently in the seam allowance only.

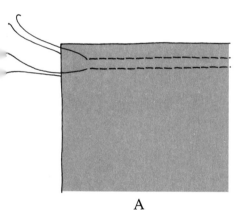

A

For lightweight fabrics with a tendency to pucker, hold the fabric taut in front and in back of the needle, especially when you start to stitch.

Pin the piece with the gathering stitches to the shorter piece, matching any seams, symbols and notches (B). Pull up only the bob-

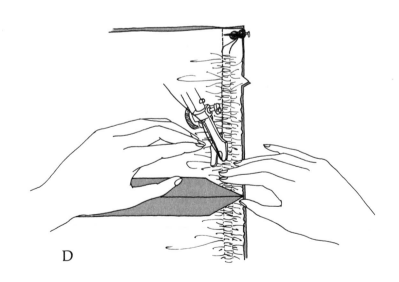

D

For gathering small areas, try this technique: Don't stop stitching at the end of the first row; instead, take two stitches across and into the seam allowance, turn and stitch the second row parallel to the first.

If the area to be gathered is very long, it's a good idea to divide it, as well as the area to which it will be joined, into four equal sections. Mark the divisions with pins. Sew separate double rows of gathering stitches for each section. Then pin layers together, matching the markings, and continue as described earlier.

BY HAND

Hand-gathering is the preferred method if you're working with delicate fabrics, small pieces, very narrow seam allowances or tricky areas where a machine may be hard to control.

Use a double strand of cotton-wrapped polyester thread (or carpet thread, for heavier fabrics) about 24" (61cm) long; do not knot the ends. Leaving 5" to 6" (12.5cm to 15cm) free at each end, make running stitches (see under HAND SEWING) about ⅛" to ¼" (3mm to 6mm) long in the seam allowance or on the gathering line.

Pin the area with the stitching to the shorter area, matching any seams, symbols and notches. Then continue as for machine gathering.

Hand Sewing

BACKSTITCH

This is a strong stitch that can be used to sew seams or to fasten the ends of threads. Work from right to left. Bring the needle to the uppermost side of the fabric. Insert it ¹⁄₁₆″ to ⅛″ (2mm to 3mm) to the right of where it came out, then bring it out the same distance to the left of where it first came out. Repeat, inserting the needle at the end of the previous stitch each time. The stitches on the wrong side will be twice as long as those on the right side (A).

RUNNING STITCH

This is probably the simplest, most basic stitch of all. Work from right to left. Weave the needle in and out of the fabric at even intervals, taking several stitches at a time before pulling the thread through (C). For a permanent seam on fine fabric, make stitches ¹⁄₁₆″ to ⅛″ (2mm to 3mm) long; for gathering, ⅛″ to ¼″ (3mm to 6 mm) long; and for basting, ¼″ to ½″ long (6mm to 13mm).

HELPFUL HINTS

- Beeswax adds strength to your thread and eliminates tangles, too. It comes in a plastic holder with slots that let you draw the thread through the wax.
- Cut thread end diagonally, then thread through the needle and knot.
- Many people like to do their hand sewing with a thimble. If you're the exception, try a rubber fingertip protector, which you can buy at an office-supply store.
- Keep a pair of thread clippers handy for cutting thread and clipping ends.

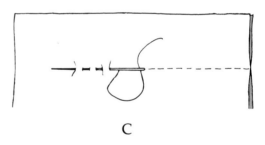

C

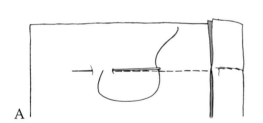

A

CATCHSTITCH

To hold batting or interfacing in place, you can use a catchstitch. Work from left to right, with the needle always pointing left. Start by taking a small stitch in the fabric at the edge of the batting. Take the next stitch about ¼″ (6mm) up and to the right of the first stitch, in the batting. Take another small stitch down and to the right, in the fabric. Continue across, alternating stitches in the fabric and the batting (B).

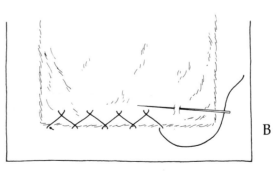

B

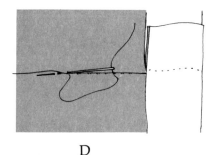

D

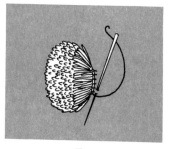

E

SLIPSTITCH

You can close openings and attach appliqués and trims almost invisibly with slipstitching. Work from right to left. Slip the needle through the folded edge about ¼" (6mm), picking up one or two threads of the layer underneath where the needle emerges; then pull the thread. Repeat, making stitches ⅛" to ¼" (3mm to 6mm) long (D). For heavy fabrics, use longer stitches.

TACK

Tacking is frequently used to fasten decorative items, such as pompons, to a background. First take a small stitch in the item being attached. Take another small stitch in the background fabric, drawing the two layers together. Take a few more stitches on each side, folding back the background fabric as needed to make the stitches (E). The stitches shouldn't show on the right side.

FRENCH TACK

This forms a loose link between two parts of a garment or a project. Use double unknotted thread to make two or three long stitches between the parts to be linked, backstitching ends to secure. Then, with the same thread, work closely spaced blanket stitches (see p. 31) over the entire length of the link (F).

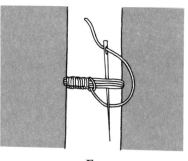

F

WHIPSTITCH

A series of tiny, slanted stitches, whipstitching is used to hold two finished edges together securely. Work from right to left. From the wrong side, bring up the needle at a right angle to the edge and ¹⁄₁₆" to ⅛" (2mm to 3mm) below it. Repeat across the edge, making stitches ¹⁄₁₆" (2mm) apart or closer together (G).

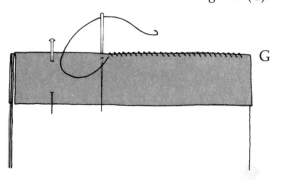

G

Hems

• *Making hems for toys or dolls is a simple matter, since you don't have to worry about marking for evenness or sewing invisibly (unless you prefer to do it that way). For the projects in this book, hems are machine-stitched, and are usually not more than ⅝" (15mm) wide.* •

MACHINE-STITCHED HEM

Turn the hem up along the hemline and press. Then turn the raw edge under ⅛" to ¼" (3mm to 6mm) and press again. Stitch close to the second fold (A).

NARROW HEM

Turn up the hem along the hemline or seamline and press. Turn the raw edge under until it meets the crease and press again. Stitch close to the second fold (B).

If you have a narrow-hem attachment for your sewing machine, you can turn and stitch hems on lightweight fabrics in one step. To help fabric feed smoothly, prefold the fabric for about 1" (25mm) in front of the foot (C).

HEMS ON KNIT FABRICS

Turn up the hem on the hemline and press. Straight-stitch or zig-zag ¼" (6mm) from the fold. Since knits don't ravel, you can trim the excess close to the stitching (D).

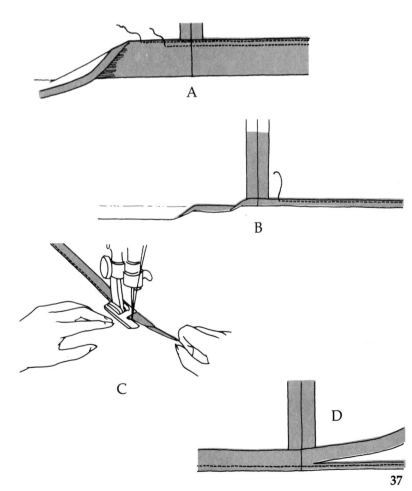

Interfacing

• *Interfacing give body and stability to the areas where they are used. On toys and dolls, shoes, hats, wings and feet are often interfaced to add needed firmness. There are two main types of interfacing—fusible and sew-in.* •

FUSIBLE

In this book, all projects that use interfacing call for fusible types. These come by the yard or in packaged, fixed amounts. Fusibles save time, especially if you're interfacing a very small area. Woven, nonwoven or knitted varieties are available in different weights. The interfacing you choose depends on the fabric you are using and on the desired effect. Since most fusible interfacings require heat, steam and pressure, they cannot be used on all fabrics. To be sure that your fabric and interfacing are compatible, always test-fuse a sample first with scraps. This sample will tell you whether you have chosen the correct interfacing weight, as well as whether interfacing can be fused successfully to your fabric without affecting the outward appearance.

Some fusible interfacings can be stretched in one direction and are stable in the other; the bolt hang-tag or packaging should give you this information. If your interfac-ing stretches in one direction, be sure to cut it making the best use of its stability.

Cut fusible interfacing using the pattern pieces indicated in your project instructions. Then trim the seam allowances to ⅛" (3mm) outside the seamline, and trim corners diagonally to reduce bulk (A). Place the interfacing, adhesive (shiny) side down, on the wrong side of the fabric piece to be interfaced. On large pieces, fuse-baste in place by touching the tip of the iron to the interfacing every 3" to 4" (7.5cm to 10cm). Following the manufacturer's instructions, fuse the interfacing in place.

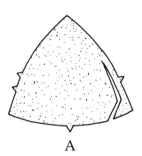

A

SEW-IN

If you have chosen a fabric for your project that cannot take the heat and steam required for fusible interfacings, you may substitute a sew-in interfacing. This type also comes in woven and nonwoven versions, in several weights, and may be used with any fabric. Like fusible interfacing, sew-ins may have directional stretch; the same comments apply.

Cut sew-in interfacing using the required pattern pieces and trimming corners only; do not trim the seam allowances. Pin the interfacing to the wrong side of the fabric piece to be interfaced. Machine-baste the interfacing in place, ⅛" (3mm) away from the seamline in the seam allowance (B). Now trim the interfacing close to the stitching (C).

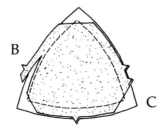

Machine Stitching

•*Most machines today will do more than just stitch seams. The suggestions that follow are meant to help you get the best-looking results on your craft projects.* •

SPECIAL STITCHING TECHNIQUES

Backstitching This technique prevents the ends of the seam from coming apart. Near the beginning of the seam, take a few stitches in reverse, holding the thread ends behind the needle. Stitch forward to the end of the seam, then backstitch again.

Easestitching To help join one project section to a slightly smaller one, use easestitching. With stitch length set at 6 to 8 stitches per inch (per 25mm), stitch along the seamline of the larger section only; do not backstitch. Matching markings, pin the two layers together at ends and/or markings, without pinning into the stitches. Pull up the bobbin thread to gather the fabric until the two sections fit. Adjust the fullness evenly so there are no puckers on the seamline, then pin or baste to hold the layers in place. Stitch the seam, being careful not to create any puckers.

Edgestitching To stabilize as well as decorate a finished edge, straight-stitch close to the edge. Pivot around corners carefully,

turning the flywheel by hand for maximum control. Use a small-hole throat plate for this technique.

Reinforcing This stitching should be done whenever you stitch a seam with a corner or point. Use 15 to 20 stitches per inch (per 25mm). For an inside corner, start the reinforcement about 1" (25mm) before the point, pivot at the point, and continue around the corner for another 1" (25mm). On an outside corner, if the angle is sharper than a right angle, take one or two stitches across the point before continuing to the other side.

Staystitching Because it prevents stretching and acts as a guideline for clipping curves, staystitching can save you time and trouble when sewing craft projects. Use a short stitch length, about 10 to 12 per inch (per 25mm), and stitch in the direction of the fabric grain, just inside the seamline in the seam allowance.

Topstitching Decorative as well as functional, topstitching helps keep edges flat and emphasizes lines or details. Follow your project instructions for placement of the topstitching, which is always done on the right side. To help guide your stitching and keep it an even distance from the edge or seam, use a seam guide, the edge of the presser foot or sewing tape. Use 6 to 8 stitches per inch (per 25mm) for topstitching.

Seams

● *Since seams hold your project together, it's very important that they be stitched correctly. Because fabrics differ in their handling and stitching characteristics, you should make it a rule to test-stitch your fabric before starting to work on the project. That way, you'll save time and trouble.* ●

STRAIGHT-STITCHED SEAMS

Place the right sides of the pieces together, matching edges and any notches and symbols. Pin the pieces together, placing the pins at right angles to the seamline, and with the heads in the seam allowance for easy removal (A).

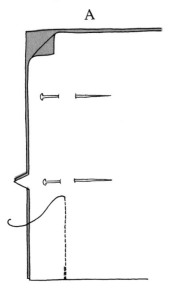

A

Place the pieces to be stitched under the presser foot so that you will be stitching with the fabric grain. The seam allowances should be to the right of the needle, the bulk of the fabric to the left. Stitch the seam width specified by your pattern or project instructions, backstitching (see under MA-CHINE STITCHING) at each end for security.

Many machines have a throat plate that is engraved with lines for different seam widths; all you have to do is align the edge of the fabric with the appropriate line as you stitch. You can also use a seam guide, which can be fastened to the throat plate for any seam width. To create your own seam guide, place a piece of masking or adhesive tape on the throat plate to the right of the presser foot, at the required distance from the needle.

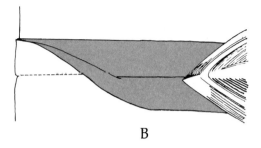

B

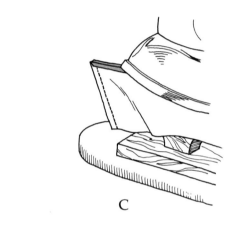

C

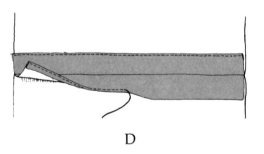

D

Pressing After stitching, seams must be pressed. First press over the seam, just as you stitched it, to blend the stitches into the fabric. Then press the seam open (B), unless your instructions specify otherwise. For craft projects, with their narrow seams and sharp corners, you may find a point presser useful (C).

Trimming Seam allowances on most craft projects are narrow— ¼″ to ⅜″ (6mm to 10mm)—so trimming may not always be necessary. See CORNERS AND CURVES for tips on trimming and grading.

SEAM FINISHES

Even though your project instructions may not specify this, it's always a good idea to finish any seams that are visible, such as those on doll clothes. The simple seam finishes that follow can add considerably to the durability of any project.

Turned and Stitched Also known as clean finishing, this seam or edge finish is fine for light- to medium-weight fabrics. After stitching the seam and pressing it open, turn each seam edge under ⅛″ (3mm) and edgestitch as you turn (see under MACHINE STITCHING) (D).

Pinked and Stitched On heavier fabrics where clean finishing could add bulk, try this method. Stitch the seam and press it open. Stitch along each seam allowance, ⅛″ (3mm) from the raw edge. Then pink the edge of each seam allowance (E).

E

Zigzagged This finish works on any fabric. Use a narrow zigzag on lightweight fabric, a wider zigzag on heavyweight fabric. Stitch the seam and press it open. Then zigzag over the raw edge of each seam allowance (F). On seams that are not pressed open, you can also zigzag the edges together, if desired.

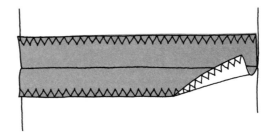

F

Mock French One of the most durable seams for doll clothes made of lightweight fabrics is the mock French seam. Stitch the seam but don't press it open. Turn the edges of the seam allowances in toward each other ⅛″ (3mm) and press. Then edgestitch the folded edges together (G). With practice, you can turn the edges in as you stitch, without pressing.

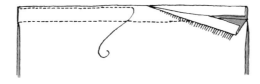

G

Stuffing

By far the most popular stuffing material is polyester fiberfill. In addition to easy handling, this material is relatively inexpensive, lightweight, washable or dry-cleanable and nonallergenic. It comes in bags of 12 to 24 ounces (340 to 680 g) or larger.

HOW TO STUFF

For small projects, pull off small tufts of fiberfill, about the size of cotton balls, and push into the item with your fingers. Where your fingers can't reach, such as corners or narrow spaces, use the eraser end of a pencil or the handle of a wooden spoon to force the stuffing into position. Fill out corners, curves and outer extremities such as hands and feet first; then finish stuffing the rest of the item with more small tufts of fiberfill.

For large projects, begin as for small ones, first filling corners, curves and extremities to establish their shapes. Continue stuffing, using larger tufts, or even small handfuls, of fiberfill until piece is the desired firmness.

Usually your project instructions or pattern tells you whether to stuff firmly or lightly. Doll bodies are often stuffed quite firmly, whereas animals may be somewhat softer.

OTHER TYPES OF STUFFING

If polyester fiberfill isn't available, or if you've run out, you can substitute shredded foam or even old nylons. The disadvantage of foam is that it's messy and, because of static electricity, tends to stick to your fingers. It also may disintegrate after a few years. Use it as you would fiberfill.

Stockings or pantyhose should be washed before being used as stuffing. Cut them into small pieces, using only the sheer parts, and work as you would for fiberfill.

Transferring Markings

• *There are many methods of transferring a design to a piece of fabric. The one you choose depends on your fabric and how you plan to execute the design. Before you decide which method to use, also check to see whether your design is reversible. Some, like monograms, are not, so you may have to reverse the design before transferring it. If your project is not washable, it's best to use a transfer method that will be hidden by the finished design.* •

Begin by tracing the design onto tracing paper, which you can buy at art supply shops. Pick one of the methods that follow for transferring the design to fabric. All of the items mentioned can be bought at needlework/craft shops or fabric shops.

the preferred method of marking pattern symbols, such as ●'s, ▲'s and ■'s, and placement lines on your fabric pieces. Most pattern markings should be transferred to the wrong side of the project pieces.

DRESSMAKER'S CARBON PAPER AND TRACING WHEEL

You can use a dressmaker's carbon and tracing wheel on any smooth-surfaced fabric. Choose a color close to that of your fabric, but still visible against it. Place the carbon, colored side down, between the fabric and the traced design. Go over the design with the tracing wheel to transfer it (A). In addition to transferring designs, dressmaker's carbon is often

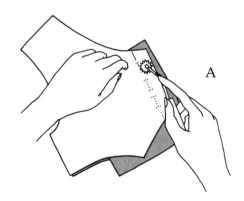

A

TAILOR'S TACKS

Use this method to transfer markings, such as facial features on fur animals, on fabrics that might be marred by a tracing wheel, or where other markings would disappear. Use a long double strand of thread—don't knot it—and take a small running stitch through the pattern and fabric at the desired marking. Then sew another stitch, crossing over the first. At the same time, pull the thread until a large loop forms. Move to the next marking, leaving a loose thread between markings (B). Clip the loops and the long threads. Remove the pattern carefully, roll the fabric back gently, and clip the threads between the pattern and fabric, leaving tufts on either side (C). Be careful not to pull the threads out of the fabric after clipping them.

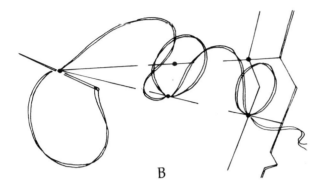

B

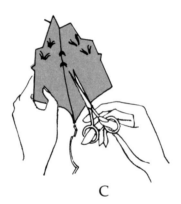

C

Trims

• While the projects in this book are mainly trimmed with lace and/or ribbon, you needn't restrict yourself to these. If you have other trims on hand, you may certainly use them in place of, or in addition to, the trim specified for the project. Be sure that you have enough yardage and that the care qualities are the same as those of the fabrics used for your project. When it comes to toys and dolls, you can be as creative as you like! •

LACE

Flat Flat lace, available in many widths, comes with one or both edges scalloped or both straight; one edge may be raw.

To use flat lace as a band trim, center it over the marked placement line and pin it in place, or use basting tape or glue stick (see under ADHESIVE). Then edge-stitch (see under MACHINE STITCHING) the lace along the straight or scalloped edges (A). To use flat lace at an edge, turn the edge under ¼" (6mm) and press. Then lap the pressed edge ⅛" (3mm) over the lace and stitch close to the pressed edge, through the lace (B).

A

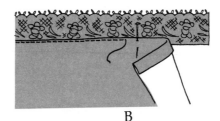

B

Pregathered This lace ruffling is already gathered and bound at one edge. It is flexible and will go around curves easily. To apply pregathered lace to an edge, lap the pressed edge of the project over the bound edge of the lace and stitch as for flat lace (C).

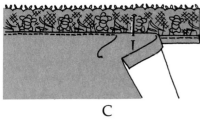

C

Eyelet Eyelet comes in several different forms, including flat with one finished edge, flat with two finished edges and pregathered. Apply eyelet as you would lace.

RIBBON

The most popular ribbons are made of satin or grosgrain, though velvets, jacquards and taffetas are also available. Ribbons come as narrow as $1/16''$ (2mm); the most common widths for toys and dolls range from $1/8''$ (3mm) to $1/2''$ (13mm).

Stitching Press your ribbon first to remove any creases or wrinkles. Then pin it in place, centering over placement lines, if any; or use disappearing basting tape or glue stick (see under ADHESIVES). Stitch ribbon in place close to both long edges (D). Very narrow ribbon may be stitched through the center. If ends are to be caught in a seam, no further finishing is necessary.

Finishing Ends If ribbon ends will not be caught in a seam, cut the ribbon $1/2''$ to $1''$ (13mm to 25mm) longer than the area to which it will be applied. Turn the ends under $1/4''$ to $1/2''$ (6mm to 13mm) (E) and either edgestitch or slipstitch (see under HAND SEWING) them in place.

The ends of ribbon bows should be finished by trimming them diagonally.

E

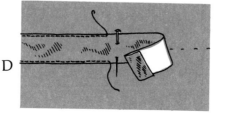

D

CORDING

You can purchase cording or make your own. To make your own, you'll need filler cord and fabric. Cut the fabric on the true bias into strips wide enough to wrap around the filler cord, plus 1" (25mm) for seam allowances, and long enough for the amount of filler cord you plan to cover. Enclose the filler cord in the bias strip. Use a zipper foot and 8 to 10 stitches per inch (per 25mm) to stitch close to the filler cord (F), stretching the bias very slightly as you stitch. Trim the seam allowances to match those of your project. Apply the cording according to pattern instructions.

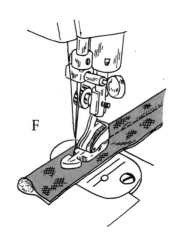

F

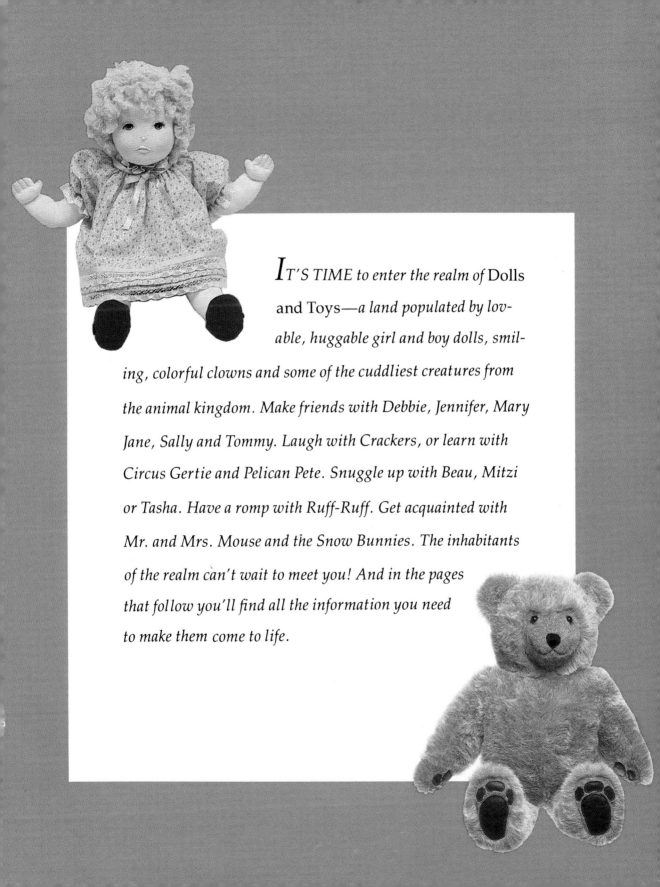

*I*T'S TIME *to enter the realm of* Dolls *and* Toys—*a land populated by lovable, huggable girl and boy dolls, smiling, colorful clowns and some of the cuddliest creatures from the animal kingdom. Make friends with Debbie, Jennifer, Mary Jane, Sally and Tommy. Laugh with Crackers, or learn with Circus Gertie and Pelican Pete. Snuggle up with Beau, Mitzi or Tasha. Have a romp with Ruff-Ruff. Get acquainted with Mr. and Mrs. Mouse and the Snow Bunnies. The inhabitants of the realm can't wait to meet you! And in the pages that follow you'll find all the information you need to make them come to life.*

Darlin' Debbie, p. 58

Dress Me Jennifer and Friend, p. 50

Mary Jane, p. 64

Sally Hug-Me-Tight, p. 71

Crackers the Clown, p. 85

Tommy, p. 93

Circus Gertie, p. 76

Pelican Pete and
His School of Fish, p. 128

Mr. and Mrs. Mouse, p. 117

Mitzi the Cat, p. 120

Ruff-Ruff the Dog, p. 124

Snow Bunnies, p. 109

Beau Bear, p. 102

Beau Bear, p. 106

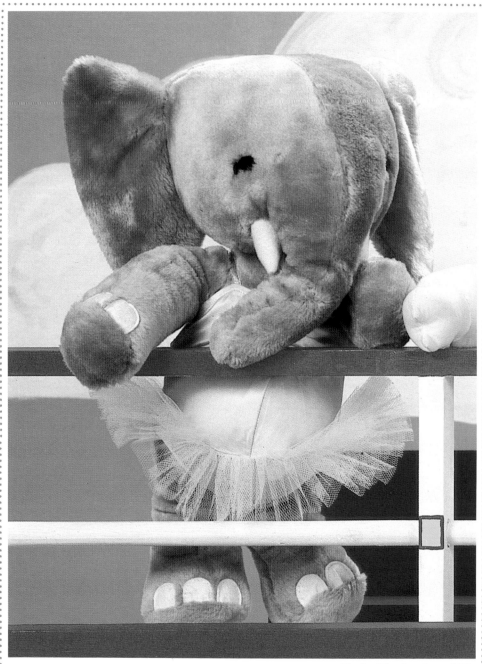

Tasha Elephant, p. 111

Dolls
& Toys

Dress Me Jennifer and Friend

• *Meet the perfect companion—Dress Me Jennifer! To make Jennifer's body, you can use unbleached muslin or other closely woven fabric. For her nightgown and matching bloomers, gingham, chambray, plissé or even lightweight flannel would be fine. You'll find that a can of antistatic spray is a real help in keeping flyaway yarn for hair under control.* •

MATERIALS NEEDED

Doll

⅝ yd (0.60m) of 45″ (115cm) fabric

2 oz (56g) of 4-ply yarn for hair

1 skein each of pink and black embroidery floss

11″ × 15″ (28cm × 38cm) piece of cardboard for making hair

transparent tape

¼ yd (0.25m) of seam binding to match yarn

carpet thread

glue

1½ lbs (680g) of polyester fiberfill

powdered blusher

Nightgown and panties

¾ yd (0.70m) of 45″ (115cm) fabric

1⅜ yds (1.30m) of ⅜″ (10mm) lace ruffling

⅞ yd (0.80m) of ⅝″ (15mm) eyelet ruffling

⅞ yd (0.80m) of ½″ (13mm) single-fold bias tape

1⅜ yds (1.30m) of ¼″ (6mm) elastic

two ½″ (13mm) buttons

Bunny slippers

6″ × 10″ (15cm × 25.5cm) remnant of curly pile fabric

9″ × 12″ (23cm × 30.5cm) piece of pink felt for ears and soles

Finished size: approximately 19″ (48.5cm)

four ⅜" (10mm) ball buttons for eyes

carpet thread

Bear

4" × 7" (10 cm × 18cm) remnant of light brown felt

1" (25mm) square of pink felt (use scrap of slipper felt)

small amount of fiberfill

glue

red and black waterproof markers

Pattern pieces are found on pp. 140–146.

CUTTING INFORMATION

Doll fabric: 1 head; 2 head sides; 2 body fronts; 1 body back; 2 inside legs; 2 outside legs; 4 arms; 2 foot soles

Nightgown/panties fabric: 2 fronts; 1 back; 2 sleeves; 4 yoke fronts; 2 yoke backs; 2 panties

Slipper fabrics: pile—2 fronts and 2 backs; felt—2 soles and 8 ears

Note: For cutting pile fabric, see under Fabrics.

Bear fabric: 2 brown felt bears; 1 pink felt bow tie

HOW-TO

Trace pattern pieces (enlarge if necessary) and transfer all pattern markings. All seam allowances are ¼" (6mm) except for bear. Press all seams open unless otherwise instructed.

Note: *For sewing with pile fabrics, see under* FABRICS.

Doll

1 Easestitch (see under MACHINE STITCHING) the head sides between small ●'s (A).

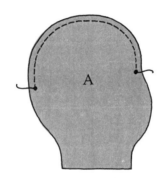

2 Pin the head sides to head, right sides together, adjusting ease between the small ●'s. Stitch (B). Clip curves (see CORNERS AND CURVES), then turn and press.

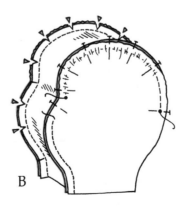

3 Reinforce (see under MACHINE STITCHING) the body fronts by stitching through the large ●'s. With right sides together, stitch the body fronts along center front (C).

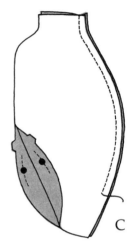

4 Stitch the darts on the body back and press toward the notched edges (D).

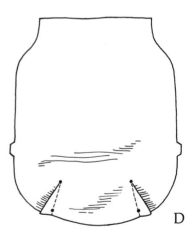

5 With right sides together, stitch the body front to the body back along the side edges. Leave the bottom of the body open between large ●'s. Clip to large ●'s (E).

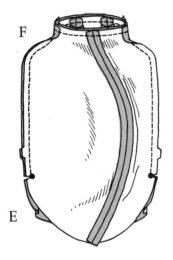

6 With right sides together, insert the head into the neck edge of the body, placing small ●'s at the shoulder seams. Be sure the head front is at the front of the body. Pin in place, then stitch the neck seam (F). Turn the head/body right side out.

7 With right sides together, stitch the arms together in pairs, leaving an opening between small ●'s (G). Clip inner curves and turn right side out. Stuff (see STUFFING)

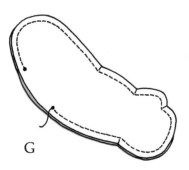

with fiberfill. Turn in the raw edges and slipstitch (see under HAND SEWING) the opening closed.

8 With right sides together, pin one inside leg to one outside leg. Stitch front and back seams, leaving back open between small ●'s; clip curves (H). With right sides

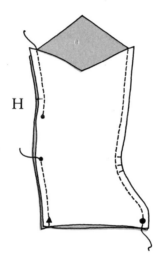

together, pin one foot sole to the bottom of the leg, matching all symbols and clipping and easing to fit. Stitch the seam (I). Repeat

for the other leg. Turn the legs right side out.

9 Fold the top of each leg in half, bringing the seams together. Make two rows of gathering stitches (see GATHERING) at the upper edge (J).

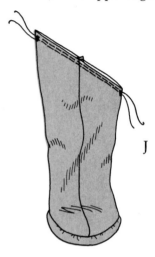

10 With toes facing the body and raw edges matching, pin the gathered edge of the legs to the body front between symbols. Stitch, keeping the body back free (K).

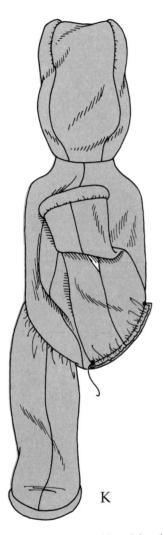

K

(see under EMBROIDERY); then outline them in backstitch. With 3 strands of pink floss, embroider the mouth in stem stitch. Apply powdered blush to cheeks, to nose area and to knees. With 3 strands of pink floss, work straight stitches along the stitching lines on the hands (L).

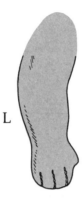

L

14 Cut a 2" × 10" (5cm × 25.5 cm) piece of cardboard. Without overlapping strands, wind the yarn closely around the short side of the cardboard until the width measures 6" (15cm); yarn should be quite thick. Do not use up more than a fourth of the yarn. Place a piece of tape over yarn at one edge, then cut yarn loops at other edge (M). Remove the cardboard. Keeping yarn doubled, stitch through tape and yarn, then remove tape.

15 Center the stitched edge of the yarn over the placement line on the head front, starting and ending at ■'s. Sew securely in place, using carpet thread (N). Now lift the yarn and cover the area near the stitching with glue (see under ADHESIVES). When glue is sticky, carefully replace the yarn, using a knitting needle or similar implement to help separate the strands. When glue is dry, trim bangs as desired.

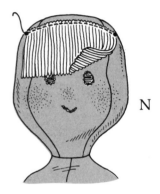

N

16 Cut a 9" × 15" (23cm × 38cm) piece of cardboard. Without overlapping strands, wind yarn lengthwise around cardboard, close together, until width is 3" (7.5cm). Leave a 1" (25mm) space, then begin a new section and wind closely until width is 2¼"(6cm). Place tape across entire edge and cut loops at other edge, as before;

11 Stuff the body and head firmly. On the body back, turn the raw edge under and slipstitch in place over leg/body seam. Stuff the legs firmly through the openings in the back seams, then slipstitch the openings closed.

12 Pin the arms to body, hands pointing forward, along placement lines. Slipstitch the arms in place around the top edges.

13 Using 3 strands of black floss, embroider the eyes in satin stitch

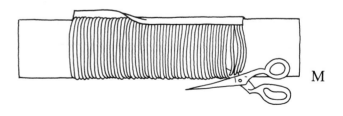

M

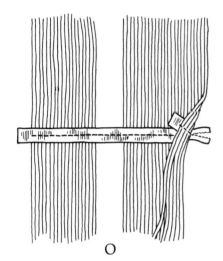

O

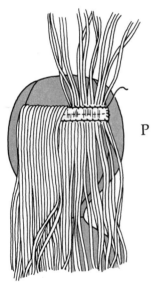

P

remove cardboard. Open out the yarn and turn over so tape is underneath. Cut seam binding 1" (25mm) longer than total width of yarn. Center the seam binding over the tape and yarn, with ends extending evenly. Stitch through all layers, then remove tape (O). Fold the yarn in half along the seam binding. Cut yarn sections apart at the middle of the space.

17 Place the wider section on the head back, centering the seam binding over the placement line and turning the ends under ½" (13mm). Sew the seam binding to the head along both edges, tacking (see under HAND SEWING) securely at each end (P). Glue the upper part of the yarn to the head as for bangs. Apply the narrower yarn section to the top of the head

in the same way, placing the seam binding over the head center marking between the bangs and back hair placement line (Q). When glue dries, trim hair as desired.

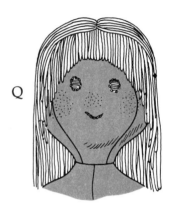

Q

Panties

1 On each section, apply a bias tape casing (see under CASINGS) between placement lines. Finish the lower edge of each section with eyelet ruffling (see under TRIMS).

2 With right sides together, stitch the center front and center back seams (A). Press each open.

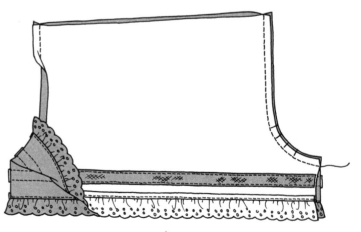

A

3 Insert an 8″ (20.5cm) length of elastic (see under ELASTIC) in each casing, securing the ends with pins (B). With right sides together, stitch the inner leg seam, including ends of ruffling (C).

4 At upper edge, make a casing at foldline, turning the raw edge under ¼″ (6mm) (D). Insert a 15″ (38cm) length of elastic, lap ends ½″ (13mm) and stitch securely. Stitch the opening closed, stretching elastic as you stitch.

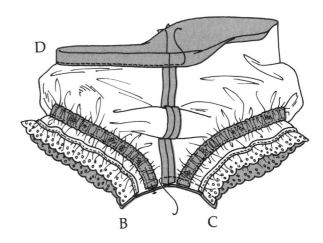

Nightgown

1 Finish lower edges of sleeves with lace ruffling as you did on the Panties, step 1. Apply a 5″ (15.5cm) length of elastic directly over placement line of each sleeve.

2 With right sides together, pin a sleeve to each nightgown front along armhole edge; stitch (A). Pin and stitch sleeve to back in same way.

3 With right sides together, stitch each side and sleeve in one continuous seam, pivoting at underarm seam (B).

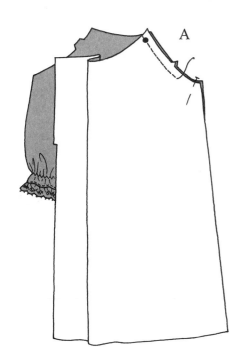

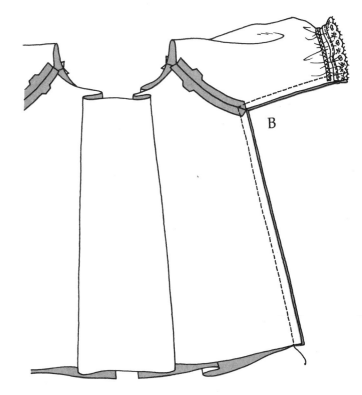

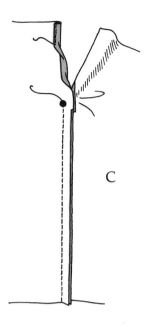

C

4 Beginning at lower edge, stitch the center front seam as far as the large ●. Above the large ●, narrow-hem (see under HEMS) the opening edges, tapering to nothing below the large ● (C). Make two rows of gathering stitches at the upper edge of the nightgown (see under GATHERING).

5 With right sides together, stitch one yoke front to each side of one yoke back at shoulders. (Remaining yoke pieces will be used as facings.) With edges even, pin the bound edge of lace ruffling to the right side of the yoke, along the upper and lower edges; turn the ends of the ruffling ¼" (6mm) to the right side and baste (D).

6 With right sides together, pin the lower edge of the yoke to the upper edge of the nightgown, matching small ●●'s on the nightgown to shoulder seams. Adjust gathers evenly, then stitch. Press seam toward yoke. On the outside, topstitch close to the lower edge of the yoke (E).

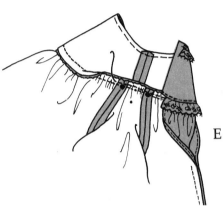

E

D

7 Assemble yoke facing as for yoke. Press the lower edge under ¼"(6mm), clipping as needed. With right sides together, pin the facing to the yoke along the front and neck opening edges. Stitch, making sure to keep the ends of the lace free. Trim corners and clip curves (F). Turn the yoke inside;

F

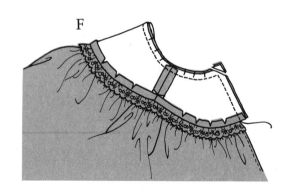

press. Slipstitch the lower edge of the facing over the yoke/nightgown seam.

8 Turn up the hem at hemline, turning the raw edge under ¼" (6mm); press. Slipstitch in place.

Make thread loops (see under FASTENERS) on the right front yoke between the small ●'s. Sew buttons to the left front yoke opposite loops.

Slippers

1 Stitch the dart on each slipper front; press to one side. With right sides together, stitch the front to the back (A).

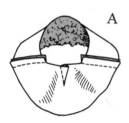

A

2 With right sides together, pin the sole to the slipper as in step 8 of the doll, matching symbols and clipping and easing to fit; stitch the seam. Turn right side out.

3 For each ear, whipstitch (see under HAND SEWING) two ear sections together; repeat, making four ears in all. Using carpet thread, slipstitch two ears to each slipper at placement lines. Also using carpet thread, sew two button eyes to each slipper below the ears (B).

B

Bear

1 Whipstitch bear pieces together, leaving an opening (A) at the top of the head for stuffing. Stuff lightly, then whipstitch the opening closed.

2 Spread a thin layer of clear-drying glue over the face area; let it dry (this technique helps prevent the marker from smearing). Using waterproof markers, draw black eyes and nose and red mouth along placement lines. Glue pink bow tie over small ● (B).

A

B

57

Darlin' Debbie

• With her clasped hands and demure expression, Darlin' Debbie is a real sweetheart. Think how perfect she would look on a little girl's dresser. And here's a plus: because there are only five pattern pieces and a few easy seams, this is a very good project for a beginner or for a sewer who's in a hurry. You can make her head from a lightweight, stable knit or gauze, and her body from a soft fabric such as velveteen or lightweight cotton. Although we show Darlin' Debbie "wearing" a woven solid, she'd look just as fetching in a dainty print. •

Finished size: approximately 16" (41cm).

MATERIALS NEEDED

⅜ yd (0.35m) of 45" (115cm) fabric for doll body

¼ yd (0.25m) of 45" or 60" (115cm or 150cm) contrasting fabric for head and hands

5" × 2½" (12.5cm × 6.5cm) remnant of fleece for hands

remnant of pink embroidery floss for nose and 1 skein to match hair

1¼ yds (1.15m) of 1¼" (32mm) flat lace

1½ yds (1.40m) of ¼" (6mm) satin ribbon

3 oz (90g) of sport or baby yarn for hair

10" × 12" (25.5cm × 30.5cm) piece of lightweight cardboard for making hair and for bottom

transparent tape

glue

heavy thread

1 lb (450g) of polyester fiberfill

powdered blusher

Pattern pieces are found on pp. 138–139.

CUTTING INFORMATION

Body fabric: 2 bodies; 1 bottom; 1 casing

Contrasting fabric: 1 head; 4 hands

Fleece: 2 hands

HOW-TO

Trace pattern pieces (enlarge if necessary) and transfer all pattern markings. All seam allowances are ¼" (6mm). Press seams open unless otherwise instructed.

Note: *For tips on using yarn for doll's hair, see* Dress Me Jennifer and Friend, *pp. 53–54.*

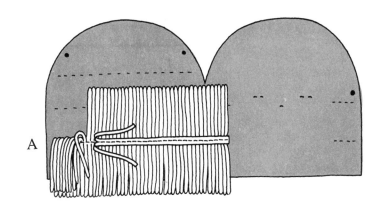

1 Cut a 2" × 10" (5 cm × 25.5 cm) strip from cardboard. Following the instructions in Dress Me Jennifer, step 14, p. 53), make a 7½" (19cm) width of yarn hair. Open out the yarn and, with the tape side up, center it over the lowest placement line on head back, leaving ¼" (6mm) seam allowance free of yarn. Stitch tape through the center. Remove tape and turn the yarn down over the stitching (A).

Repeat this step twice, once for the center placement line and once for the upper placement line, making hair measure 5¾" (14.5cm) across for the upper line.

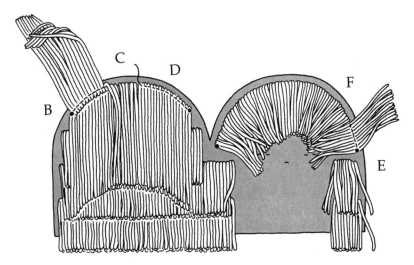

2 For the top layer, make two 5¾" (14.5cm) widths of hair; cut along the tape. Open out one width and, with the yarn facing toward the head, position the cut edge along the top of the head back between small ●'s, ¼" (6mm) from edge; stitch (B). With the yarn facing away from the head, apply a second width of yarn along top of the head back, lapping slightly over stitching on first layer. Stitch, then turn the yarn down over the stitching (C). Using heavy thread, tack (see under HAND SEWING) the yarn to the head along the curve between small ●'s (D).

For hair at side of face, make two separate 1" (25mm) wide sections as in step 1. Center and stitch the yarn over placement lines on the head front as you did on the head back, leaving the seam allowance free (E). Turn yarn down over stitching as before. For bangs, make a 9¼" (23.5cm) width of hair. Open out and position taped center of yarn between small ●'s on head front, ¼" (6mm) from edge (F). Stitch through all layers along center of tape. Turn yarn down over stitching and tack upper edge in place as you did on the back.

3 Baste one piece of fleece to the wrong side of one right hand piece. Pin the other right hand piece to the fleece-backed piece with right sides together and

G

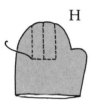

H

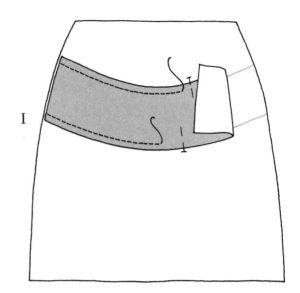

I

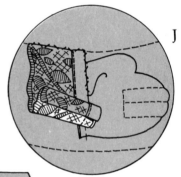

J

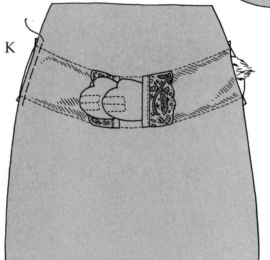

K

stitch. Clip the thumb corner and trim the fleece close to the stitching (G). Turn and press the hand. To form fingers, stitch along the stitching lines through all layers (H). Make the left hand in the same way.

4 On the wrong side of one body piece, center and pin the casing over the marked placement lines. Stitch ¼" (6mm) from both long edges (I).

5 Cut lace and ribbon each 5" (12.5cm) long. Position the ribbon over the straight edge of the lace and stitch the ribbon in place close to both long edges. Cut the ribbon/lace in half.

6 Pin one hand, thumb up, to the right side of the front along one placement line; stitch ⅛" (3mm) from raw edge through all layers. Position the straight edge of one ribbon/lace piece over the stitching on the hand, overlapping slightly. Turn the raw edges under ¼" (6mm) and slipstitch (see

under HAND SEWING) in place all around (J). Stitch the second hand along the other placement line and apply ribbon/lace as for first hand.

7 Stuff the arm casings firmly (see under STUFFING), using small amounts of stuffing at a time. Baste across ends of casing (K).

8 With right sides together, pin the front to the back along the right-hand edge; stitch (L) and press open.

9 Cut lace and ribbon the same length as the lower edge of the joined body pieces. Pin the lace with the straight edge 1½″ (3.8cm) from the lower edge of the body. Stitch close to the straight edge. Pin the ribbon over the straight edge of the lace. Stitch in place, close to both long edges (M).

10 With right sides together, stitch the head to the body, keeping the hair free (N). (Hair is not shown in this illustration). Clip and press the seam toward the body.

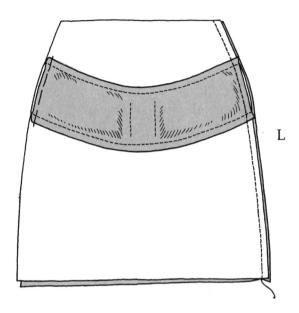

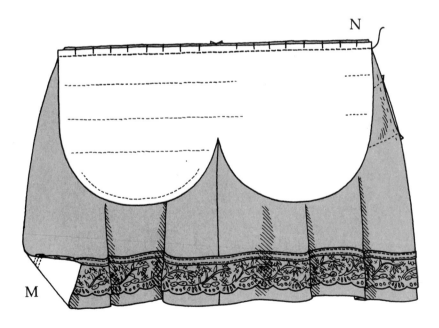

11 With right sides together, pin front to back around the head and the remaining side seam. Carefully stitch, keeping yarn hair and lace free (O).

12 With right sides together, pin the bottom to the lower edge of the body, clipping the body as needed to fit and matching small ●'s. Stitch, keeping lace free and leaving a 5" (12.5cm) opening in the back for turning (P). Turn the doll right side out.

13 Stuff the head almost full, using small amounts of fiberfill at a time and pushing seam allowances to one side. Pack firmly. Using heavy thread in a sewing needle, make a line of running stitches (see under HAND SEWING) around the neck, ½" (13mm) above the neck seam. Pull tight, keeping the ends free to knot. Before knotting, add extra stuffing to fill out the doll's chin and then tie thread ends in a secure square knot. Trim the ends close to the knot. Finish stuffing the body.

14 Cut cardboard ¼" (6mm) smaller all around than bottom pattern piece. Insert the cardboard to form a flat bottom. Slipstitch the opening closed.

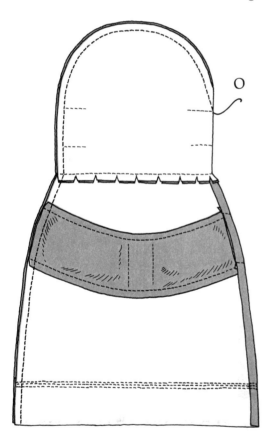

O

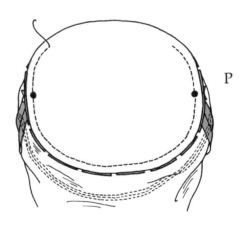

P

15 Make eyes, using 4 strands of embroidery floss in a color to match hair. Insert needle in center of each eye between stitching lines, leaving ¾″ (20mm) of floss hanging (Q). Make a stitch to right side of eye (R), then bring needle up at outer left edge of eye (S). Insert needle again at right edge of eye (T) and bring needle up at center (U), leaving ¾″ (20mm) of floss hanging.

Separate the strands of floss with the point of the needle and trim into an arc shape. Glue (see under ADHESIVES) strands in place (V). To make nose, use 3 strands of pink floss, and take 3 or 4 small stitches on nose stitching line. Apply powdered blusher to doll's cheeks.

16 Cut a 14″ (35.5cm) length of lace. With right sides together, join the ends to form a circle. Make one row of gathering stitches (see under GATHERING) by hand ⅛″ (3mm) from long straight edge. Slip the lace collar over the doll's head and pull the gathering thread until collar fits loosely around doll's neck (W). Tie and cut thread ends.

17 Trim yarn around the face to a pleasing shape. Using your fingers as a comb, arrange the hair neatly. Tie the remaining ribbon around the head through the hair, covering the part and forming a bow to one side (X).

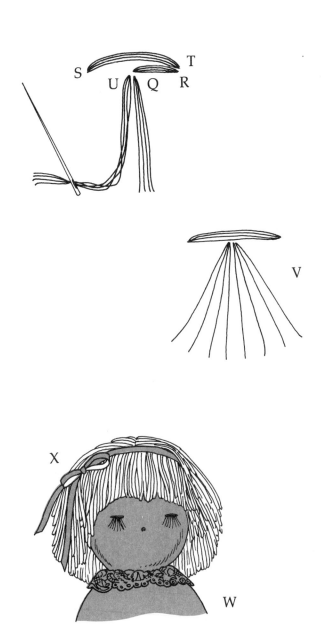

Mary Jane

• *This cuddly cutie is perfect for just about any child. An especially appealing feature is her tousled head—easily achieved with crinkly bouclé yarn. We suggest using a stretchy fabric for this toddler doll's face; that way you can mold her features with strategically placed stuffing and stitches. Her body can be made from woven fabric such as muslin or cotton poplin, and her dress (with matching panties) from any medium-weight cotton or blend.*•

MATERIALS NEEDED

Doll

⅝ yd (0.60 m) of 45″ (115cm) fabric for body

6″ × 8″ (15cm × 20.5cm) remnant of lightweight knit fabric with crosswise stretch *or* flesh-colored opaque pantyhose for face

6″ × 8″ (15cm × 20.5cm) piece of polyester batting

1 skein each of white, black, light gray and dark gray embroidery floss

2 oz (56g) of heavy bouclé yarn for hair

6″ × 11¼″ (15cm × 28.5cm) piece of cardboard for making hair

1½ lbs (680g) of polyester fiberfill

carpet thread

glue

pair of false eyelashes

fine-tip black permanent marker

powdered blusher

Dress and panties

⅞ yd (0.80m) of 45″ (115cm) fabric

3 yds (2.75m) of ⅜″ (10mm) ribbon

4½ yds (4.15m) of ¾″ (20mm) flat lace

1½ yds (1.40m) of ⅜″ (10mm) elastic

Shoes

12″ × 12″ (30.5cm × 30.5cm) remnant of felt

Finished size: approximately 20″ (51cm)

6″ × 12″ (15cm × 28.5cm) piece of fusible web

⅛ yd (0.15m) of ½″ (13mm) elastic

two ¼″ (6mm) buttons

Pattern pieces are found on pp. 147–152.

CUTTING INFORMATION

Doll body fabric: 1 back; 1 front; 4 arms; 4 legs; 2 foot soles; 2 head sides; 1 rectangle 3½″ × 9⅝″ (9cm × 24.4cm) for head back

Face fabric: 1 face. *Note:* If necessary, dye face fabric to match body fabric before cutting. To do this, soak fabric in hot tea until it is the desired shade, keeping in mind that fabric looks darker when it's wet. Rinse thoroughly with cold water and let dry. If using pantyhose, cut piece from upper leg; dyeing is not necessary.

Batting: 1 face

Dress/panties fabric: 2 dress front/backs; 2 sleeves; 2 panties

Shoe fabric: Cut felt remnant in half, then fuse halves together with fusible web, following manufacturer's directions. Cut pieces as follows from fused fabric: 2 fronts; 2 backs; 2 soles; 2 straps

HOW-TO

Trace pattern pieces (enlarge if necessary) and transfer all pattern markings. All seam allowances are ¼″ (6mm).

Doll

Note: *Press all seams to one side.*

1 With right sides together, pin each pair of arms together; stitch, leaving the straight edge open. Clip (see under CORNERS AND CURVES) inner curves and corners (A). Turn right side out. Stuff the hand only (see under STUFFING), using a small amount of fiberfill. Stitch along the finger stitching lines, through all layers. Using double thread, sew a running stitch (see under HAND SEWING) along the wrist stitching line, pulling up the thread to gather slightly; tie thread ends and cut. Stuff the arm firmly to within ½″ (13mm) of the open edges. Baste the raw edges together ¼″ (6mm) from the opening.

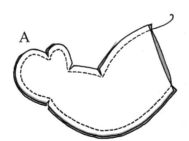

A

2 Stitch the darts on the body front and press them toward the center. Pin the arms to the body front between large ● and small ●; baste (B).

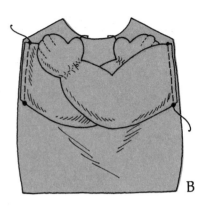

B

3 Stitch the darts on the body back and press toward center. With right sides together, fold the back along the foldline. Then stitch along the seamline and the stitching line, ending at small ●'s. (C).

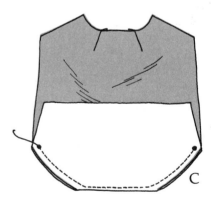

C

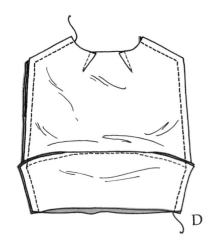

D

4 With right sides together, stitch the body back to the front, leaving the neck and lower edges open (D). Turn the body right side out. On the outside, edgestitch (see under MACHINE STITCHING) the body close to the body/arm seams, through all layers (E).

5 Leaving both top and bottom edges open, stitch the legs and clip as for arms. Pin soles to legs as for Dress Me Jennifer and Friend, Step 8, p. 52, and stitch. Turn legs right side out. Stuff the legs firmly to within ½" (13mm) of top edge, adding a compact ball of stuffing to create a plump knee. Fold the top of the leg in half, bringing the front and back seams together; baste ¼" (6mm) from opening (F).

6 Using double thread, take four ½" (13mm) long stitches through each foot to form toes; pull the end stitch tighter than the others to create little toe (G).

7 With toes facing the body, pin the top edge of the legs to the lower edge of the body front, keeping the back edge of the body free; stitch (H). Press the seams toward the body. Turn under the lower edge of body back along the seamline. Pin this edge over the leg/body front seam and slipstitch (see under HAND SEWING) in place. Edgestitch body near seam, as for arms. Stuff the body firmly, up to the neck seamline.

8 In the cardboard, cut a lengthwise-centered notch ½" (13mm) wide and 9¼" (23.5cm) long. Wind yarn closely around the cardboard template as shown, filling it up completely. Using thread to match yarn, machine-stitch through the center of the template (I). Slip the row of curls off the template and set aside. Make two more rows of curls in the same way.

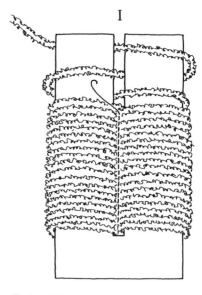

I

Easestitch (see under MACHINE STITCHING) along the seamline of each long edge of the head back. Press the head back in half lengthwise, then press in half lengthwise again. Open out. Pressed creases are the placement lines for the hair.

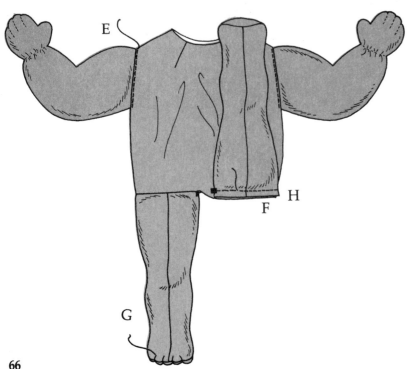

E

H

F

G

To apply yarn hair, pin curls to the head back piece, centering each row over a placement line; stitch over the previous stitching (J). For each head side, make a row of curls as long as each placement line. Starting at the bottom, apply rows of curls as for the head back (K). Make one more full-length row of curls for use around face and set aside.

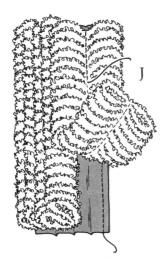

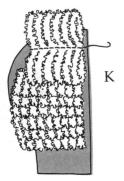

9 With right sides together, pin the head back to head sides, easing the back to fit. Keeping the hair free, stitch both seams (L).

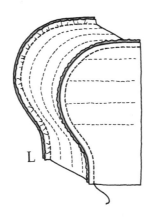

10 Trim the batting along the face seamline and lower stitching line to form an oval. Pin batting to wrong side of face and catchstitch (see under HAND SEWING) in place. Make two rows of gathering stitches (see under GATHERING) at the lower edge of the face between small ●'s. With right sides together, stitch the face to the head back/sides, keeping the hair free (M). Turn the head right side out. Stuff firmly.

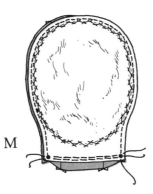

11 To form the nose, using double thread, bring the needle up from inside of head at nose stitching line. Make a running stitch on the stitching line; then pull up the thread, keeping some batting in the nose. Fasten thread securely.

Work the eyelids in the same way, but do not pull thread to gather. Join the stitching lines by making back and forth running stitches just above and below first stitching lines; pull up the thread slightly as you sew, keeping some batting in the eyelids (N).

Using two strands of embroidery floss, embroider the eyes as follows: with dark gray, work stem stitch (see under EMBROIDERY) along the stitching lines for eyes. Then fill in eye with satin stitch, using dark gray for upper half and light gray for lower half; for eye's center, work black padded satin stitch in the opposite direction, adding white satin-stitch highlights (O). Using black marker, outline lower half of eye just below the stitching (P).

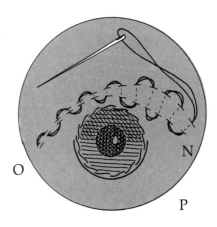

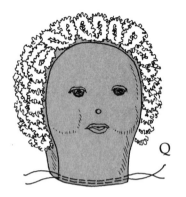

To make cheeks, insert compact balls of fiberfill into cheek areas. Make mouth in same way as eyelids (Q).

Trim the eyelashes and glue (see under ADHESIVES) in place. To form the chin, use carpet thread to make two rows of running stitches along lower stitching lines. Pull threads so stitching measures about 2½" (6.5mm); fasten securely. Add more stuffing to fill out chin. Redden cheeks with blusher (R).

12 On the head, turn the seam allowance under at the lower edge. Position the head over the neck opening on body, with the turned edge ¼" from raw edge and small ●●'s at shoulders. Adjust the gathers. Using double thread and small, closely spaced stitches, slipstitch the head to the body (S). Using double thread and backstitch, sew the reserved row of curls around the face, over face/side seam (T).

Dress and Panties

Note: *Press all seams open.*

1 Press the lower edge of each sleeve under ¼" (6mm). Cut the lace to fit. On the right side, lap the lace over the pressed edge. After pinning it in place, stitch the lace close to the straight edge (A).

Apply a 6" (15cm) length of ⅜" (10mm) elastic (see under ELASTIC)

directly to the wrong side of each sleeve, placing one edge along the pressed-under raw edge of the sleeve and covering the hem allowance (B).

2 With right sides together, stitch sleeves to front and back sections, leaving one seam open (C). Finish

the neck edge with lace and a 12″ (30.5cm) length of elastic as for sleeves. Stitch the remaining seam. Stitch one side/sleeve seam (D).

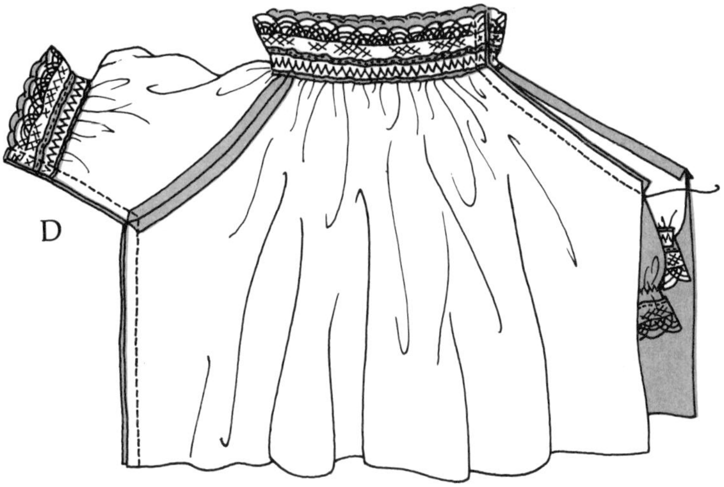

3 On the right side, form a tuck near the lower edge of the dress by bringing lines of small ●'s together; stitch, then press the tuck toward the lower edge. Pin the upper edge of the lace, cut to fit, along the placement line; stitch. Pin ribbon, cut to fit, just above the lace; edgestitch both long edges in place. Narrow-hem the lower edge of the dress (see under HEMS). Apply another length of lace to the lower edge of the dress, keeping the tuck free (E). Stitch the remaining side/sleeve seam. Turn the dress right side out.

4 Cut ribbon 30″ (76cm) long, trimming ends diagonally. Tack (see under HAND SEWING) the center of the ribbon to the center back of the neck edge (F). When the doll is dressed, bring the ribbon ends around to the front and tie in a bow.

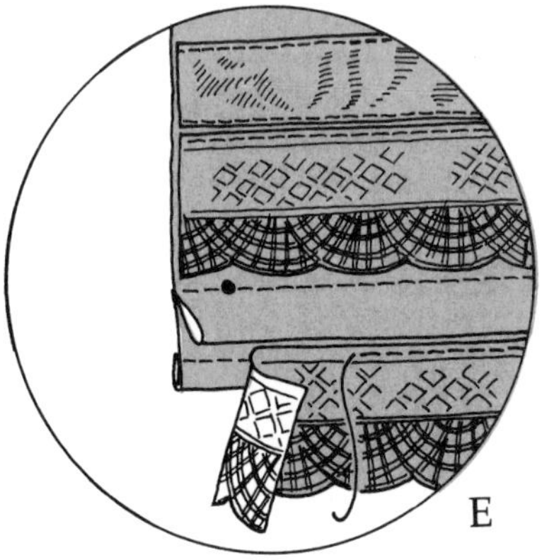

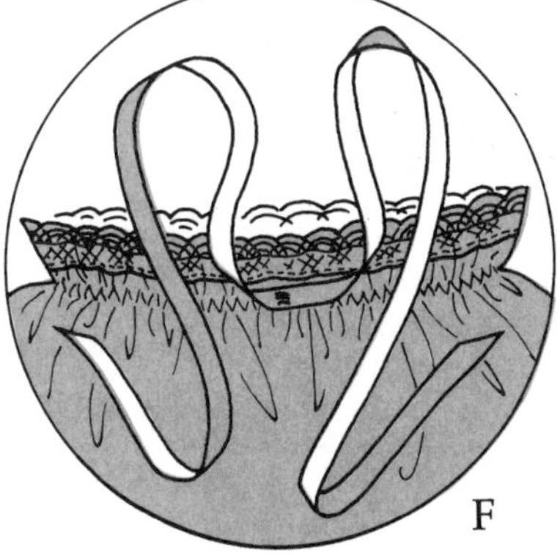

5 Finish the lower edges of the panties as for dress sleeves, using 6″ (15cm) lengths of elastic. With right sides together, stitch the center front and center back seams of the panties (G).

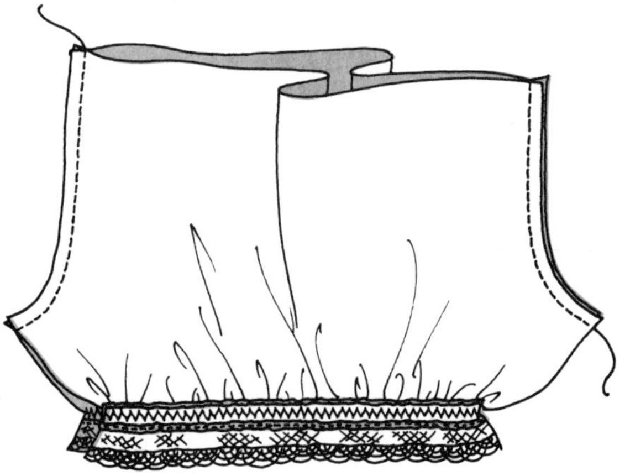

6 Omitting lace, finish the upper edge of the panties as for the dress neckline, beginning and ending at center back; use a 12" (30.5cm) length of elastic, lapping the ends ¼" (6mm) and stitching securely. Stitch the inner leg seams; clip the inner curves (H). Turn the panties right side out. For each panty leg, cut ribbon 17½" (44.5cm) long. Trim ends diagonally and tack ribbon to center back. Bring the ribbon ends to the front and tie in a bow.

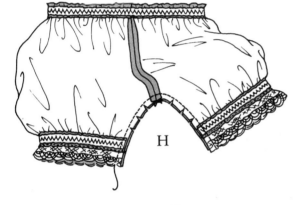

H

Shoes

1 On each front and back, edge-stitch the edge without symbols (A).

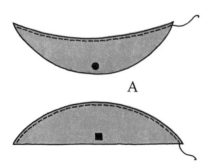

A

2 With right sides together and matching symbols, stitch the back to the sole. Stitch the front to the sole, lapping the ends over the back (B).

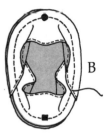

B

3 Cut two pieces of ½" (13mm) elastic each 1" (25mm) long. Stitch one end of elastic to the straight end of the strap, lapping edges ¼" (6mm). Pin the free end of elastic to the sole over the back, next to the front; stitch in place (C). Trim the elastic end to the shape of the sole. Be sure to make a left and right shoe by stitching elastic to the opposite sides of the shoes. Turn shoes right side out.

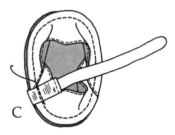

C

4 Tack the strap to shoe back on the inside. Sew the curved end of the strap to outside of back near the front. Sew a button to the curved end of the strap (D).

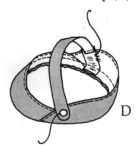

D

Sally Hug-Me-Tight

• *Whoever said you can never have too many dolls certainly knew what she was talking about. Who could resist adding this appealing doll to a growing collection? We've named her Sally Hug-Me-Tight, and the reason should be obvious. Not only does Sally have lots of old-fashioned charm, but she's quite easy to make. So is her dress, which is cut in one piece. And though you can't see them here, she's got matching panties, too. For Sally's body, you can use all-cotton muslin or any medium-weight cotton blend in pale pink, peach or off-white. For her dress, pick your favorite calico or challis print.* •

Finished size: approximately 18½" (47cm)

MATERIALS NEEDED

Doll

⅝ yd (0.60m) of 35" or 45" (90cm or 115cm) fabric

4 oz (115g) of 2-ply yarn for hair

1 skein of pink embroidery floss for nose and 1 skein to match hair

7" × 14" (18cm × 35.5cm) piece of cardboard for making hair

transparent tape

1½ lbs (680g) of polyester fiberfill

1 yd (1.00m) of ¼" (6mm) satin ribbon

carpet thread

glue

rubber bands

powdered blusher

Dress and panties

⅞ yd (0.80m) of 35" or 45" (90cm or 115cm) fabric

1¼ yds (1.20m) of ¼" (6mm) elastic

1½ yds (1.40m) of ⅜" (10mm) flat lace edging

Pattern pieces are found on pp. 163–165.

CUTTING INFORMATION

Doll fabric: 1 body front; 1 body back; 1 bottom; 4 arms; 4 legs

Dress/panties fabric: 1 dress front/back; 2 panties; two 4" × 19" (10cm × 48cm) crosswise strips for ruffles

HOW-TO

Trace pattern pieces (enlarge if necessary) and transfer all pattern markings. All seam allowances are ¼" (6mm). Press seams open unless otherwise instructed.

Note: *For tips on using yarn for doll's hair, see* Dress Me Jennifer and Friend, *pp. 53–54.*

Doll

1 With right sides together, pin the bottom to the back at the lower edge and stitch the seam (A). Press the seam toward the back.

2 With right sides together, fold the front and back in half lengthwise. Press the head sections only as far as the small ●'s (B). Open each flat. These creases serve as placement lines for hair.

3 Following the directions in Dress Me Jennifer, step 14, p. 53, make one 5" (12.5cm) and one 1¼" (32mm) width of yarn hair with these changes: wind the yarn around the *long* side of the cardboard and, after taping and cutting, *open out* the yarn to a single thickness and stitch through the center of the tape.

4 Place the stitching on the narrower yarn section over the crease line on the right side of the body front; stitch through the yarn and the head, over the previous stitching (C).

Apply the other yarn section to the head back in the same way.

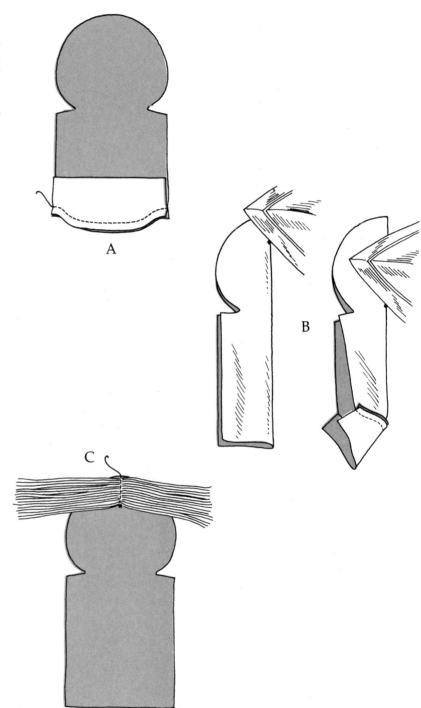

5 With right sides together, pin each pair of arms and legs together; stitch the seam, leaving the top edges open (D). Turn the arms and legs right side out.

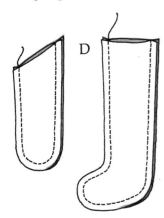

6 Stuff both arms and legs with fiberfill (see under STUFFING), inserting small amounts at a time. While stuffing, push seam allowances to one side. Stuff firmly, to within ¾″ (20mm) of the top edge.

Bring the top edges of the arms together with seams at the sides (E), and stitch together ¼″ (6mm) from raw edges. Repeat with legs, but bring seams together at the center of the top edges (F).

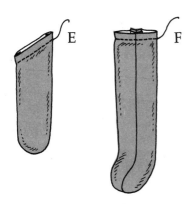

7 Pin the arms to front, matching symbols. Be sure to keep the hair free by guiding it toward the center of the body, away from the seam allowances. Stitch the arms in place (G).

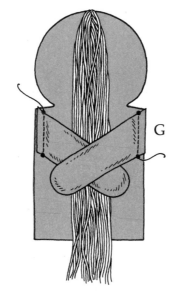

8 With right sides together, pin the front to the back, matching raw edges and symbols and again keeping hair free. Stitch, leaving the bottom edge open and pivoting at small ●'s at the neck corners (H). Reinforce (see under MACHINE STITCHING) the neck corners by stitching again over the first stitching. Clip diagonally to small ●'s (I).

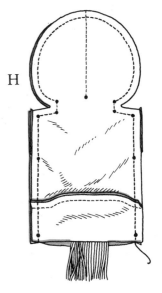

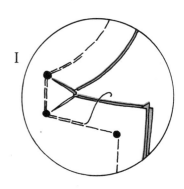

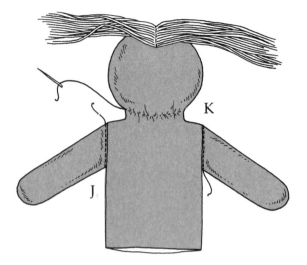

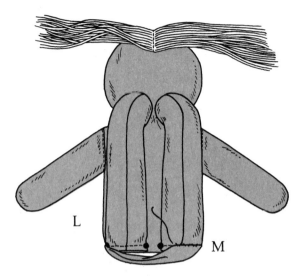

9 Turn the body right side out. Using straight or zigzag stitching, stitch over the arm/body seams, through all layers (J).

10 Stuff the head firmly through the bottom opening, creating a nice, round shape. When the head is nearly complete, use carpet thread in a sewing needle to make a line of running stitches (see under HAND SEWING) along the stitching line on the front. Pull the thread taut to form a chin (K), and fasten ends securely with a square knot. Insert additional stuffing to round out the chin and back of head.

11 Pin the legs to the body front, with toes facing the body and matching large ●'s. Stitch, keeping the lower back edge free (L). Finish stuffing the body. Turn under the raw edge at the lower back and slipstitch (see under HAND SEWING) in place over the leg/body seam (M).

12 To make facial features, follow Darlin' Debbie, step 15, p. 63. Apply powdered blusher to cheeks.

13 Bring the yarn hair to the front of the head next to the face. Divide each side into three parts and braid, securing the ends with rubber bands. Trim the ends even. To keep the hair in place, sew it to the side of the head, catching the braid, head and some of the stuffing (N). Cut the ribbon in half and tie a bow around each braid (O).

Dress

1 Finish the edges of the sleeves with lace edging (see under TRIMS). Cut 5″ (12.5cm) of elastic for each sleeve. Apply elastic directly to the wrong side of each sleeve, ½″ (13mm) from pressed edge (see under ELASTIC).

2 Narrow-hem (see under HEMS) one long edge of each ruffle. Make two rows of gathering stitches (see under GATHERING) at the other long edge. With right sides together, pin the gathered edge of one ruffle to each lower edge of the dress (A). Adjust the gathers evenly and stitch the seam (B). Press the seams toward the dress.

3 Staystitch (see under MACHINE STITCHING) the neck edge of the dress ⅜″ (10mm) from edge. Press the neck edge under ⅜″ (10mm), clipping as needed (C). Cut lace ½″ (13mm) longer than the measurement of the neck edge. Then finish the neck edge with lace, turning under and lapping the end ¼″ (6mm) over start.

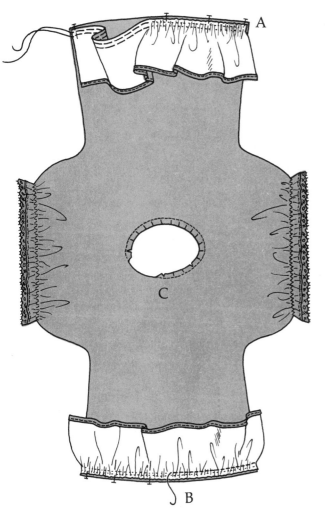

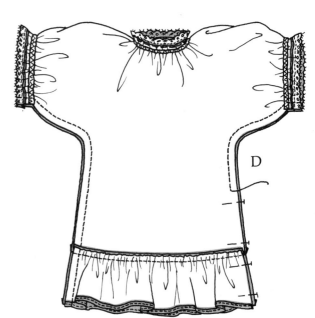

Panties

1 Finish the lower edge of each panty section with lace and elastic as for Mary Jane Dress and Panties, step 1, p. 68.

2 With right sides together, stitch the center front and center back seams.

3 With right sides together, stitch inner leg seam, including lace.

4 At top edge, make a casing, pressing under ¼″ (6mm), then ½″ (13mm) (see under CASINGS). Insert a 12½″ (32cm) piece of elastic in the casing.

4 Cut elastic 10½″ (26.6cm) long. Lap the ends ½″ (6mm) and stitch to form a ring. Divide into quarters with pins. Divide the neck edge of the dress into 4 equal sections and mark with pins. Matching markings, apply elastic directly to the wrong side of the dress, ⅛″ (3mm) from neck edge.

5 With right sides together, pin and stitch each side and underarm of dress in one continuous seam (D). Clip curves at underarms.

6 Turn the dress right side out. Topstitch (see under MACHINE STITCHING) ¼″ (6mm) above dress/ruffle seam, through all layers (E).

Circus Gertie

• *Button her, zip her, snap her, buckle her, lace her, tie her . . . in short, Gertie can virtually provide a three-ring circus! Preschoolers everywhere will be encouraged by Gertie's cheerful grin as their little fingers practice—and learn— important skills.* •

Finished size: approximately 25" (63.5cm)

MATERIALS NEEDED

Doll

- ¾ yd (0.70m) of 45" (115 cm) fabric for body
- 3" × 4" (7.5cm × 10cm) black felt remnant for eyes and hand trim
- 3" × 3½" (7.5cm × 9cm) red felt remnant for nose and mouth
- 2" × 3½" (5cm × 9cm) pink felt remnant for cheeks
- 2 oz (56g) of 4-ply yarn for hair
- 13" × 15" (33cm × 38cm) piece of cardboard for making hair
- 20" (51cm) piece of seam binding in color to match hair
- 1 skein of black embroidery floss
- 1¼ lbs (570g) of polyester fiberfill
- 1 yd (1.00m) of ⅜" (10mm) ribbon
- glue
- rubber bands

Jumpsuit

- ⅝ yd of 45" (115cm) fabric for front, back and straps
- ⅜ yd (0.40m) of contrasting 45" (115cm) fabric for bodice and sleeves
- ¼ yd (0.25m) of ½" (13mm) single-fold bias tape
- ¾ yd (0.70m) of ¼" (6mm) elastic
- 9" (23cm) zipper
- ¾ yd (0.70m) of 1½" (38mm) grosgrain ribbon
- size 2/0 snap fastener
- two 1⅛" (28mm) overall fasteners
- ⅝" (15mm) button
- 6" × 6" (15cm × 15cm) felt remnant for flowers

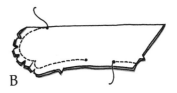

Collar and hat

⅜ yd (0.40m) of 45" (115cm) fabric

¾ yd (0.70m) of fusible interfacing

Shoes

13" × 15" (33cm × 38cm) felt remnant

⅜ yd (0.40m) of ¼" (6mm) elastic

sixteen ¼" (6mm) metal eyelets

1 pair of 24" (61cm) shoelaces

Pattern pieces are found on pp. 186–191.

CUTTING INFORMATION

Doll fabric: 4 heads; 4 bodies; 2 arms; 4 legs

Black felt: 2 eyes; 6 hand trims

Red felt: 1 mouth; 1 nose

Pink felt: 2 cheeks

Jumpsuit fabric: 2 lower fronts: 2 backs; two 3" × 6½" (7.5cm × 16.5cm) straps

Contrasting fabric: 2 upper fronts; 2 sleeves

Collar and hat fabric: 2 collars; 4 crowns; 2 brims

Shoe felt: 4 shoes

Flower felt: 4 flowers

Interfacing: 4 hat crowns; 1 hat brim; 1 collar; 4 shoes; 2 flowers

HOW-TO

Trace pattern pieces (enlarge if necessary) and transfer all pattern markings. All seam allowances are ⅜" (10mm). Press seams open unless otherwise instructed.

Note: *For tips on using yarn for hair, see* Dress Me Jennifer and Friend, *pp. 53–54.*

Doll

1 With right sides together, pin the double-notched (center) edges of two head pieces together; stitch to form the head front. For the head back, pin and stitch the remaining head pieces along the center seam, leaving open below large ●. With right sides together, pin the head back to the head front and stitch, leaving the lower edge open (A). Clip and notch curves (see under CORNERS AND CURVES) as needed. Press seams open as far as possible. Turn the head right side out.

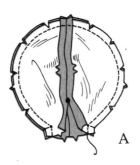

2 With right sides together, fold each arm along the foldline, matching the raw edges. Stitch, leaving openings along the upper edge and between small ●'s. Clip corners and curves (B). Turn the arms right side out and baste the upper raw edges together.

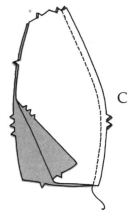

3 With right sides together, pin two legs together and stitch as you did the arms, leaving openings along the upper edge and between small ●'s; clip curves. Repeat with the remaining legs. Turn the legs right side out and baste the upper edges together as you did the arms.

4 For body front, pin the center edges of two body pieces and stitch with right sides together (C). For body back, repeat with remaining body pieces, leaving an opening above large ●. Staystitch (see under MACHINE STITCHING) the neck edge of the front and back ¼" (6mm) from the raw edge.

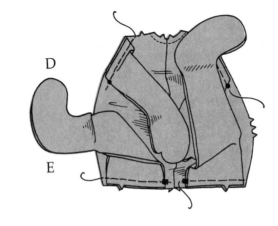

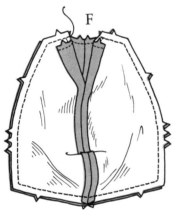

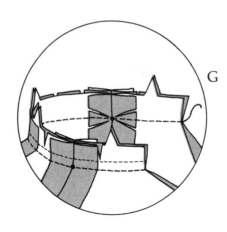

5 With thumbs facing down, pin the arms to the right side of the body front, matching large ●'s and notches; baste (D). Pin the legs to the lower edge of the body front, matching ■'s and notches; then baste (E).

6 With right sides together, pin the body back to the body front, enclosing the arms and legs. Stitch, leaving the curved neck edge open and being careful not to catch the hands and feet (F).

7 With right sides together, pin head to body along the neck edges, matching the seams and small ●'s, and clipping as needed. Stitch the neck seam (G). Turn body right side out. Stuff (see under STUFFING) the head, body, arms and legs firmly. Turn all opening edges to the inside and slipstitch (see under HAND SEWING) closed.

8 Cut the cardboard into 2 pieces, one 3″ × 9″ (7.5cm × 23cm) and one 8⅛″ × 15″ (20.7cm × 38cm). To make yarn hair, follow Dress Me Jennifer, steps 14 to 17, pp. 53–54. Using the smaller cardboard, make 9″ (23cm) wide bangs as for Jennifer, step 14. Then sew to the head over the front/back seam between small ●'s as for Jennifer, step 15, omitting reference to gluing.

9 Using the remaining yarn and the larger cardboard, wind yarn as for Jennifer, step 16, *except* fill up the cardboard completely instead of leaving a space, and do not fold the yarn in half after attaching it to the seam binding. Sew this section of hair to the head back along the center back seam between small ●'s as for the narrower section of hair in Jennifer, step 17. Smooth out the hair on the head back and bring some of the back hair over the head front to hide the base of the bangs; glue in place (H). Divide the hair on each side of the head into 3 parts and braid (I), securing the ends with rubber bands. Trim ends even and trim bangs as desired. Cut the ⅜" (10mm) wide ribbon in half and tie bows around the braids (J).

10 Glue (see under ADHESIVES) the eyes, nose and cheeks to the head front along placement lines. Embroider the mouth line in stem stitch (see under EMBROIDERY), using 2 strands of floss. Then glue the mouth in place (K). Glue the hand trims in place along the placement lines on the arms (L). *Note: If desired for greater security, pin features in place, then whipstitch* (see under HAND SEWING).

Jumpsuit

1 On each lower front, staystitch ¼" (6mm) from the upper edge. Then turn the upper edge under along the foldline, clipping to the staystitching as needed and folding in the extra fullness at the corner; press (A).

2 Lap the lower front over the lower edge of the upper front, matching the pressed edge to the placement line. Pin in place; then stitch close to the pressed edge (B). To reinforce (see under MACHINE STITCHING) the inner corner (bottom of zipper opening) on the front, stitch around the corner along the seamline, using small machine stitches. Then clip diagonally into the corner (C).

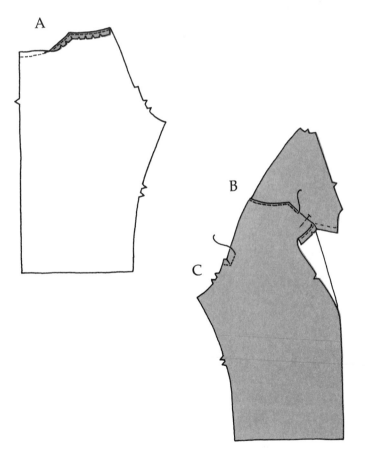

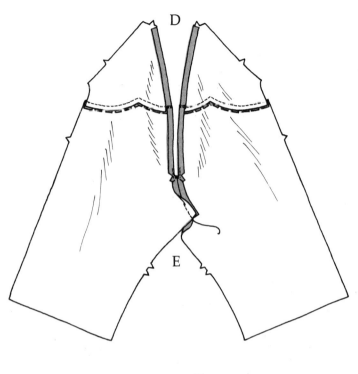

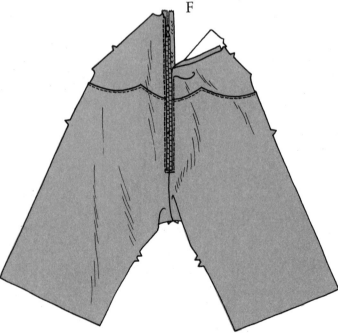

3 With right sides together, pin and stitch the fronts as far as large ● (D). Press the seam open and press the bottom of the zipper opening down; then press the center front edges above the large ● to the wrong side along the seamline (E). Turn the front right side up.

4 Center the closed zipper, face up, under the pressed front opening edges, placing the pull tab ⅛" (3mm) below the neck seamline. Pin or tape the zipper in place; then, using a zipper foot, edge-stitch (see under MACHINE STITCH-ING) close to the pressed edges (F). With right sides together, pin and stitch the center back seam; press open.

5 Finish the lower edge of the sleeves with an ⅛" (3mm) narrow hem (see under HEMS). Cut two 4¾" (12cm) pieces of elastic and apply them directly (see under ELASTIC) to the wrong sides of the sleeves along the placement line.

With right sides together, pin the sleeves to the armhole edges of the jumpsuit front and back, matching notches; stitch, then stitch again over the first stitching and press open (G). Staystitch around the neckline as you did on the doll body (H).

6 Trim away the seam allowance of the collar interfacing. Following the manufacturer's instructions, fuse the interfacing to the wrong side of one collar piece. With right sides together, pin the interfaced collar to the remaining collar piece and stitch around the outer curved edges, leaving the notched edge open (I). Trim and notch the seam allowances (J), and turn the collar right side out. Press the collar, then baste the raw edges together.

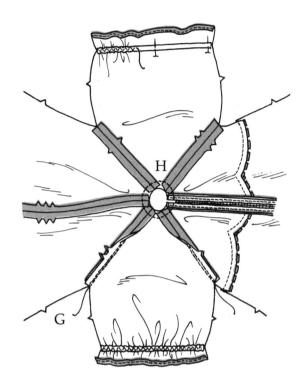

7 With the interfaced side up, pin the collar to the jumpsuit neck edge, matching notches, centers and small ●'s, and clipping the neck edge as needed. Baste the collar in place (K). Using single-fold bias tape as a facing (see under BIAS TAPE), apply the collar to the neck edge.

8 With right sides together, pin and stitch the inner leg seams (L). Finish the lower edges of the legs and apply a 6½" (16.5cm) piece of elastic to each leg as you did on the sleeves.

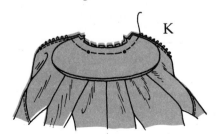

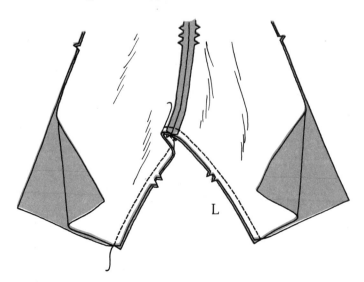

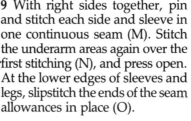

9 With right sides together, pin and stitch each side and sleeve in one continuous seam (M). Stitch the underarm areas again over the first stitching (N), and press open. At the lower edges of sleeves and legs, slipstitch the ends of the seam allowances in place (O).

10 With right sides together, fold each strap in half lengthwise. Stitch along one short end and the long edge. Trim seam allowances and corners and turn the straps right side out. Turn the raw ends in along the seamline, then press the straps. Baste the pressed edges together. Lift the jumpsuit collar and pin the basted ends of the straps to the sleeves along placement lines; stitch in place (P). Turn the collar down over the straps.

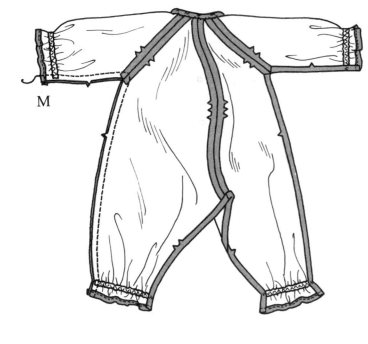

M

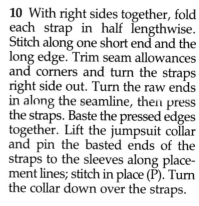

P

11 Sew the overall fastener buttons to the jumpsuit front at the markings. Following the manufacturer's instructions, insert the free end of each strap into a fastener, adjust to fit, and then stitch the strap end in place through all layers, using a zipper foot (Q).

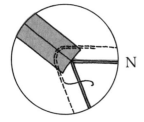

N

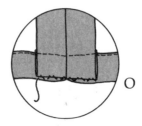

O

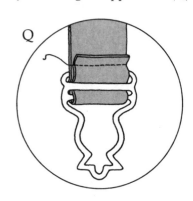

Q

Button the fasteners and sew the remaining button to the left strap, about 1" (25mm) above the top of the fastener (R).

12 Trim the seam allowances of the flower interfacing and fuse to the wrong sides of two felt flowers. With wrong sides together, pin corresponding flowers to the interfaced ones, matching edges and markings. Stitch close to edges. Make a buttonhole (see under FASTENERS) in one flower (S), then button it onto the left strap (T).

Sew the socket half of the snap to the other flower and the ball half to the right front leg of the jumpsuit at marking; snap the flower in place.

13 Cut the 1½" (38mm) ribbon in half. Press one end of each half under ¼" (6mm). Gather (see under GATHERING) the pressed edge tightly and fasten thread securely. Pin the gathered ends of the ribbon to the upper fronts at ■'s under the collar; tack (see under HAND SEWING) in place securely (U). Tie the ribbon in a bow and trim the ends diagonally.

Shoes

1 Trim the interfacing seam allowances and fuse to the wrong side of each shoe piece. Following the manufacturer's instructions, apply four eyelets to each shoe piece at the markings. With right sides together, pin the shoes together in pairs. Stitch, leaving top edges open (A). Trim the seam allowances and notch and clip the curves and corners (B). Turn the shoes right side out and press.

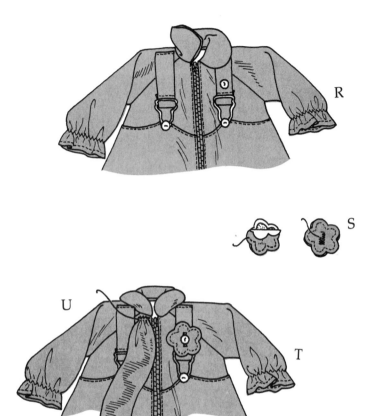

2 To form a casing on each shoe, turn the upper edge to the inside along the foldline, then stitch close to raw edge, leaving an opening to insert the elastic. Cut two 5¼" (13.3cm) pieces of elastic and insert one into each casing; finish ends (see under ELASTIC).

3 Insert shoelaces through eyelets, with ends even at top eyelets. Tie laces in a bow (C).

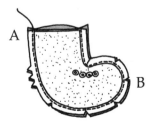

Hat

1 Interface each crown piece as you did the collar. With right sides together, pin and stitch two crown pieces along the double-notched edges. Repeat with the remaining crown pieces. Then stitch the crowns together along the center front and center back (A).

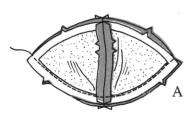

2 Trimming seam allowances and the area between the center front V-shaped stitching lines, interface one brim as you did the other pieces. With right sides together, pin and stitch the center back seam of the interfaced brim (B).

3 On the notched edge of the interfaced brim, turn the seam allowance to the wrong side, clipping as needed, and press in place (C).

4 On the other brim, staystitch ¼" (6mm) from the notched edge. Then stitch the center back seam. With right sides together, pin the brims along the unnotched edges and stitch along the seamline and the center front stitching lines, leaving the edge with notches open (D).

Slash the center front between the stitching lines close to the point of the V-shape, then trim close to the stitching (E). Turn the brim right side out and press.

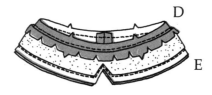

5 With right sides together, pin the notched edge of the uninterfaced brim to the lower edge of the crown, matching centers and notches, placing small ●●'s at side seams and clipping the brim as needed. Stitch, being careful to keep the pressed edge of the brim free (F). Trim and clip the seam; then press the seam toward the brim.

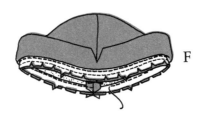

6 With the brim turned down, pin the pressed edge of the brim over the brim/crown seam; edgestitch in place (G). Then edgestitch the other edge of the brim (H). Turn the hat right side out. Place the hat on the doll's head and tack in place at side seams, if desired.

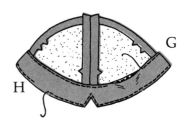

Crackers the Clown

• *Hurry, hurry, hurry—the circus is in town! And the main attraction is (you guessed it) Crackers the Clown. This soft, floppy doll is a riot of color in his removable jumpsuit, collar and hat. He'll be prepared for rough-and-tumble play if you use sturdy, washable cotton or cotton-blend fabrics for both body and clothes. Small-scale prints and/or solids in bright, primary colors will add to his appeal.*•

Finished size: approximately 19" (48cm)

MATERIALS NEEDED

Clown

⅝ yd (0.60m) of 45" (115cm) fabric for head, arms and body

10" × 10" (25.5cm × 25.5cm) remnants of two contrasting colors for legs

1 skein each of blue, green, red and white embroidery floss

3½ oz (100g) skein of bulky acrylic rug yarn for hair

4" × 14" (10cm × 35.5cm) piece of cardboard for making hair

1 lb (450g) of polyester fiberfill

1 oz (28g) of red 4-ply acrylic yarn for nose pompon

1" × 3" (25mm × 7.5cm) piece of cardboard for making pompon

Jumpsuit, hat and collar

⅝ yd (0.60m) of 45" (115cm) print or solid fabric for jumpsuit and hat

⅝ yd (0.60m) of 45" (115cm) contrasting print or solid fabric for jumpsuit and hat

3" × 5" (7.5cm × 12.5cm) contrasting remnant for patches

½ yd (0.50m) of 45" fabric for collar

4-ply acrylic yarn: 1 oz (28g) of yellow and 2 oz (56g) of blue for pompons

2" × 3" (5cm × 7.5cm) piece of cardboard for making pompons

1 package each of red, yellow, blue and green ¼" (6mm) double-fold bias tape

1½ yds (1.40m) of ¼" (6mm) elastic

2 hooks and eyes

Pattern pieces are found on pp. 197–200.

CUTTING INFORMATION

Clown fabric: 2 head fronts; 2 head backs; 1 body front; 1 body back; 4 arms

Clown remnants: 2 legs from each

Jumpsuit/hat fabric: 1 front, 1 back and 2 hats

Contrasting jumpsuit/hat fabric: 1 front, 1 back and 2 hats

Patch remnant: two 1⅝" × 2" (4cm × 5cm) patches

Collar fabric: two 6" × 43½" (15cm × 110.5cm) collars

HOW-TO

Trace pattern pieces (enlarge if necessary) and transfer all pattern markings. All seam allowances are ¼" (6mm). Press seams open unless otherwise instructed.

Clown

1 With right sides together, pin the head fronts together along the edges with the single notch and stitch the seam. Stitch the triple-notched edges of the head back the same way. With right sides together, pin the head front to the head back. Matching the double notches, stitch, leaving the lower (neck) edge open (A). Turn the head right side out.

2 Staystitch (see under MACHINE STITCHING) the lower edges of the body front and body back (B). Then stitch the darts on the body back and press them open (C).

3 With right sides together, pin the body front to the body back at the shoulders; stitch, easing the back to fit and ending at large ●'s (D). Do not turn.

4 With right sides together, insert the head into the body at the neck opening. Matching the head side seams to the body shoulder seams, pin the head in place, then stitch (E).

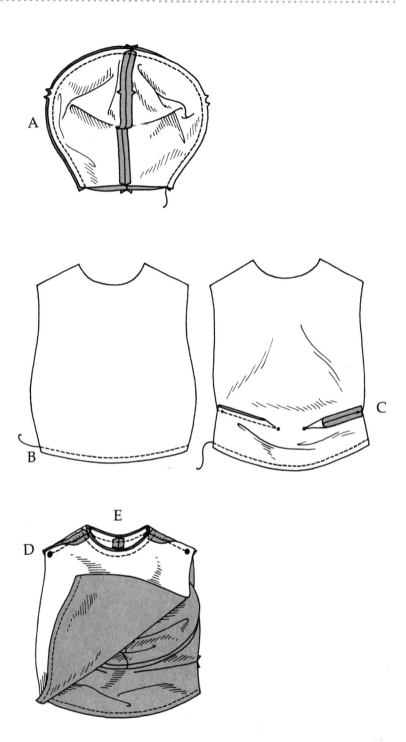

5 With right sides together, pin the arms together in pairs and stitch, leaving the upper edge open. Clip the inside corners and curves (see under CORNERS AND CURVES) (F). Turn the arms right side out and stuff firmly (see under STUFFING) to within ½" (13mm) of the top. Baste the upper edges together ¼" (6mm) from the raw edge.

6 Pull the body back away from the front. With thumbs facing down, pin the arms to the body front only, between symbols, and baste (G). With right sides together and keeping the hands free, pin the body back to the front at the side edges, enclosing the arms; stitch, ending at ■'s (H). Turn the body and head right side out.

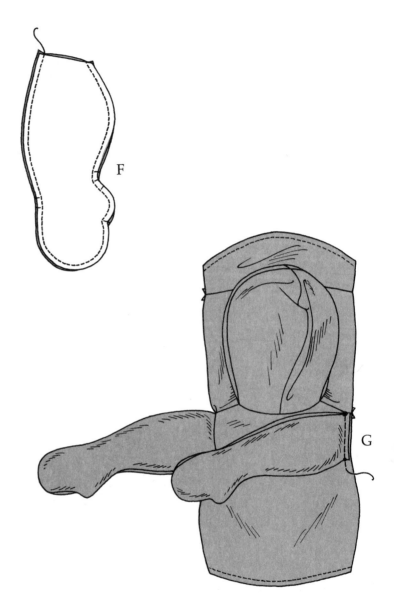

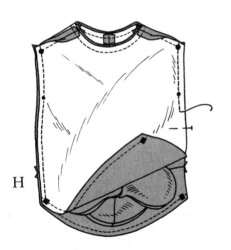

7 Pairing matching colors, stitch and stuff the legs as you did the arms, *except* after stuffing, bring the leg seams together at centers; then baste the upper edges together ¼" (6mm) from the raw edge. With toes facing the body front, pin the legs to the lower edge of the body front only, matching symbols; stitch the legs in place (I). Stuff the body and head firmly. On the back, turn the lower edge under and slipstitch (see under HAND SEWING) in place over the leg/front seam.

8 Using 3 strands of floss, embroider (see under EMBROIDERY) clown's face along placement lines as follows: eyes—green satin stitch; eyebrows—3 rows of blue stem stitch; lips—red satin stitch; mouth outline and opening—white stem stitch; cheeks—white satin stitch outlined with red stem stitch (J). Make a nose pompon using the red yarn (directions follow), and tack (see under HAND SEWING) in place at the marking (K).

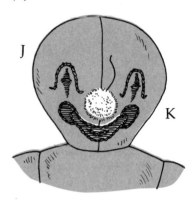

To make pompon, wind yarn around the 1" side of the small cardboard about 100 times. Slip a short length of yarn under the wrapped yarn at one edge and tie tightly. Cut the yarn at the opposite edge (L). Shake the pompon to fluff it, then trim all around to 1¼" (3.2cm) in diameter.

9 To make hair, use the rug yarn and see Mary Jane, step 8, for the method used. To prepare the cardboard template, cut a centered notch 1″ (25mm) wide and 12″ (30.5cm) long in the large cardboard. Make 2 rows of curls, one 8″ (20.5cm) long and the other 9″ (23cm) long. Center the curls over the placement lines, placing the longer row on the lower placement line. Using matching double thread and a backstitch (see under HAND SEWING), sew the curls in place along the previous stitching (M).

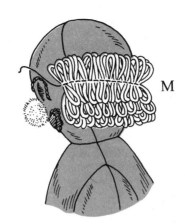

Jumpsuit

1 Matching placement lines, zig-zag a patch to the left front and the right back of the jumpsuit. With right sides together, pin the jumpsuit fronts together along the centers; stitch the seam (A). Pin the backs together in the same way, but stitch from the lower edge to the large ● only (B).

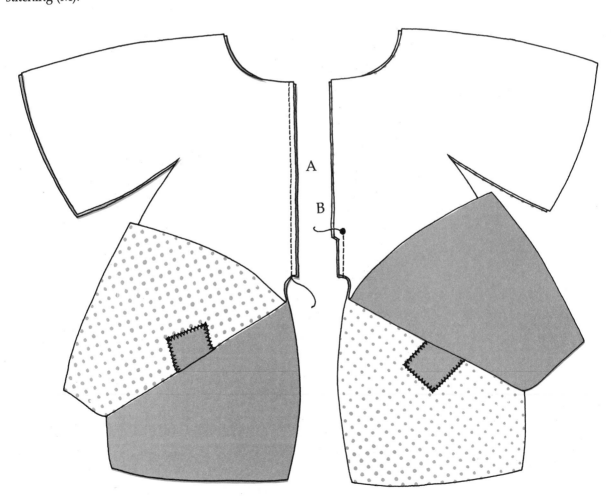

2 With right sides together, pin the back to the front along the shoulder/upper sleeve edges and stitch the seams.

3 Cut red bias tape to fit the jumpsuit neck edge. Open out all but one fold and press, then use this piece to make a casing (see CASINGS) along the neck edge. Insert a 7" (18cm) piece of elastic (see ELASTIC) in the casing (C).

4 Finish the back opening edges with a ⅛" (3mm) narrow hem (see under HEMS), squaring off stitching ¼" (6mm) below large ●.

5 Using green bias tape, bind (see under BIAS TAPE) the lower edges of the sleeves. Then apply 6" (15cm) lengths of elastic directly to each sleeve along the placement line (see under ELASTIC) (D).

6 With right sides together, pin the jumpsuit back to the front along the side/sleeve edges; stitch each side in one continuous seam (E). At the underarms, stitch over the previous stitching to reinforce, then clip into the corner (F).

7 Using blue bias tape and 7" (18cm) lengths of elastic, finish the

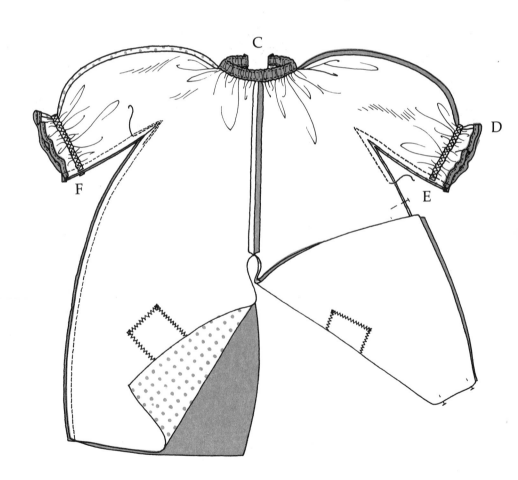

leg edges as you did the sleeves (G). With right sides together, pin and stitch the inner leg seams (H).

8 Using the 2″ × 3″ (5cm × 7.5cm) cardboard and 4-ply yarn, make one yellow and two blue pompons as in the clown, step 8, winding the yarn about 180 times around the 2″ (5cm) side of the cardboard. Trim the pompon to about 3½″ (9cm) in diameter. Tack (see under HAND SEWING) 2 pompons to the front of the jumpsuit, a yellow one at the upper small ● and a blue one at the lower small ●. Set aside the remaining pompon.

9 Sew a hook and eye (see under FASTENERS) to the back neck edges.

Hat

1 With right sides together, pin 2 contrasting hat pieces together along their straight edges and stitch, breaking stitching at large ● (A). Trim the seam (B). For the lining, repeat this step with the remaining hat pieces. Turn only the lining right side out.

2 With wrong sides together, insert the hat in the lining, match-

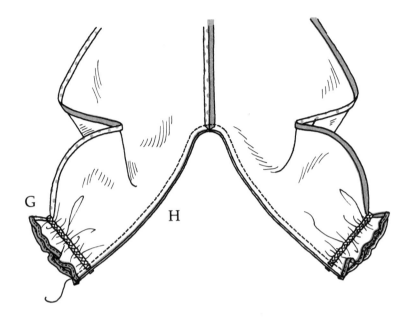

ing seams. Baste together along the lower edge (C). Do not turn.

3 Cut red bias tape ½″ longer than the lower edge of the hat. Press all but one fold open. Apply the bias tape as you would for a facing (see under BIAS TAPE) to the *lining* side of the lower edge. Begin and end at a seam, turning the

ends back ¼″ (6mm). Turn the hat right side out, bringing the tape to the right side of the hat. Pin the folded edge of the tape in place and edgestitch (see under MACHINE STITCHING) through all layers (D). Slipstitch the turned ends of the tape together. Sew the reserved blue pompon to the top of the hat at large ●.

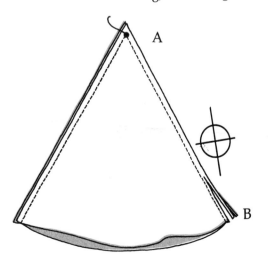

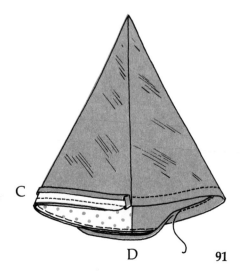

Collar

1 Bind the long edges of one collar piece, using blue bias tape at one edge and red at the other. Repeat for the other collar, using yellow and green (A). Finish each end of the collar with a ⅛" (3mm) narrow hem (B).

2 With wrong sides up and edges matching, baste the collars together lengthwise along the centers. Cut yellow bias tape ½" (13mm) longer than the collar, open out the center fold and press. Centering the tape over the basting on the wrong side, make a casing (see under CASINGS), turning the ends under ¼" (6mm) and stitching through all layers (C).

3 Cut a 15" (38cm) piece of elastic and insert it in the casing. Try the collar on the clown to adjust elastic length, then stitch ¼" (6mm) from each end to secure the elastic. Slipstitch the casing ends closed, then sew the hook and eye to casing ends.

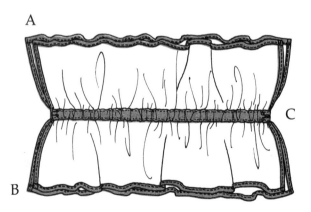

Tommy

• No collection of toys would be complete without a boy doll. This young fellow, named Tommy, sports a casual outfit—shirt, rolled-up jeans, zippered jacket and running shoes—all removable. Use a flesh-toned stretch knit fabric such as jersey or tricot for Tommy's body and a lightweight knit for his shirt. His pants and jacket can be made of sturdy woven fabrics such as denim, poplin, corduroy or lightweight gabardine. And for his shoes, pick a nonraveling suede- or leatherlike fabric, and some really colorful shoelaces! •

Finished size: approximately 24" (61cm)

MATERIALS NEEDED

Doll

⅝ yd (0.60m) of 45" (115 cm) or ½ yd (0.50m) of 72" (180cm) stretchable knit fabric for body

2" × 2" (5cm × 5cm) felt remnant for eyes

70 yd (67m) skein of rug yarn for hair

6½" × 10" (16.5 cm × 25.5.cm) piece of cardboard for making hair

⅜ yd (0.40m) of seam binding to match hair

1 skein each of red and black embroidery floss

¼ yd (0.25m) of fusible interfacing glue

1 lb (450g) of polyester fiberfill

1 pair of purchased baby socks (3-month size)

Shirt

⅜ yd (0.40m) of 45" (115cm) stretchable single knit or jersey

⅜ yd (0.40m) of ⅛" (3mm) elastic

3 hammer-on snaps

Pants

⅝ yd (0.60m) of 45" (115cm) denim, corduroy or poplin

½ yd (0.50m) of ¼" (6mm) elastic

1 hook and eye

Jacket

½ yd (0.50m) of 45" (115cm) denim, corduroy or poplin

3" × 3" (7.6cm × 7.6cm) remnant for appliqué

3 no-sew snaps

10" (25.5cm) separating zipper

Shoes

10" × 14" (25.5cm × 35.5cm) remnant of synthetic suede or leather

1 package double-fold bias tape

1 pair of 20" (51cm) shoelaces

small hole punch or awl

Pattern pieces are found on pp. 153–162.

CUTTING INFORMATION

Doll fabric: 1 face; 2 head sides; 2 head backs; 2 body fronts; 2 body backs; 2 arms; 2 inside legs; 2 outside legs; 2 foot soles; 1¾" (45mm) circle for nose

Felt remnant: 2 eyes

Fusible interfacing: 1 face; 2 foot soles

Shirt fabric: 2 backs; 1 front; 2 sleeves; 1 collar

Pants fabric: 2 front/back pieces

Jacket fabric: 1 back; 2 fronts; 2 sleeves; 2 front facings; two 2¼" × 7¼" (5.7cm × 18.5cm) crosswise strips for cuffs; one 2¼" × 10¼" (5.7cm × 26cm) crosswise strip for collar; one 2¼" × 16⅝" (5.7cm × 42.3cm) crosswise strip for waistband

Jacket remnant: 1 appliqué

Shoe fabric: 4 sides; 2 toes; 2 tongues; 2 soles

HOW-TO

Trace pattern pieces (enlarge if necessary) and transfer all pattern markings. All seam allowances are ⅜" (10mm). Press all seams open unless otherwise instructed.

Doll

1 Following the manufacturer's instructions, fuse the interfacing to the wrong side of the doll's face. Using 3 strands of floss and stem stitch (see under EMBROIDERY), embroider the eyes in black and the mouth in red. Glue (see under ADHESIVES) felt eyes inside the placement lines (A).

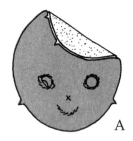

A

Using double thread, sew running stitches (see under HAND SEWING) around the nose, ⅜" from the edge. Draw up the thread slightly, forming a hollow ball and tucking in the seam allowance. Stuff with a bit of fiberfill; then draw up the thread tightly, fasten securely and cut. Center the nose over the X on the face and sew in place by hand (B).

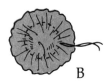

B

2 With right sides together, pin the head back sections together along the edges with triple notches and stitch the seam, leaving it open below the large ● (C). With right sides together and matching double notches, pin and stitch the head sides to the head back (D).

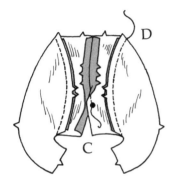

3 With right sides together, pin the short single-notched edges of the head sides together and stitch the seam (E).

4 Staystitch (see under MACHINE STITCHING) all raw edges of the head back/side along the seamlines (F).

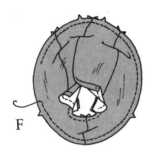

5 With right sides together, pin the face to the head back/side, clipping (see under CORNERS AND CURVES) as needed. Baste, then stitch the seam (G). Press the seam toward the face.

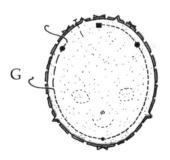

6 Make arms as for Circus Gertie, step 2, p. 77. Make legs as for Dress Me Jennifer and Friend, step 8, p. 52, fusing interfacing to wrong side of each sole before assembling. After turning, fold the top of each leg in half, bringing the seams together; then baste the top edges together.

To assemble and stuff the doll, follow Circus Gertie, steps 4 to 7, pp. 77–78.

To make hair, cut cardboard crosswise into 4" and 6" (10cm and 15cm) pieces. Following Jennifer, step 14, p. 53, use the 6½" (16.5cm) side of the smaller cardboard to make a section of hair 5¼" (13.3cm) wide for bangs, and sew to the front of the head between large ●'s. Using the short side of the larger cardboard for winding yarn, follow Jennifer, step 16, pp. 53–54, to make two separate sections of hair 5" (12.5cm) wide (do not leave a space); after taping, do not fold in half but leave hair opened out. Sew the taped center of one section along the center back seam of head between ■ and ▲. Next sew the second section on top of the first. Glue the lower layer of hair to the head near the center back seam, keeping strands close together.

7 On the front of the doll, glue some of the hair to the head at the side of the face (H). Trim the hair and bangs to the desired length (I).

Shirt

1 On each back section, press the opening edge under ¼" and stitch. With right sides together, pin backs to front at shoulders and stitch; press seams open (A). Staystitch around the neck edge (B).

2 With right sides together, fold the collar in half along the roll line. Stitch the ends; trim and turn the collar right side out. Press the collar, then baste the raw edges together. Pin the collar along the neck edge of the shirt on the right side, matching symbols and placing the small ●●'s at shoulder seams; clip the neck edges as needed. Baste.

3 Turn the back opening edges to the right side along the foldlines and pin to the neck edge, over the ends of the collar. Stitch across the entire neck edge; then stitch again, ¼" (6mm) away, in the seam allowance (C).

4 Turn the self-facings to the inside, turning the collar seam toward the shirt; press (D). Baste across the lower edges of the self-facings (E).

5 On each sleeve, stitch a casing (see under CASINGS), turning the raw edge under ⅛" (3mm) and the casing under along the foldline. Insert a 4⅝" (11.7cm) length of ⅛" (3mm) elastic (see under ELASTIC) in each casing; baste across the ends to secure.

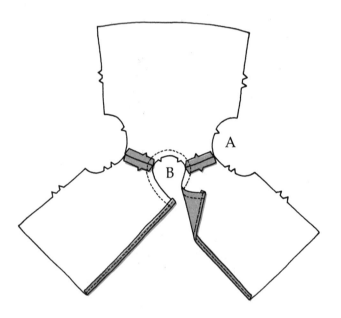

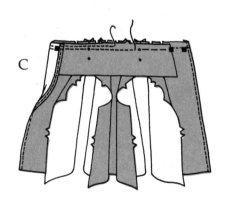

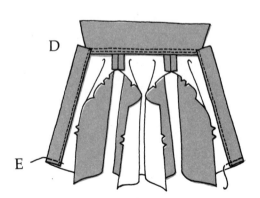

6 With right sides together, pin sleeves to armhole edges, matching notches and placing large ●'s at shoulders; then stitch. Stitch again ¼" (6mm) away (F). Press the seams toward the sleeves.

7 Stitch each side and sleeve in one continuous seam (G). Turn under the lower edge of the shirt ¼" (6mm) and press; then stitch in place. Following manufacturer's instructions, apply snaps (see under FASTENERS) along the back opening edges at small ●'s.

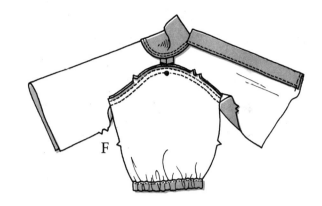

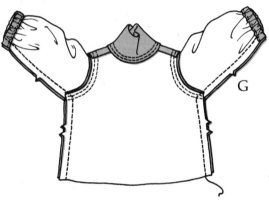

Pants

1 With right sides together, pin the pants sections together along the triple-notched edges of the center back. Stitch, leaving an opening above the large ●. Stitch again ¼" away, ending ½" (13mm) from large ● (A). Above the large ●, finish the opening with a ³⁄₁₆" (5mm) narrow hem (see under HEMS), tapering to nothing below the large ● (B). Stitch the center front seam, then stitch again ¼" (6mm) away (C).

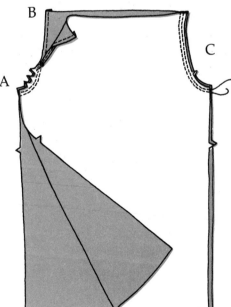

2 At the upper edge, make a casing as you did on the shirt sleeves and insert a 13½" (34cm) length of ¼" (6mm) elastic, so ends are even with back opening edges. Try the pants on the doll to adjust the fit of the elastic. On the outside, topstitch (see under MACHINE STITCHING) the back opening edges over the previous stitching (D).

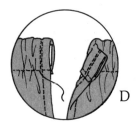

3 Turn and press the lower edge of each pants leg ⅜" (10mm) to the right side; stitch. To form cuff, turn 1¾" (4.5cm) to the right side (E) and press.

4 Stitch the inner leg seam, then stitch again as for sleeve seams (F).

5 Sew a hook and eye (see under FASTENERS) to the back opening.

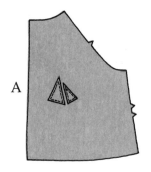

Jacket

1 Machine stitch the appliqué (see under APPLIQUÉ) to the left front along placement lines (A).

2 Make two rows of gathering stitches (see under GATHERING) along the lower edge of each sleeve between the seamlines (B). With right sides together, pin the sleeves to the fronts and back along the armhole edges. Double-stitch as for shirt sleeve seams, step 6 (C). Press the seams toward the sleeves. Staystitch the neck edge (D).

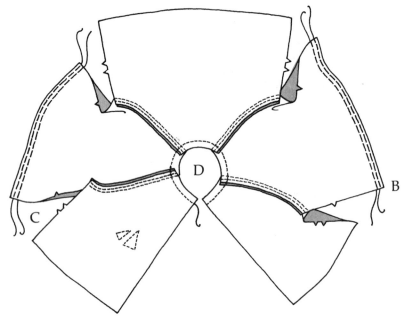

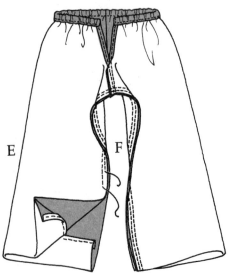

3 With right sides together, pin the fronts to the back along the side and the sleeve edges. Stitch each side in one continuous seam, leaving open below ■'s (E). Clip the front seam allowances ¼" (6mm) above ■. Beginning at ■'s, stitch again as before; press seams toward the back (F).

the raw edges. Trim and clip into the inner corners (H). Turn the cuffs right side out and press. Baste the raw edges together.

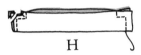

H

collar, then baste the raw edges together. Fold the collar in half crosswise to mark the center back, then unfold. Beginning and ending at the center front seamline, pin the collar along the neck edge of the jacket on the right side, matching center backs and clipping the neck edge of the jacket as needed; baste (J).

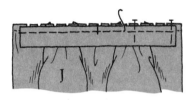

J

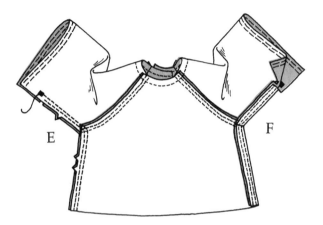

E

F

4 On each sleeve, press the sleeve opening under, turning raw edges under ⅛" (3mm) and stitching, pivoting across ■ (G).

6 Matching the raw edges, pin a cuff to the lower edge of each sleeve, adjusting the gathers to fit. Double-stitch the seams (I). Press the seams toward the sleeves.

8 Place the closed zipper face down on the outside of the right front, with the teeth over the seam line and the bottom stop at the large ●. Using a zipper foot, machine-baste, being careful to keep the end of the collar free (K). The zipper extends above the neck edge. Baste the other side of the zipper to the left front in the same way.

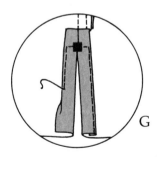

G

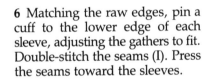

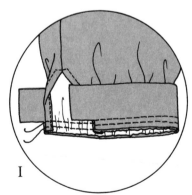

I

K

5 Fold each cuff in half lengthwise with right sides together. Starting at the fold, stitch across each end to within ⅜" (10mm) of the raw edges; pivot and stitch along the seamline for ½" (13mm), then pivot again and stitch up to

7 Fold the collar in half lengthwise with right sides together. Stitch across the collar ends, trim and turn right side out. Press the

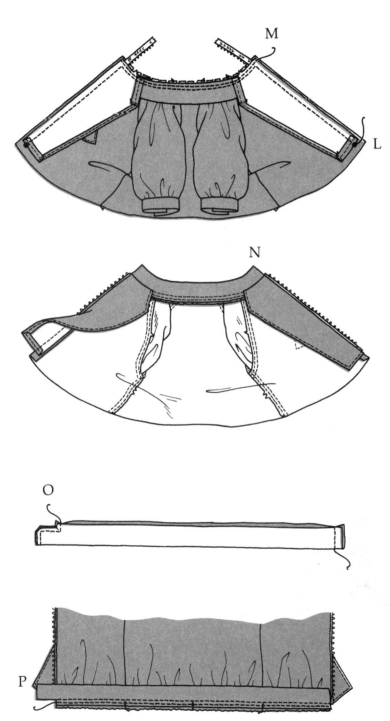

9 Finish the outer edge of each front facing as you did in step 1 of the shirt. Turn the shoulder and lower edges of each facing to the wrong side along the seamline and stitch.

10 Open the zipper. With right sides together, pin the facings to the front over the zipper and collar. Using a zipper foot, stitch the facing and collar seam, beginning and ending at large ●'s (L). Stitch the neck edge again. Cut off the excess zipper tape (M).

11 Turn facings to the inside, turning the neck seam toward the jacket, and press (N).

12 Fold the waistband in half lengthwise with right sides together. Stitch across one end. On the other end, stitch as for cuff, step 5, stitching for 1" (25mm) after first pivot (O). Trim and clip the waistband; turn it right side out and press and baste raw edges together as you did for the cuff. Fold the waistband in half crosswise and mark the center back. Then fold each side in half crosswise again *between ends of stitching* and center back and mark for side seams.

13 Open out the front facings of the jacket. Make two rows of gathering stitches at the lower edge. With the waistband extension at the left front, pin the waistband to the lower edge of the jacket on the outside, matching the center back and side seam markings and adjusting the gathers to fit. Double-stitch the seam as you did for the cuff, keeping the front facings free (P). Press the seam toward the jacket. Turn the front facings to the inside and slipstitch (see under HAND SEWING) the lower ends over the waistband/jacket seam and the shoulder edges over the shoulder seams.

14 Apply snaps to cuffs and waistband, about ⅜″ (10mm) from ends.

Shoes

Note: *For sewing with synthetic suede and leather, see under* FABRICS.

1 Cut lengths of bias tape to fit the placement lines. On each shoe side, center bias tape over the placement lines and edgestitch (see under MACHINE STITCHING) close to both long edges (A). With right sides together, pin or tape two shoe sides along the center back edges and stitch (B). Repeat with the remaining shoe side sections. Press the seam open.

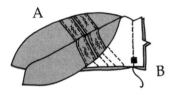

2 Bind (see under BIAS TAPE) the upper edges of both shoe side sections, toes and tongues. Matching the placement lines, pin or tape the wrong side of the toe to the right side of the shoe sides; machine-baste or tape (C).

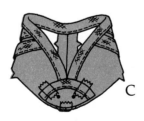

3 Turn the shoes wrong side out. Pin or tape the right side of the tongue to the wrong side of the toe at the lower edge; machine-baste or tape (D).

4 Turn shoes right side out. Stitch the toes along the lower edge of the binding, through toe, shoe sides and tongue. Then staystitch around the lower edge of each shoe (E).

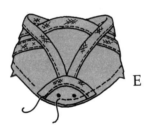

5 With right sides together, pin a sole to each assembled shoe, matching the symbols and notches and clipping the shoe as needed. Double-stitch the seam as on other clothes; trim (F). Press seam toward shoe. Turn shoes right side out.

6 Punch holes at small ●'s, through the shoe sides only (G). Insert shoelaces.

Beau Bear

• *Here he is . . . our nattily attired bear-around-town. There's no friendlier bear to be found in the realm of Dolls and Toys. Kids, no matter how young or old, will take to Beau right away. And who can help falling in love with his wardrobe: an elegant vest, a floppy bow tie and a jaunty, visored cap. In the likeness of a real bear, Beau's face is sheared to show up his fine features; read on to learn this useful technique.*•

Finished size: 23″ (58.5cm)

MATERIALS NEEDED

Bear

⅝ yd (0.60m) of 60″ (150cm) wide, 1¼″ (32mm) deep pile fabric for body

5″ × 7″ (12.5cm × 18cm) remnant of synthetic leather or suede or felt for paws

remnants of black and brown embroidery floss

carpet thread

black permanent marker

1½ lbs (680g) of polyester fiberfill

two ½″ (13mm) ball buttons

Vest

⅜ yd (0.40m) of 45″ (115cm) fabric

three ⅝″ (15mm) buttons

Cap

⅜ yd (0.40m) of 45″ (115cm) fabric

¾ yd (0.70m) of fusible interfacing

Bow tie and vest lining

¾ yd (0.70m) of 45″ (115cm) contrasting fabric

⅜ yd (0.40m) of ¼″ (6mm) elastic

Pattern pieces are found on pp. 178–185.

CUTTING INFORMATION

Pile fabric: 2 head fronts; 2 head backs; 2 inner arms; 2 outer arms; 2 inner legs; 2 outer legs; 2 body fronts; 2 body backs; 2 soles; 4 ears

Note: *For cutting pile fabrics, see under* FABRICS.

Synthetic leather, suede or felt: 2 front paws; 2 hind paws

Vest fabric: 2 fronts; 1 back

Cap fabric: 1 crown; 2 visors; one 8⅝″ (22cm) diameter circle for top; two 1½″ × 23¾″ (38mm × 60.5cm) strips for band

Contrasting fabric: 2 vest fronts and 1 vest back for lining; 1 rectangle 10⅝″ × 26″ (26.9cm × 66cm) for bow tie

Interfacing: 1 cap top; 1 cap band; 2 visors (see sizes above)

HOW-TO

Trace pattern pieces (enlarge if necessary) and transfer all pattern markings. Press seams open unless otherwise instructed.

Note: *For sewing with pile fabrics, see under* FABRICS.

Bear

Seam allowances are ¼" (6mm).

1 With scissors, trim pile to ¼" (6mm) as far as the trim line on the head front and the inner arm, and on the entire sole (A).

2 With right sides together, pin one inner leg along the front and back edges. Stitch, leaving an opening between the small ●'s and ending at ■ and ¼" (6mm) above the lower edge (B). Repeat with the remaining leg sections.

3 Pin the hind paws to the right side of the soles along the placement lines; baste before stitching in place close to the paw edges (C). With right sides together, pin a sole to the lower edge of each leg, matching symbols, easing to fit and clipping if needed; stitch the seam (D). Turn legs right side out.

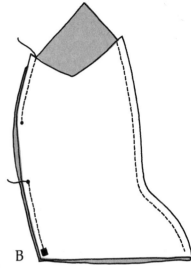

B

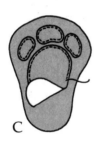

C

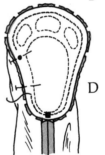

D

4 Bring the upper edges of each leg together, matching ▲'s and basting closed. With the front leg seam facing the body front, pin the basted edge of one leg to one body front, matching symbols. Baste in place. With right sides together, pin one body back over the body front, enclosing the leg; stitch the side seam and the shoulder seam and press open. Staystitch (see under MACHINE STITCHING) the neck edge along the seamline (E). Repeat for the remaining body front and back.

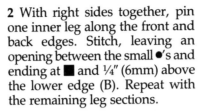

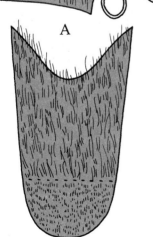

A

E

5 Apply the front paws to the inner arms as you did for the soles. Pin and stitch the inner and outer arms together, leaving the upper edges open (F). Turn the arms right side out.

6 With right sides together, pin the arm into the armhole, placing large ● at the shoulder seam and small ●●●'s at the side seam, and easing the arm to fit between small ●'s. Stitch along seamline, then stitch again ⅛″ (3mm) away in the seam allowance (G). Repeat for the other arm.

7 Now pin the body fronts and the body backs together along the center seamlines. Starting at the front neck edge, stitch the center front and center back seams, pivoting at small ● and ending at large ● (H). Press the seams open.

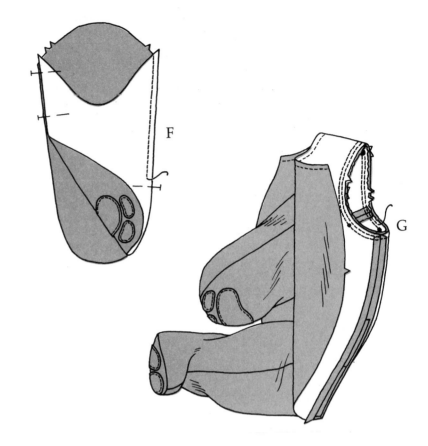

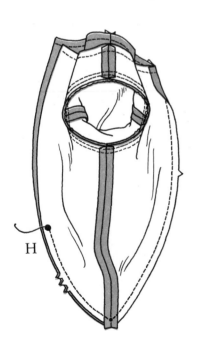

8 On each head front, stitch the neck dart and slash it to within ¼″ (6mm) of the point. Trim the pile from the dart and press it open (I).

Stitch along stitching lines of mouth opening, using small stitches and pivoting at small ●. Slash along the slash line close to small ● (J).

With right sides together, pin the head fronts along the front edges only, leaving neck and back edges open. Stitch the front seam, stopping and starting the stitching at the mouth opening (K). Press the seam open.

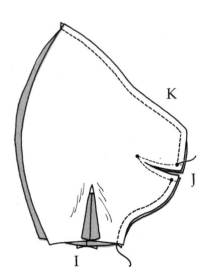

9 With right sides together, bring the slashed edges of the mouth opening together, matching and centering seams, and stitch between small ●'s (L). Press the mouth seam open.

10 With right sides together, stitch the ears together in pairs. Turn right side out. Matching small ●'s, pin and baste the ears to the head front (M). With right sides together, pin the head back sections along the center back edge only. Starting at the upper edge, stitch to the large ● (N).

11 With right sides together, pin the head front to the head back. Starting and ending at large ●'s stitch, leaving the neck edge open (O). Turn the head right side out. With right sides together, insert the head in the body. Pin around the neck edge, matching symbols and clipping the body neck edge to staystitching as needed. Stitch the seam (P). Turn right side out.

Stuff (see under STUFFING) the legs to the top of the leg seams, then slipstitch (see under HAND SEWING) the openings closed. Now stuff the arms, body and head lightly, and slipstitch the opening closed. Use only enough stuffing to create a nice soft, rounded shape. Beau Bear should be somewhat floppy; it adds to his appeal.

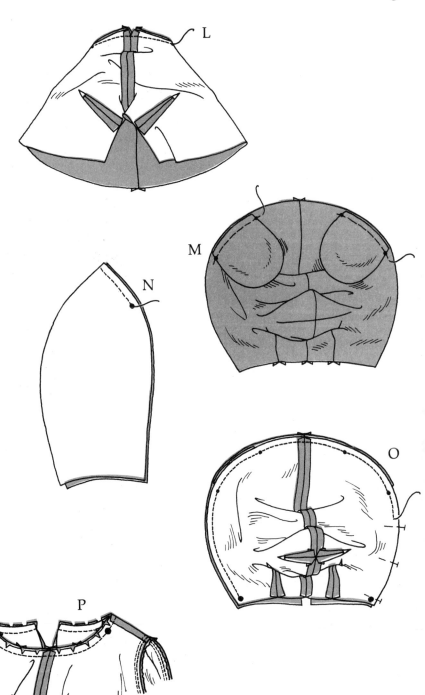

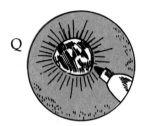

12 Using carpet thread, sew ball buttons securely to the bear's face at the markings. Using a marker, make short strokes radiating from the eyes all around, after testing first on a scrap (Q).

13 Embroider (see under EMBROIDERY) the nose and mouth, using 6 strands of floss in the needle. Work the nose in black satin stitch within the marked stitching line on the snout; and work the mouth in brown with a couching stitch (R).

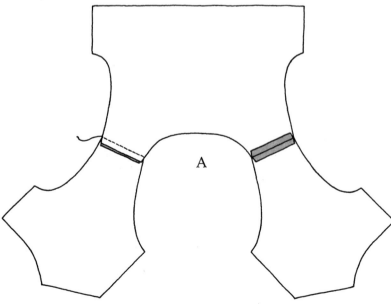

Vest

Seam allowances are ⅜" (10mm).

1 With right sides together, pin the fronts to the back at the shoulders. Stitch, then press seams open (A). Repeat for lining pieces.

2 On lining, press side seam allowances under. With right sides together, pin the vest and lining sections together and stitch seams along all edges *except* side edges (B). Trim the seam allowances and corners and clip the curves (C). Turn the vest right side out by pulling the fronts through the shoulders and out one side opening of the back. Press the edges.

3 With right sides together, pin the vest fronts and the backs together at the side edges. Stitch, keeping the lining edges free (D). Slipstitch the pressed lining edges together over the seams. Edge-stitch (see under MACHINE STITCHING) close to all edges of vest. Make buttonholes (see under FASTENERS) on the left front and sew buttons to the right front, at the markings.

Cap

Seam allowances are ⅜" (10mm).

1 To mark the cap bands, fold each in half crosswise and press the fold to mark the center. Open out and measure 3⅝" (9.2cm) away from each side of the center along one long edge; mark with ■'s on the seamline. To mark center of top, fold in half and press a tiny crease at each end of fold.

Trim away the seam allowances on all interfacing pieces. Following the manufacturer's instructions, fuse interfacing to the wrong side of the top, one band and both visors.

2 Staystitch unmarked long edge of crown. Form pleats on the right side of the crown by folding along the line of small ●'s and bringing the fold to the line of large ●'s. Baste across the lower edge of pleats (A). With right sides to-

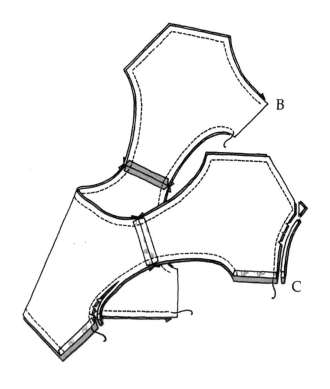

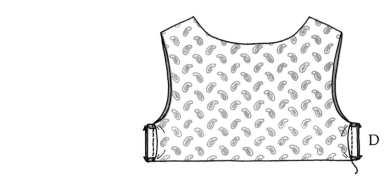

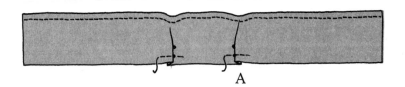

gether, stitch the ends of the crown together to form a ring. Press the seam open.

3 With right sides together, pin the staystitched edge of the crown to the top with the seam at one crease mark for the center back, clipping as needed; then stitch (B). Press the seam open, notching the seam allowance of the top so it will lie flat. Turn right side out. Edgestitch close to the seam on either side.

6 On the other band, turn the unmarked long edge under along the seamline and press. With right sides together and matching ■'s, pin the unpressed edge of the other band to the interfaced band, enclosing the visor, and stitch (D). Press the seam open (visor down and visor seam allowance toward crown) and, with right sides together, stitch the ends of the band together (E). Turn the band right side out and press.

7 With right sides together and matching seams, pin the interfaced band to the crown and stitch (F). Trim the seam allowances and press the seam toward the band (G). Slipstitch the pressed edge of the band over the band/crown seam. Turn the cap right side out and edgestitch close to both long edges of band.

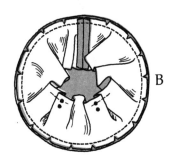

B

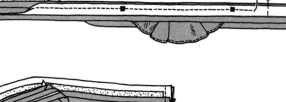

D

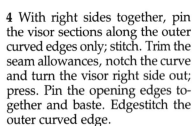

4 With right sides together, pin the visor sections along the outer curved edges only; stitch. Trim the seam allowances, notch the curve and turn the visor right side out; press. Pin the opening edges together and baste. Edgestitch the outer curved edge.

5 Matching ■'s, pin the visor to the right side of the interfaced band. Baste in place (C).

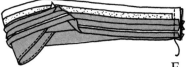

E

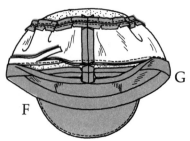

F

G

Bow Tie

Seam allowances are ⅜" (10mm).

1 With right sides together, fold the bow tie in half lengthwise. Stitch edges together, leaving an opening along one long edge. Trim the corners diagonally, turn right side out and press. Slipstitch the opening closed.

2 Pin elastic snugly around bear's neck. Allowing ½" (13mm) at each end for lapping, trim excess. Remove elastic, lap ends and stitch securely. Tie the bow tie around the elastic (A).

C

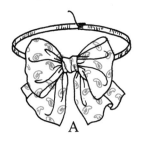

A

Snow Bunnies

• *These furry rabbits are so adorable they're offered in two sizes. That way, you won't have to choose between them! Since each bunny has only four pattern pieces, it's a good beginner's project. You can use a short- or long-pile fabric, depending on how fuzzy you want your critters to be. For the ear lining and the bottom, we suggest wool tweed, corduroy or velveteen in a color that harmonizes with the "fur."* •

Finished sizes (including ears): large bunny—approximately 12″ high × 11″ long (30.5cm × 28cm); small bunny—approximately 7½″ high × 8″ long (19cm × 20.5cm)

MATERIALS NEEDED

Large bunny

15″ × 20″ (38cm × 51cm) remnant of pile fabric for body and ears

2″ × 2″ (5cm × 5cm) remnant of contrasting pile fabric for tail

9″ × 11″ (23cm × 28cm) remnant of fabric for bottom and ear lining

Small bunny

11″ × 13″ (28cm × 33cm) remnant of pile fabric for body and ears

2″ × 2″ (5cm × 5cm) remnant of contrasting pile fabric for tail

6″ × 8″ (15cm × 20.5cm) remnant of fabric for bottom and ear lining

Both bunnies

1 skein of pink embroidery floss

polyester fiberfill: 12 oz (340g) for large; 8 oz (225g) for small

carpet thread

black permanent marker

½″ (13mm) ball buttons for eyes: 2 for each bunny

⅜″ (10mm) ribbon: 1 yd (1.00m) for large; ¾ yd (0.70m) for small

Pattern pieces are found on pp. 176–177.

CUTTING INFORMATION

Note: *For cutting pile fabric, see under* FABRICS.

For small bunny, cut pattern pieces ignoring grid. For large bunny, enlarge patterns with grid. Then follow cutting instructions for either bunny.

Main pile fabric: 2 bodies; 2 ears

Contrasting pile fabric: 1 tail

Fabric: 1 bottom; 2 ear linings

HOW-TO

Trace pattern pieces (enlarge if necessary) and transfer all pattern markings. All seam allowances are ¼" (6mm). Press seams open unless otherwise instructed.

Note: *For sewing with pile fabrics, see under* FABRICS.

1 With right sides together, pin the bodies together along the curved edges only. Stitch, leaving an opening between large ●'s (A). Clip inner corners.

2 With right sides together, pin the bottom to the lower edge of the body, matching symbols, easing the body to fit and clipping as needed. Stitch, leaving an opening for turning (B). Turn the body right side out.

3 With right sides together, stitch one ear to one lining, leaving the bottom open (C). Repeat with the remaining ear and lining. Trim the points and turn the ears right side out. With the lining side up, fold the sides of the ears toward each other along the foldlines and baste the folds in place. With lower edges even and backs of ears together, baste the ears to each other at the lower edge (D).

4 Turn in the raw edges of the head opening between large ●'s. Insert the ears into the opening, so all raw edges are even. Using carpet thread, slipstitch (see under HAND SEWING) the ears in place and the opening closed (E).

5 Stuff the bunny somewhat firmly (see under STUFFING). Slipstitch the opening closed. Using carpet thread, sew the tail to the back of the bunny.

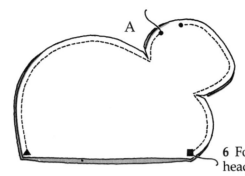

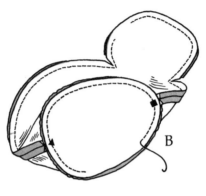

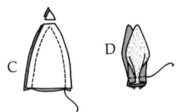

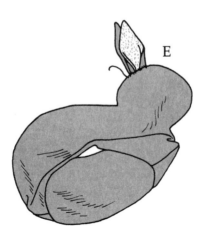

6 For eyes, sew the buttons to the head at the markings, using carpet thread. Sew the buttons to each other, taking stitches through the head without pulling them too tightly (F). Fasten the thread securely. With permanent marker, darken the pile around the eyes as for Beau Bear, step 12, p. 106.

7 Using 6 strands of floss, embroider the nose in satin stitch (see under EMBROIDERY), filling in the area inside the stitching lines (G). Tie a ribbon bow around bunny's neck, trimming the ribbon ends diagonally (H).

8 Make the whiskers at the small ●'s, using double carpet thread: Take a small stitch, leaving 1½" (38mm) hanging free at each end (I); knot securely. Trim the whiskers evenly.

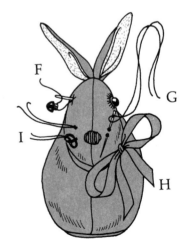

Tasha Elephant

• Artistic and outgoing, Tasha is the perfect choice for social director of the S.S. Happiness *crew. What's more, she'll be just as much at home on dry land in any young collector's menagerie. For Tasha's body, we suggest a short-pile fabric in a nice shade of elephant gray. You can use felt for her tusks and nails; just be sure it's "ivory"! Tasha's tutu, which goes on and off easily thanks to snap fasteners, would be splendid in either satin or polished cotton. •*

Tasha Elephant is a member of the S.S. *Happiness* crew. Both are trademarks of Determined Productions, Inc.

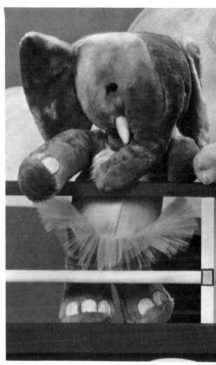

Finished size: approximately 20″ (51cm)

MATERIALS NEEDED

Elephant

½ yd (0.50m) of 60″ (150cm) short-pile fabric for body

9″ × 12″ (23cm × 30.5cm) piece of felt for tusks and nails

1 skein of black crewel yarn

1 lb (450g) of polyester fiberfill

Tutu

⅜ yd (0.40m) of 45″ (115cm) fabric

¼ yd (0.30m) of 108″ (275cm) net for ruffle

½ yd (0.50m) of ¼″ (6mm) ribbon

2 snap fasteners

Pattern pieces are found on pp. 192–196.

CUTTING INFORMATION

Note: *For cutting pile fabric, see under* FABRICS.

Pile fabric: 2 head fronts; 2 head backs; 2 body fronts; 2 body backs; 2 arms; 2 hooves; 2 soles; 4 ears; 1 nose; 1 tail

Felt: 2 tusks; 12 nails

Tutu fabric: 2 fronts; 2 backs; 1 front facing; 1 back facing

Net: 5 ″ × 108″ (12.5cm × 275cm) strip

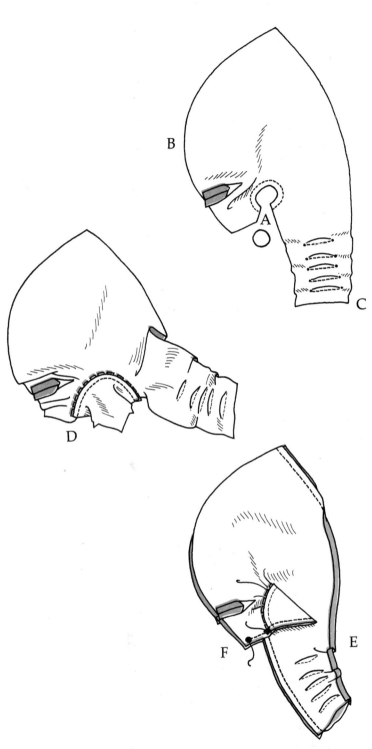

HOW-TO

Trace pattern pieces (enlarge if necessary) and transfer all pattern markings. All seam allowances are ¼" (6mm). Press all seam allowances open unless otherwise instructed.

Note: *For sewing with pile fabrics, see under* FABRICS.

Elephant

1 Staystitch (see under MACHINE STITCHING) the circle on each head front, using small stitches ¼" (6mm) away from cutting line. After staystitching, slash on slash line and cut out the circle on the cutting line (A). Stitch the large dart on each head front and press open (B). Then stitch the darts on each trunk and press them toward the head (C).

2 With right sides together, pin the curved edge of one tusk to one head front along the staystitched circle, clipping (see under CORNERS AND CURVES) head as needed (D) and stitch. Repeat with other tusk and head front.

3 With right sides together, fold tusk in half, matching notches on tusk and ■'s on head. Stitch from tip to ■ (E). Now stitch the center front seam, the under-tusk seam between large ● and ■, and the trunk seam from lower edge to ■ (F). Press the center front and trunk seams open.

4 With right sides together, pin the nose to the end of the trunk, and, matching the small ●'s, stitch, easing the trunk to fit (G).

5 Stitch and press the darts on the ears as you did on the head front. With right sides together pin two ears along outer curved edges and stitch, leaving open between large ● and ■. Repeat with the remaining ears. Turn the ears right side out and baste the raw edges together.

6 Pin an ear to each head back, matching symbols. Baste between symbols (H). With right sides together, pin the head backs along the center back edge and stitch from the upper edge to ▲; press open (I).

7 With right sides together, pin the head back to the head front, matching symbols and seams and easing the back to fit; stitch (J). Turn the head right side out.

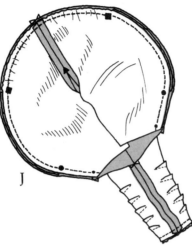

8 On each body front, stitch the leg dart. Trim the dart to ¼" (6mm) and press it open (K).

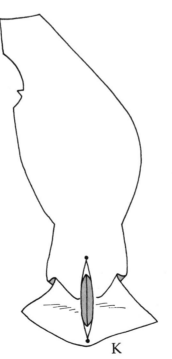

9 Matching placement lines, pin three nails to the bottom of each leg, centering the middle one over the dart seamline. Stitch the nails in place close to the curved edges (L). With right sides together, pin the body fronts along the center front edges. Stitch from the upper edge to the large ● and press open (M).

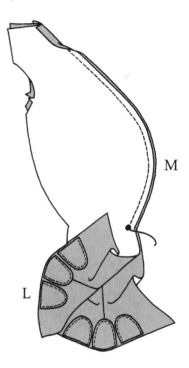

10 With right sides together, fold the tail in half and stitch, leaving the short straight end open. Trim the seam allowances close to the stitching and turn the tail right side out. Baste the raw edges together.

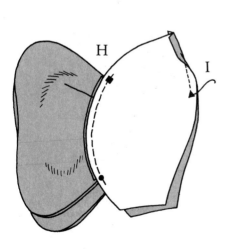

113

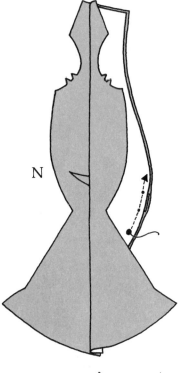

11 Pin the tail to one body back between small ●'s and baste. With right sides together, pin the body backs along the centers and stitch between the ▲ and large ● only (N).

12 With right sides together and matching symbols, pin the body front to the body back at the shoulders, sides and inner leg edges; stitch, ending the inner leg seams at large ●'s (O). Pin and stitch the soles to the ends of the legs, matching large ●'s and small ●'s and easing to fit (P). Turn the body right side out.

13 On the arms, stitch, trim and press the darts as you did on the legs; then stitch the nails in place. With right sides together, pin and stitch the arm seams, leaving the top and bottom edges open. Join the hooves to the lower edges of the arms as you did the soles to the legs.

14 Pin and stitch arms in place as for Beau Bear, step 6, p. 104.

15 Turn the head right side out. With right sides together, pin the head to the body along the neck opening, matching the seams, and stitch (Q). Using small amounts of fiberfill at a time, stuff (see under STUFFING) the legs, arms, tusks and trunk firmly. Then stuff the body and head firmly. Turn in the opening edges along the center back and slipstitch (see under HAND SEWING) the opening closed.

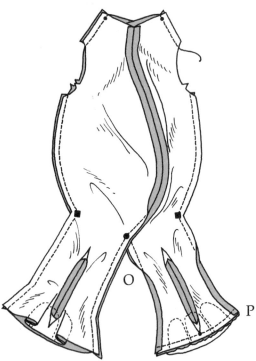

16 Split the crewel yarn into separate strands and use one strand in the needle. Embroider (see under EMBROIDERY) the eyes in satin stitch, filling in the area indicated by the placement lines. Work stem stitch over the seam under the tusks, forming a V under the base of the trunk (R).

Tutu

1 On each front, make one row of gathering stitches (see GATHERING) between small ●'s; pull up the gathers to 1″ (25mm) and knot the thread ends securely (A). Then, with right sides together, pin the fronts along the center edges and stitch the seam (B).

2 With right sides together, pin the back sections along center edges. Stitch, leaving an opening between ▲'s for the tail. Press the seam open, pressing opening edges under along the seamline. On the right side, edgestitch (see under MACHINE STITCHING) around the opening (C).

3 With right sides together, pin the back to the front along the sides; stitch and press open. Stitch the crotch seam.

4 Cut two 9″ (23cm) lengths of ribbon. Pin one end of each ribbon to the front of the tutu at ■'s and baste (D).

5 With right sides together, pin the front facing to the back facing at the sides; stitch and press open. Press the lower edge of the facing ¼″ (6mm) to the wrong side and stitch close to the pressed edge. With right sides together, pin the facing to the upper edge of the tutu, matching seams. Stitch the seam (E). Turn the facing to the

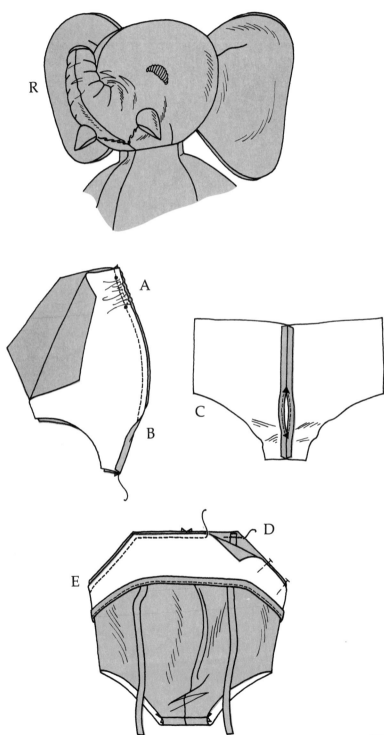

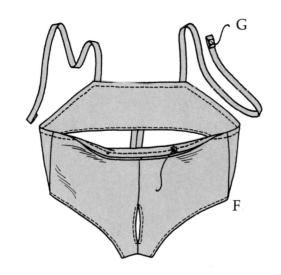

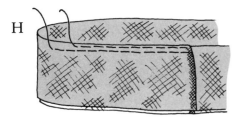

inside and press. Stitch ¼" (6mm) from the upper edge of the tutu. Finish the lower edges of the legs as you did the facing (F).

6 Turn the free ends of the ribbons under ½" (13mm). Sew the snaps (see under FASTENERS) to the ribbons and to the tutu facing at small ●'s (G).

7 Stitch the ends of the net strip together. With wrong sides together, fold the strip in half lengthwise. Make two rows of gathering stitches ¼" and ⅛" (6mm and 3mm) from the folded edge and gather (H).

8 With raw edges of net toward top of tutu, pin the net strip to the tutu, placing the gathers along the placement line and adjusting them to fit. Turn the tutu wrong side out and stitch the net in place; then turn the tutu right side out and turn the net down over the stitching (I).

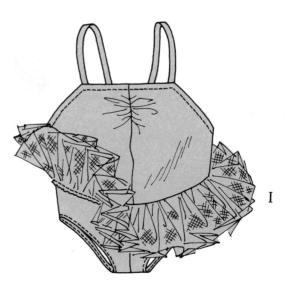

Mr. and Mrs. Mouse

• These tiny creatures can be made entirely from remnants—mostly scraps of felt, plus some calico for Mrs. Mouse's dress and a bit of solid white for her apron. Since the pieces are so small, you'll want to cut very accurately and use small machine stitches—12 to 15 per inch (per 25mm)—for assembling. On all felt pieces, there's no need to finish edges, since felt doesn't ravel! •

MATERIALS NEEDED

Each mouse

- 8″ × 12″ (20.5cm × 30.5cm) piece of gray felt
- 2″ × 2″ (5cm × 5cm) piece of cardboard for bottom
- 1 skein each of red and black embroidery floss
- 1 oz (28g) of polyester fiberfill

Mrs. Mouse

- 8″ × 9″ (20.5cm × 23cm) remnant for dress
- 3″ × 5″ (7.5cm × 12.5cm) remnant for apron
- ⅜ yd (0.40m) of ⅝″ (15mm) flat eyelet

Mr. Mouse

- 3″ × 6″ (7.5cm × 15cm) felt remnant for vest
- 1″ × 2″ (25mm × 5cm) felt remnant for bow tie

Pattern pieces are found on pp. 170–171.

CUTTING INFORMATION

Note: *For cutting felt fabric, see under* FABRICS.

Gray felt (each mouse): 2 bodies; 1 body front; 4 arms; 4 legs; 2 ears; 4 paws; 1 bottom; 1 strip ⅛″ × 5″ (3mm × 12.5cm) for tail

Dress fabric: 1 front; 2 backs

Apron fabric: 2″ × 4″ (5cm × 10cm) rectangle

Vest fabric: 1 vest

Bow tie fabric: 1 bow tie

Finished size: approximately 4¾″ (12cm)

HOW-TO

Trace pattern pieces (enlarge if necessary) and transfer all pattern markings. All seam allowances are ¼" (6mm) Press seams open unless otherwise instructed.

For sewing with felt, see under FABRICS.

Mouse

1 Staystitch (see under MACHINE STITCHING) the curved edges of the body sections. With right sides together, pin the body sections together along the curved edges with symbols. Starting at lower edge, stitch as far as large ●, leaving an opening between small ●'s (A). Matching large ●'s, pin and stitch the body to the body front, breaking stitching at large ● and clipping the seam allowances as needed (B).

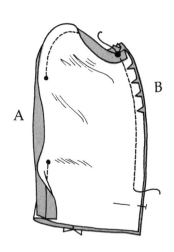

2 With right sides together, pin the bottom to the lower edge of the body; ease to fit, clip as needed and stitch (C). Turn the piece right side out. From the cardboard, cut a 1¾" (4.5cm) circle. Insert the cardboard through the body opening over the bottom. Stuff (see under STUFFING) firmly and slipstitch (see under HAND SEWING) the opening closed.

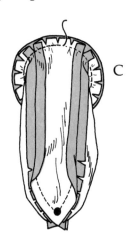

3 To make the arms and legs, pin the pieces together in pairs and stitch, leaving openings between small ●'s. Trim and clip the seams (D). Turn the arms and legs right side out and stuff each arm and leg firmly, then slipstitch the openings closed.

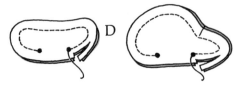

4 Matching placement lines, slipstitch the arms and legs in place (E).

5 Slash each ear along the slash line, then lap one cut edge over the other ⅛" (3mm); baste. Whipstitch (see under HAND SEWING) the ears to the mouse head at placement lines (F). Whipstitch a paw to each arm and leg (G). Slipstitch one end of the tail to the mouse at the lower end of the center back seam.

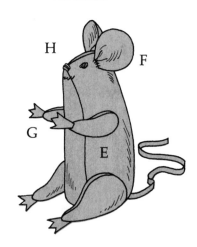

6 Using 2 strands of floss in the needle, embroider (see under EMBROIDERY) the eyes in black satin stitch and the mouth in red stem stitch, along the stitching lines (H).

Mrs. Mouse's Dress and Apron

1 With right sides together, pin the dress backs to front at shoulders, and stitch as far as small ●'s. Turn the neck edges of the dress under ¼" (6mm), press and stitch (A). Finish the lower edges of the sleeves in the same way.

2 With right sides together, pin and stitch each side and sleeve in one continuous seam, clipping as needed (B). Finish the back opening edges and the lower edges as you did the neck and sleeve edges. Turn the dress right side out and put it on the mouse. Lap the opening edges at the back of the neck and tack (see under HAND SEWING) in place.

3 Finish the sides and lower edge of the apron with a ⅛" (3mm) narrow hem (see under HEMS). Make two rows of gathering stitches and gather (see under GATHERING) the upper edge to 1¾" (4.5cm). Center the eyelet over the gathered raw edge and stitch close to the lower edge of the eyelet (C). Tie the apron around the mouse, tacking the knot in place at back.

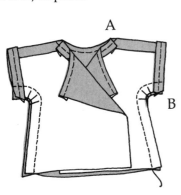

Mr. Mouse's Vest and Tie

1 Cut holes for arms along cutting lines. Put the vest on the mouse.

2 Tack the bow tie to the mouse ½" (13mm) below the mouth (A).

Mitzi the Cat

A lovable, huggable bundle of purr—that's Mitzi! She's easy to sew and a joy to have around. If you like the idea of a long-haired kitty, choose a long-pile fabric. Of, if you prefer the domestic short-haired variety, pick a short-pile fabric, in whatever cat color you like best. For Mitzi's bottom, use velvet, wool tweed or corduroy, in a tone to harmonize with her "fur." To be sure that her embroidered nose and mouth will be visible, choose floss colors that will show up against the pile, without contrasting too sharply.

MATERIALS NEEDED

⅝ yd (0.60m) of 60" (150cm) pile fabric

13" × 16" (33cm × 40.5cm) remnant of contrasting fabric for body bottom and tail bottom

1 skein each of light and dark contrasting embroidery floss

two ½" (13mm) amber ball buttons

12 oz (340g) of polyester fiberfill

carpet thread

black permanent marker

Pattern pieces are found on pp. 166–169.

CUTTING INFORMATION

Note: *For cutting pile fabric, see under* FABRICS.

Pile fabric: 1 right side; 1 left side; 1 right head front; 1 left head front; 1 right head back; 1 left head back; 1 tail; 2 ears

Contrasting fabric: 1 body bottom; 1 tail bottom

Finished size: approximately 15" (38cm) long, excluding tail

HOW-TO

Trace pattern pieces (enlarge if necessary) and transfer all pattern markings. All seam allowances are ¼" (6mm). Press seams open unless otherwise instructed.

Note: *For sewing pile fabric, see under* FABRICS.

1 Using scissors, trim the pile on all head pieces to ⅛" (3mm) as far as trim lines, tapering trimming gradually (A).

2 With right sides together, pin the left head front to the right head front at the center. Stitch front head seam, interrupting the stitching at the dart (B).

3 Now stitch the dart, leaving openings between the small ●'s for inserting the eyes (C).

4 With right sides together, pin the left head back to the right head back along the notched center edge and stitch.

5 With right sides together, pin and stitch the head front to the head back along the sharply curved upper edge, easing the back to fit and leaving the lower (neck) edge open (D). Turn the head right side out.

6 Stitch the dart on the left side piece; press it flat. With right sides together, pin the left side piece to the right side along centers; stitch to form the body (E).

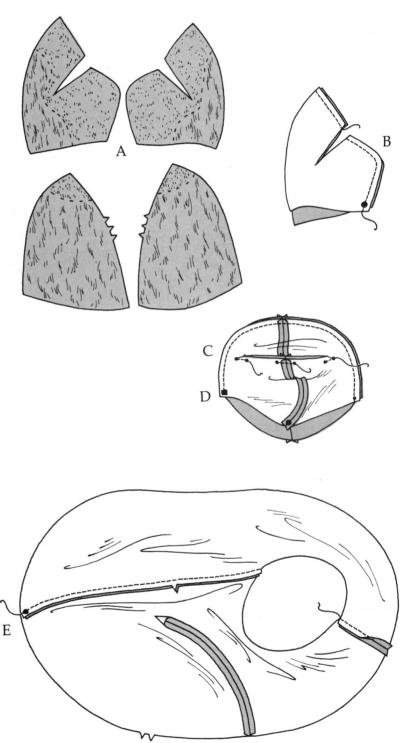

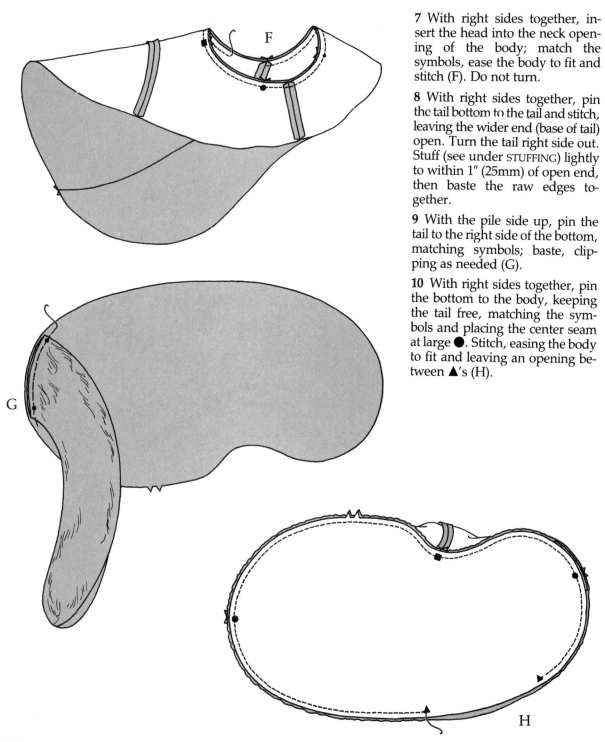

7 With right sides together, insert the head into the neck opening of the body; match the symbols, ease the body to fit and stitch (F). Do not turn.

8 With right sides together, pin the tail bottom to the tail and stitch, leaving the wider end (base of tail) open. Turn the tail right side out. Stuff (see under STUFFING) lightly to within 1" (25mm) of open end, then baste the raw edges together.

9 With the pile side up, pin the tail to the right side of the bottom, matching symbols; baste, clipping as needed (G).

10 With right sides together, pin the bottom to the body, keeping the tail free, matching the symbols and placing the center seam at large ●. Stitch, easing the body to fit and leaving an opening between ▲'s (H).

11 Turn the cat right side out. Stuff the head firmly, using small amounts of fiberfill at a time. Stuff the nose area first, then alternately stuff the cheeks. Keeping the forehead area flat and the cheeks wide, continue to stuff the head (I). Begin stuffing the body enough to establish the shape, but leave the rest for later and do not close the opening.

12 Trim the pile on the ears as you did on the head pieces, leaving long pile only along the bottoms of the ears (J). Pin the ears to the head along placement lines and slipstitch (see under HAND SEW-ING) them in place (K).

13 Insert the buttons into the eye openings on the head. Using carpet thread, sew the buttons to each other through the stuffing, with care not to pull the stitches too tight.

14 To form the bridge of the nose, pinch the fabric, along with some stuffing, together from the eye dart to the nose placement line. Using carpet thread, sew back and forth through the nose and the stuffing, to hold the shape; be careful not to pull the stitches too tight (L).

Using 6 strands of the lighter color floss, embroider (see under EMBROIDERY) the nose in satin stitch within the nose placement lines (M); with the darker color, work the mouth in couching stitch (N).

15 Using the permanent marker, outline the eyes after testing first on a scrap (O). If the cat's face needs to be adjusted, do it now by rearranging the stuffing. If desired, trim more pile from the face. Using double carpet thread, make

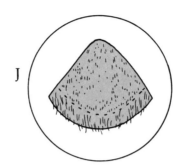

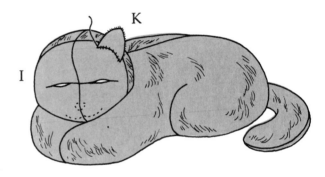

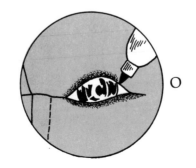

the whiskers at the markings, following the instructions in Snow Bunnies, step 8, p. 110.

16 Finish stuffing the body, keeping it fairly soft. Slipstitch the opening closed.

Ruff-Ruff the Dog

• *Our plush pooch makes a wonderful pet (and you don't even have to walk him). We show two versions of Ruff-Ruff—one made of short-pile, the other of medium-pile fabric. But if you'd really love a shaggy dog, then choose a long-pile fabric. Just be sure to follow the tips given in the instructions. The soles of Ruff-Ruff's paws can be made of contrasting fabric, such as wool flannel, corduroy or velvet.* •

MATERIALS NEEDED

⅞ yd (0.80m) of 60" (150cm) pile fabric for body

7" × 8" (18cm × 20.5cm) remnant of contrasting fabric for soles

1 skein of black embroidery floss

two ¾" (20mm) amber ball buttons

2 lbs (910g) of polyester fiberfill

carpet thread

black permanent marker

18" (46cm) collar (optional)

Pattern pieces are found on pp. 172–175.

CUTTING INFORMATION

Note: *For cutting pile fabrics, see under* FABRICS.

Pile fabric: 2 head fronts; 2 head backs; 2 ears; 2 bodies; 2 inside legs; 2 tails

Contrasting fabric: 2 front soles; 2 hind soles

Finished size: approximately 20½" (52cm) high

124

HOW-TO

Trace pattern pieces (enlarge if necessary) and transfer all pattern markings. All seam allowances are ¼" (6mm). Press seams open unless otherwise instructed.

Note: *For sewing with pile fabrics, see under* FABRICS.

1 On the head fronts, trim the pile to ⅛" (3mm) within the areas marked by the trim line and the dart line (A). Stitch the dart on each head front, then slash the dart to within ½" (13mm) of the point and press it open.

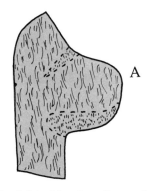

A

2 With right sides together, pin the head fronts together along the center edges and stitch the seam (B). With right sides together, pin the head backs along the notched center edges; stitch.

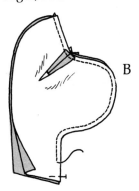

B

3 Fold each ear to the wrong side along the foldlines, then baste across the fold at upper edge. Pin the ears to the right side of the head back between large ● and ■ and stitch in place (C). With right sides together, pin the head back to the head front along the sharply curved edges. Stitch, leaving the lower (neck) edge open. Turn the head right side out.

4 With right sides together, pin and stitch the tail sections together, leaving the wide end with the symbols open. Turn the tail right side out and baste the open edges together. Then pin the tail to the right side of one body section between the symbols and baste in place, clipping as needed (D).

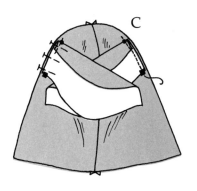

C

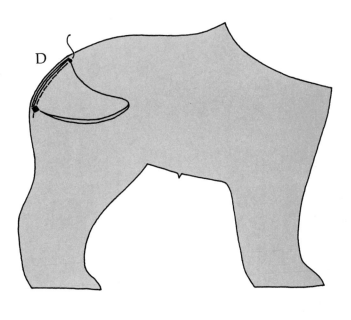

D

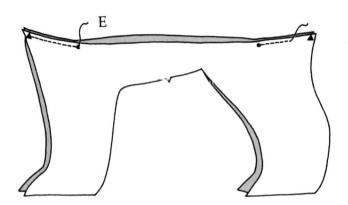

5 With right sides together, pin the inside legs along the upper edges. Stitch inside leg seam, leaving a long opening between the small ●'s (E).

6 With right sides together, pin the inside legs to the body along the leg and tummy edges. Stitch, leaving the bottoms of the feet open between the symbols, and breaking the stitching at the ▲'s at the top of the inside legs. Clip into the corner and clip curves (F).

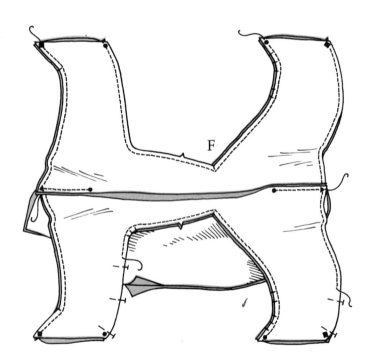

7 Pin and stitch the front and hind soles to the bottoms of the legs. To join a curve to a straight edge, see under CORNERS AND CURVES.

8 With right sides together, pin the curved center back edges of the body and the short center front edges above ▲; then stitch (G). Do not turn.

9 Attach the head to the body as for Mitzi the Cat, step 7, p. 122. Turn the dog right side out and stuff firmly (see under STUFFING). Slipstitch, (see under HAND SEWING) the opening closed.

10 Using carpet thread, sew the buttons to the dog's face at the markings (H). With small scissors, trim the pile around the button eyes. With permanent marker, darken the area around the eyes as for Beau Bear, step 12, p. 106.

11 Using black floss, embroider the nose in satin stitch (see under EMBROIDERY) within the marked placement lines; work the mouth in couching stitch along the placement lines. Using double carpet thread, make the whiskers at the markings, following instructions for Snow Bunnies, step 8, p. 110 (I).

12 To help the dog stand up solidly, use carpet thread to work a French tack (see under HAND SEWING) between the front legs and between the back legs, near the tops (J). Add a collar, if desired.

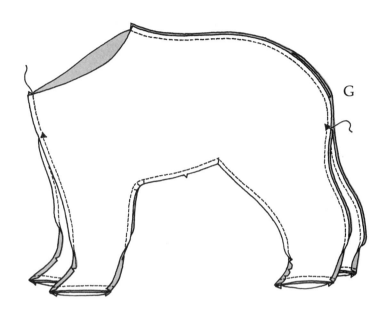

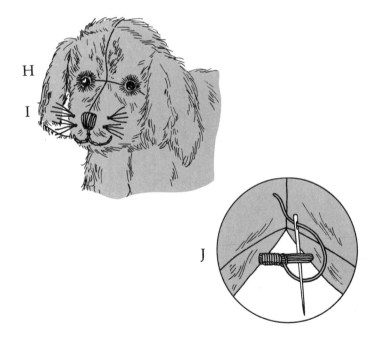

127

Pelican Pete and His School of Fish

● *You'd expect someone to learn a lot at a school of fish, right? Well, Pelican Pete, a patient and friendly teacher, can help preschoolers learn their basic numbers and colors. Choose firmly woven fabrics for Pete and his fish: poplin, broadcloth, calico and sailcloth are all suitable. Mix and match prints and solids as you like, as long as the result is colorful!* ●

Finished size: approximately 24" (61cm) high

MATERIALS NEEDED

1 yd (1.00m) of 45" (115cm) calico fabric for body, beak and pouch lining

⅜ yd (0.40m) of 45" (115cm) yellow fabric for upper beak and 1 fish

¾ yd (0.70m) of 45" (115cm) orange fabric for pouch, feet, eyes and 1 fish

¾ yd (0.70m) of 45" (115cm) green fabric for bow and 1 fish

¾ yd (0.70m) of 45" (115cm) blue fabric for bow lining and 1 fish

6" × 12" (15cm × 30.5cm) black remnant for eyeballs and 1 fish

five different 6" × 10" (15cm × 25.5cm) remnants for 5 fish

12" × 15" (30.5cm × 38cm) piece of fusible interfacing for feet

18" (46cm) zipper

1 skein each of white, black and brown embroidery floss

2 lbs (910g) of polyester fiberfill

1 yd (1.00m) of ⅜" (10mm) filler cord for cording

long darning needle

4 flat drapery weights

Pattern pieces are found on pp. 201–207.

CUTTING INFORMATION

Calico fabric: 2 bodies; 1 beak; 1 pouch for lining; 1 inset; 1 pouch bottom; 2 bottoms; 4 wings; 2 eye backs

Yellow fabric: 2 upper beaks; 2 fish

Orange fabric: 1 pouch; 1 pouch bottom; 2 feet; 2 eyelashes; 2 eyelids; 2 fish; 2 bias strips 1¾" × 20" (45mm × 51cm)

Green fabric: two 4½" × 30" (11.5cm × 76cm) bias strips for bow; 2 fish

Blue fabric: two 4½" × 30" (11.5cm × 76cm) bias strips for bow lining; 2 fish

Black remnant: 2 eyeballs; 2 fish

5 fish remnants: 2 fish from each

Fusible interfacing: 1 foot

HOW-TO

Trace pattern pieces (enlarge if necessary) and transfer all pattern markings. All seam allowances are ¼" (6mm). Press all seams open unless otherwise instructed.

Pelican

1 Reinforce (see under MACHINE STITCHING) the head area of each body section by stitching ¼" (6mm) from edge, through the small ●'s, and pivoting at the small ● at the inner corner. Clip to the small ●'s (A). Reinforce and clip the inner corner of the pouch and pouch lining in the same way.

2 Staystitch (see under MACHINE STITCHING) a scant ¼" (6mm) from the curved end of each upper beak. With right sides together, pin one upper beak to one head section between the small ●'s, clipping the beak as needed. Stitch between the small ●'s (B). Repeat with the other beak and head. Press the beaks away from the head and the seam allowances toward the head, bringing the ends of the beak seam allowances to the inside. On the outside, edgestitch (see under MACHINE STITCHING) the head close to the beak/head seam through all layers, between the small ●'s.

3 With right sides together, pin the upper beak and front head sections together. Stitch the seam. Clip the curved seam allowances and corners (C).

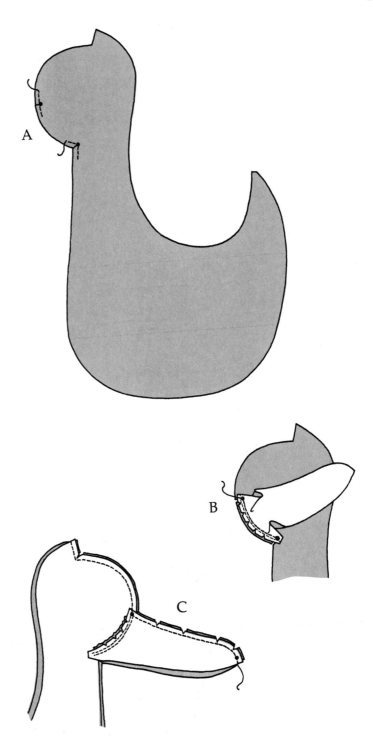

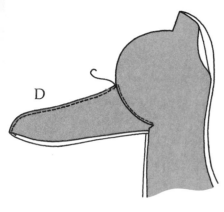

D

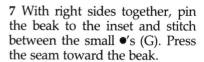

4 On the outside, with wrong sides together, edgestitch the upper beak close to the seam, through all layers, forming a ridge (D).

5 Using the narrow bias strips and the filler cord cut in half, make two lengths of cording, beginning and ending the filler cord 1" (25mm) from each end of strip (see under TRIMS).

Matching raw edges, pin one length of cording to the right side of the upper beak, with ends extending 1" (25mm) beyond small •'s; baste, using a zipper foot (E).

7 With right sides together, pin the beak to the inset and stitch between the small •'s (G). Press the seam toward the beak.

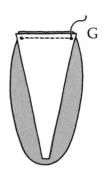

G

8 With right sides together, pin the beak to the upper beak, matching the raw edges. Using a zipper foot, stitch between the small •'s (H). Turn right side out.

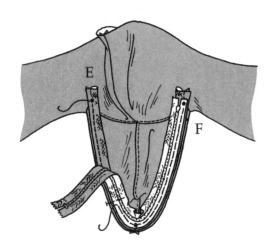

E

F

6 Fold the zipper in half, matching the lower stop to the top of the pull tab, and mark the zipper tape at the fold for center. Unfold the zipper tape and place the closed zipper face down over the cording, with edges even and the pull tab ¼" (6mm) below the small •, and the center marking of the zipper at the upper beak seam. Baste, using a zipper foot (F).

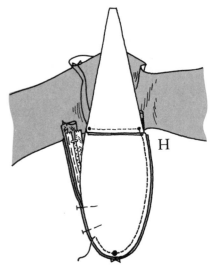

H

9 Using a pouch bottom section in a color to match the pouch, and with right sides together, pin the pouch bottom to the pouch, matching the large ●'s. Stitch from the pouch side, starting and ending at the large ●'s and pivoting at the small ● on the inner corner (I). With right sides together and matching the symbols, stitch the pouch together between large ● and ■ only (J). Turn right side out.

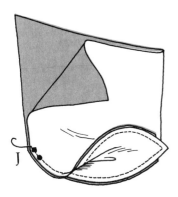

10 Pin and baste the remaining length of cording to the right side of the pouch, as you did on the upper beak. Open the zipper on the upper beak. Place the zipper face down over the pouch cording, matching the ends, edges and centers as before. Baste, using a zipper foot (K).

11 Assemble the pouch lining as you did the pouch. With right sides together, pin the lining to the pouch, with upper raw edges even. Stitch, using a zipper foot, being careful to keep the body and beak away from the stitching (L).

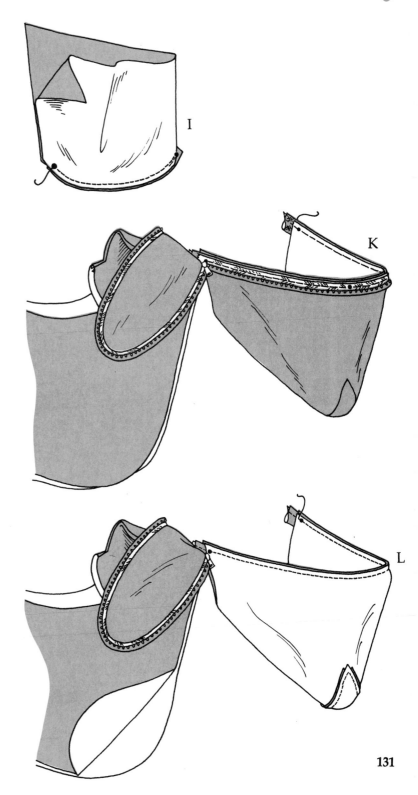

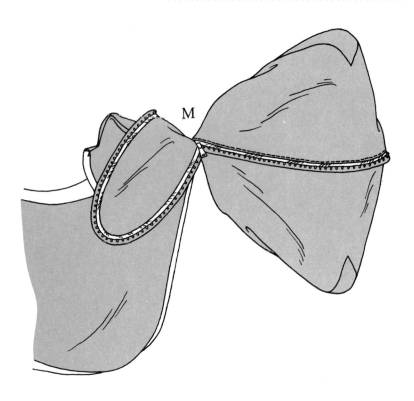

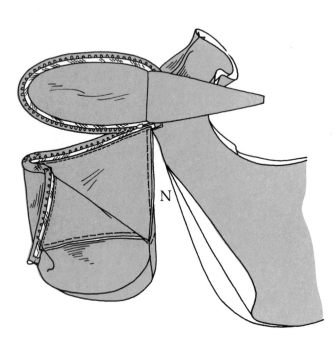

12 Open out the lining, pulling it away from the pouch. Using a zipper foot, on the inside, stitch the lining to the seam allowance, close to the seam (M).

13 Turn the pouch lining to the inside. Baste the remaining raw edges of pouch and lining together (N). Close the zipper and hand-sew the ends of the cording together (O).

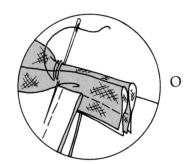

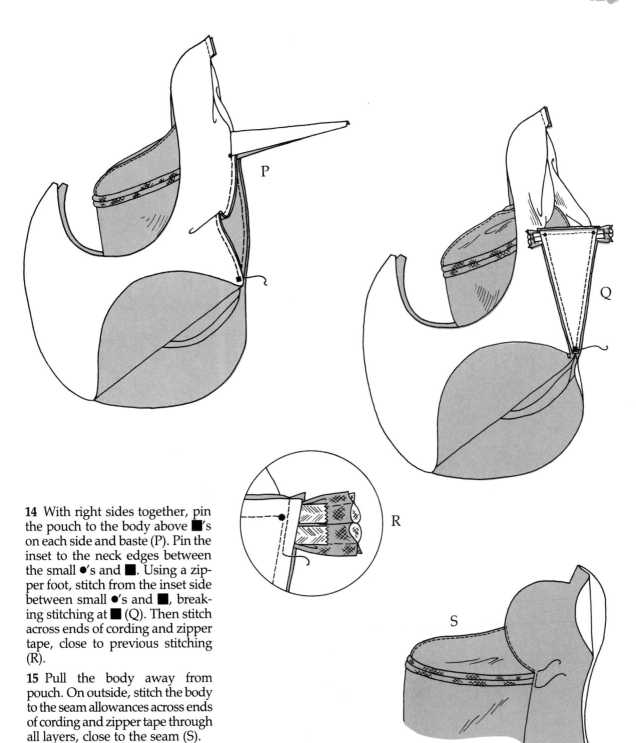

14 With right sides together, pin the pouch to the body above ■'s on each side and baste (P). Pin the inset to the neck edges between the small ●'s and ■. Using a zipper foot, stitch from the inset side between small ●'s and ■, breaking stitching at ■ (Q). Then stitch across ends of cording and zipper tape, close to previous stitching (R).

15 Pull the body away from pouch. On outside, stitch the body to the seam allowances across ends of cording and zipper tape through all layers, close to the seam (S).

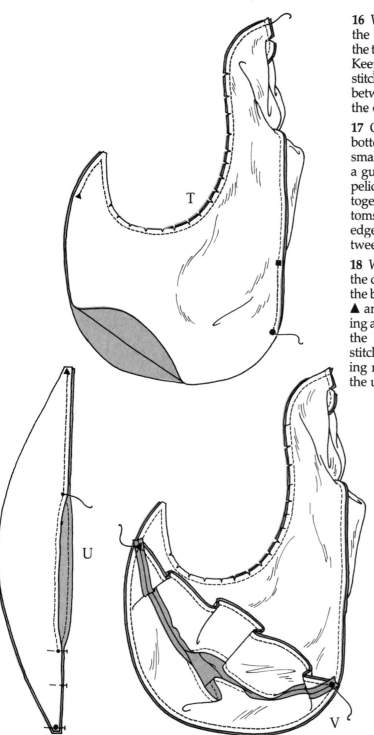

16 With right sides together, pin the body sections together along the top of the head, back and front. Keeping the pouch and beak free, stitch, leaving the lower edge open between the large ● and ▲. Clip the curves (T). Do not turn.

17 On the straight edge of each bottom section, stitch between small ●'s. This stitching serves as a guide for slipstitching after the pelican is stuffed. With right sides together, pin and stitch the bottoms together along the straight edges, leaving an opening between the small ●'s (U).

18 With right sides together, pin the curved edges of the bottom to the body between the large ● and ▲ and stitch, breaking the stitching at the large ● and ▲ (V). Turn the body right side out. Edge-stitch all remaining seams, forming ridges, as you did the top of the upper beak.

19 Stuff (see under STUFFING) the beak and head, creating a nice round shape. Stuff the neck area very firmly; then stuff the rest of the body firmly, rounding out the chest area. Turn under one raw edge of the bottom along the stitching and slipstitch (see under HAND SEWING) the turned edge over the stitching on the other edge.

20 With right sides together, pin two wings together. Stitch, leaving an opening between the small •'s (W). Repeat with the remaining pair of wings. Clip curves, turn the wings right side out and press. Stuff the wings lightly, keeping them rather flat. Slipstitch the openings closed. Stitch along the wing stitching lines for feathered effect, then edgestitch the wings all around.

21 Slipstitch the wings to each side of the body along placement lines, matching symbols (X). With double thread in a large darning needle, stab through the body at the upper small • to corresponding small • on the other side of the body; take several stitches in this way (Y), then knot the thread securely and cut it. Repeat this step at the lower small •'s.

22 Following the manufacturer's instructions, fuse interfacing to the wrong side of one foot section. Sew drapery weights to this sec-tion to help the pelican stand solidly (Z). With right sides together, pin the foot sections together and stitch, leaving an opening for turning. Clip the corners and curves. Turn the feet right side out and press. Stuff the feet lightly, keeping them as flat as possible. Slipstitch the opening closed, then edgestitch the feet as you did the wings (AA).

23 With the interfaced side on the bottom, pin the feet to the bottom of the pelican between ■'s. Turn the pelican right side up to check its balance; adjust the position of the feet if necessary. Whipstitch (see under HAND SEWING) the feet in place (BB).

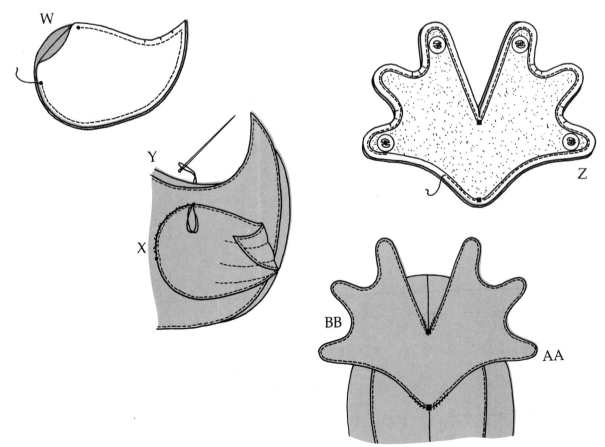

24 Fold each eyelash section along the roll line with right sides together. Stitch along each diagonal end and around the corner as far as the small ●, leaving an opening between the small ●'s. Clip to the small ●'s, trim the stitched seam allowances, turn the eyelash right side out and press it. Baste the raw opening edges together.

25 With right sides up, pin one eyelash to each eyelid, matching straight edges, and baste between small ●'s (CC).

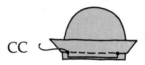

CC

26 On each eyeball section, turn under the straight edge along the seamline; baste. Make one row of hand gathering stitches on the curved edge and gather (see under GATHERING) (DD).

DD

27 With right sides together, pin the gathered edge of the eyeball to the straight edge of the eyelid, over the eyelash. Adjust the gathers, then stitch between the small ●'s (EE).

EE

28 Turn under and baste the straight edge of each eye back. With right sides together, pin the eye back to the eyelid along the curved edges. Keeping the eyelash and eyeball free, stitch the curve, leaving an opening between the small ●'s (FF).

FF

29 Turn the eyes right side out, turning the eyeball seam toward the eyelid. Edgestitch the curved edge of the eyes, keeping the eyelash free (GG). Stuff the eyes firmly, keeping the back as flat as possible. Slipstitch the openings closed.

GG

30 Pin an eye to each side of the head along the placement lines between the small ●'s. Slipstitch in place (HH). Turn each eyelash up, keeping the seam hidden, and slipstitch eyelash ends in place (II).

HH

II

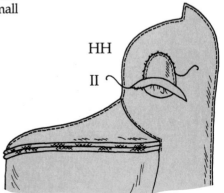

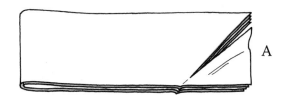

Bow

1 Place bow sections with right sides together; repeat with lining sections. Then fold each double bow and lining section in half crosswise, matching edges. Fold the ends in a 45° angle along the straight grain; press. Unfold ends, then cut both ends through both layers along the crease line (A). Unfold the bow.

2 With right sides together, join the bow sections at one end to form a long strip and stitch. Press the seam open. Repeat for the lining sections.

3 With right sides together, pin the bow to the lining and, leaving an opening for turning, stitch; trim the corners (B). Turn the bow right side out and press. Slipstitch the opening closed. Place the bow around the pelican's neck and tie in a nice, fat bow.

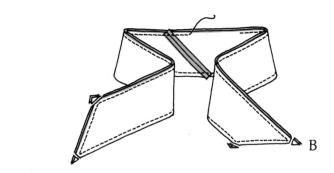

Fish

1 Transfer (see under TRANSFERRING MARKINGS) one number to the right side of one fish section of each color, having all pieces face the same way. With right sides together, pin and stitch each marked fish section to its mate, leaving an opening along the tail. Trim the fish seam allowances and clip the corners (A). Turn the fish right side out and press.

2 Stuff each fish lightly, within the body section only; do not stuff the fins and tail. Slipstitch the opening closed.

3 Topstitch (see under MACHINE STITCHING) the fins and tail along the stitching lines.

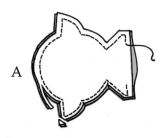

4 Using 3 strands of floss, on each fish embroider the number, mouth and eye in chain stitch (see under EMBROIDERY). To work the eye, start in the center and work around until the eye is the desired size (B).

5 Place completed fishes in pelican's pouch.

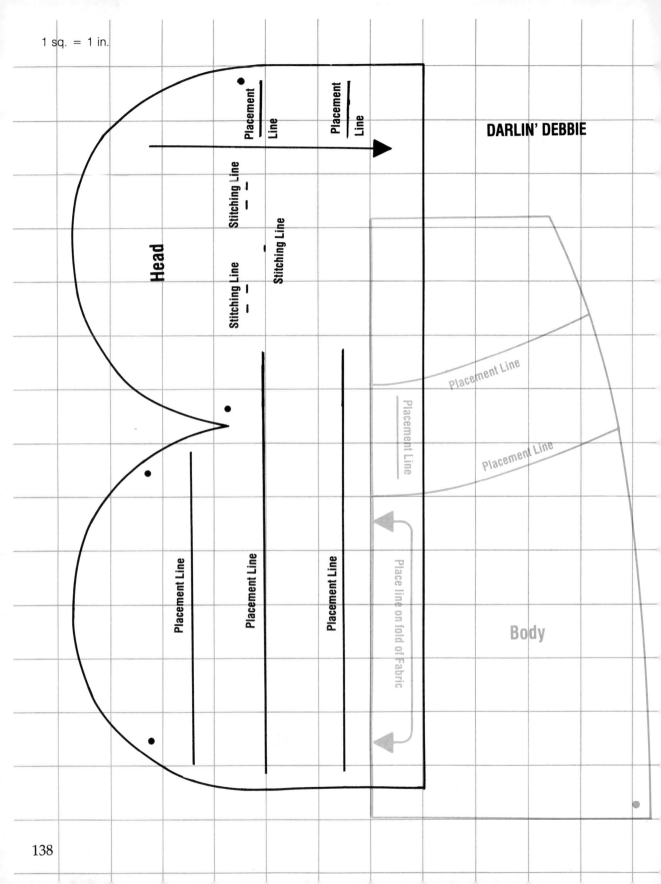

1 sq. = 1 in.

DARLIN' DEBBIE

Head

Placement Line

Placement Line

Stitching Line

Stitching Line

Stitching Line

Stitching Line

Placement Line

Placement Line

Placement Line

Placement Line

Placement Line

Placement Line

Place line on fold of Fabric

Body

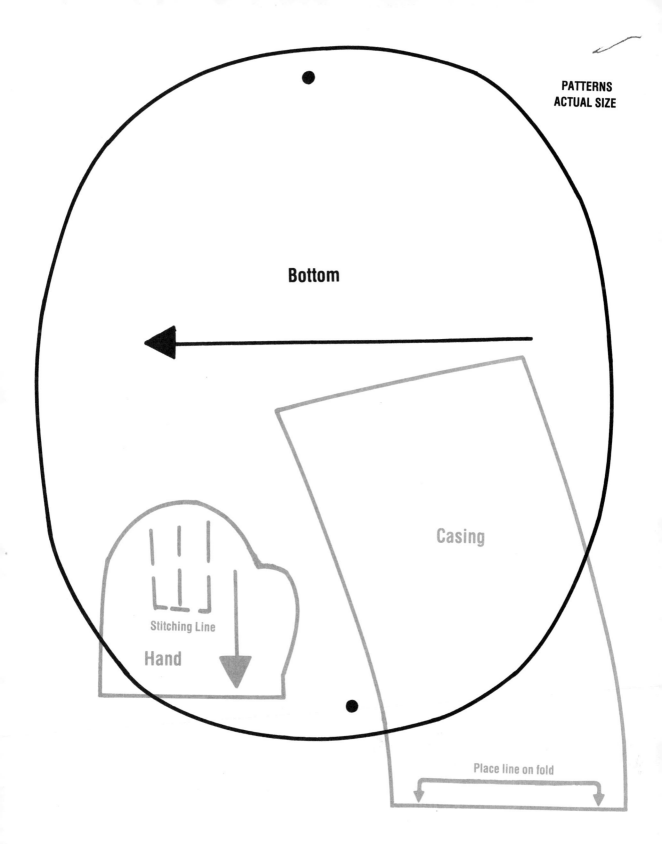

PATTERNS
ACTUAL SIZE

Bottom

Casing

Stitching Line

Hand

Place line on fold

139

1 sq. = 1 in.

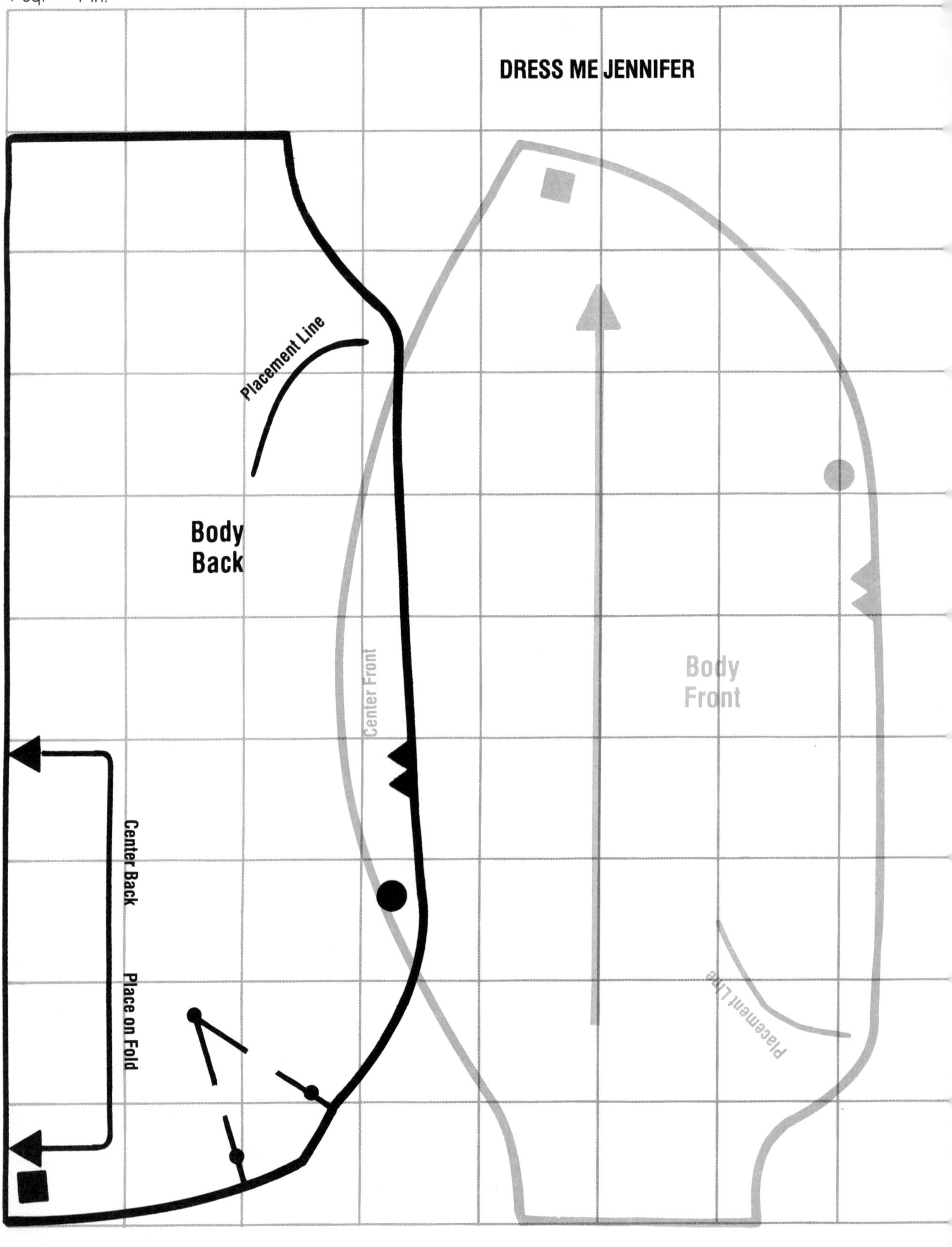

DRESS ME JENNIFER

Placement Line

**Body
Back**

Center Front

**Body
Front**

Center Back

Place on Fold

Placement Line

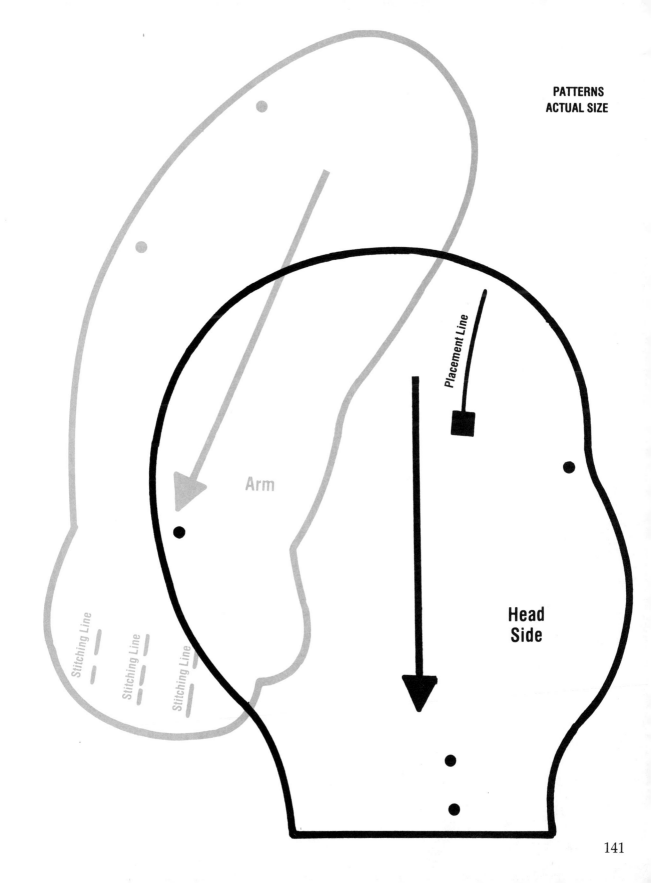

PATTERNS
ACTUAL SIZE

Placement Line

Arm

Stitching Line
Stitching Line
Stitching Line

Head
Side

141

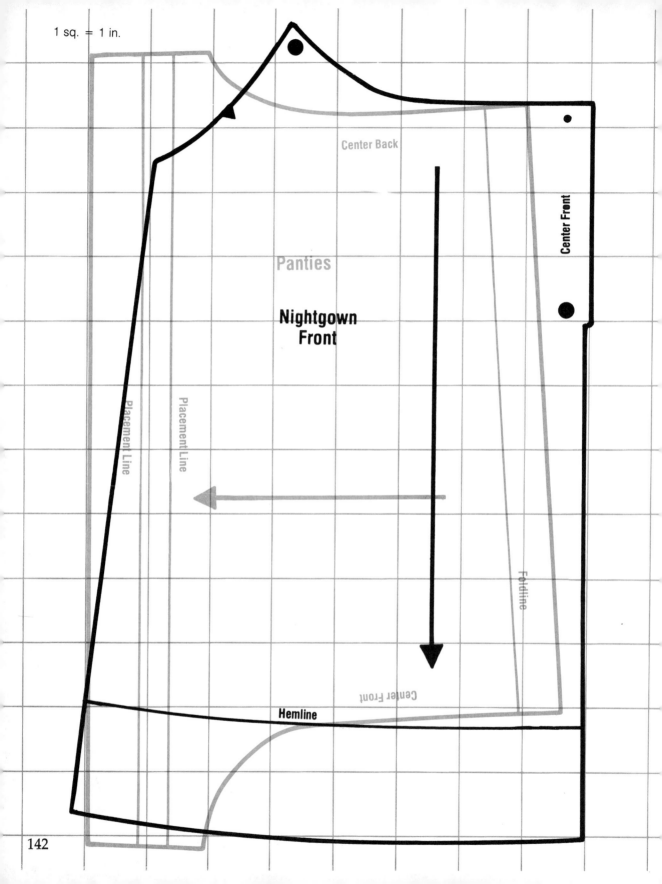

1 sq. = 1 in.

Center Back

Center Front

Panties

**Nightgown
Front**

Placement Line

Placement Line

Foldline

Center Front

Hemline

142

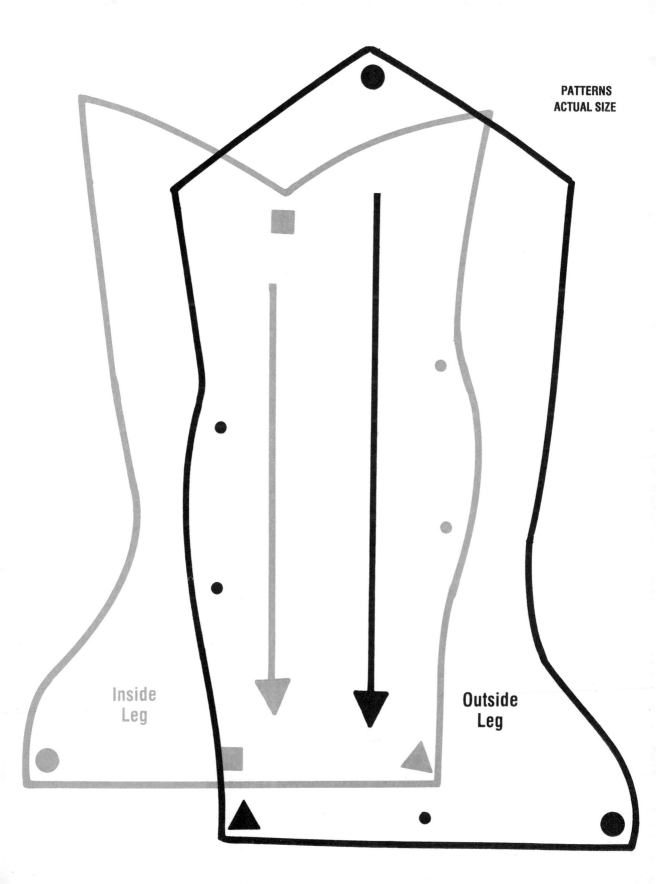

PATTERNS
ACTUAL SIZE

Inside
Leg

Outside
Leg

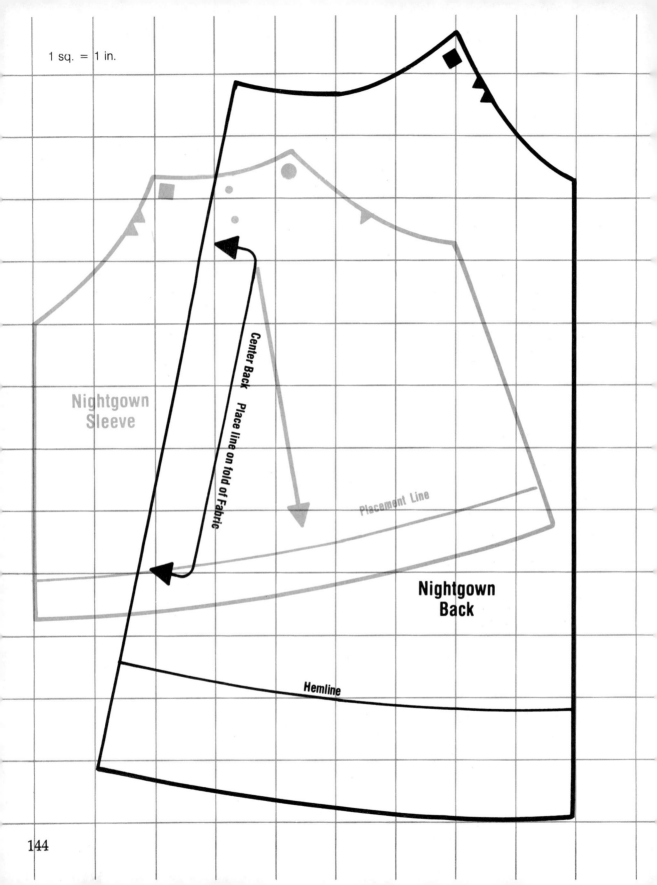

1 sq. = 1 in.

Nightgown
Sleeve

Center Back

Place line on fold of Fabric

Placement Line

Nightgown
Back

Hemline

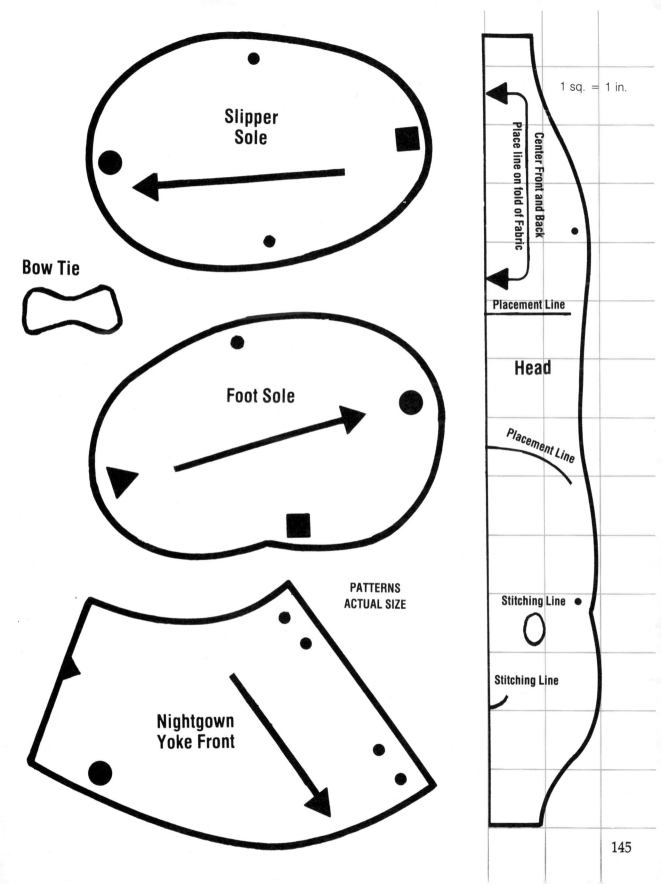

Slipper Sole

Bow Tie

Foot Sole

PATTERNS
ACTUAL SIZE

Nightgown
Yoke Front

1 sq. = 1 in.

Center Front and Back

Place line on fold of Fabric

Placement Line

Head

Placement Line

Stitching Line

Stitching Line

145

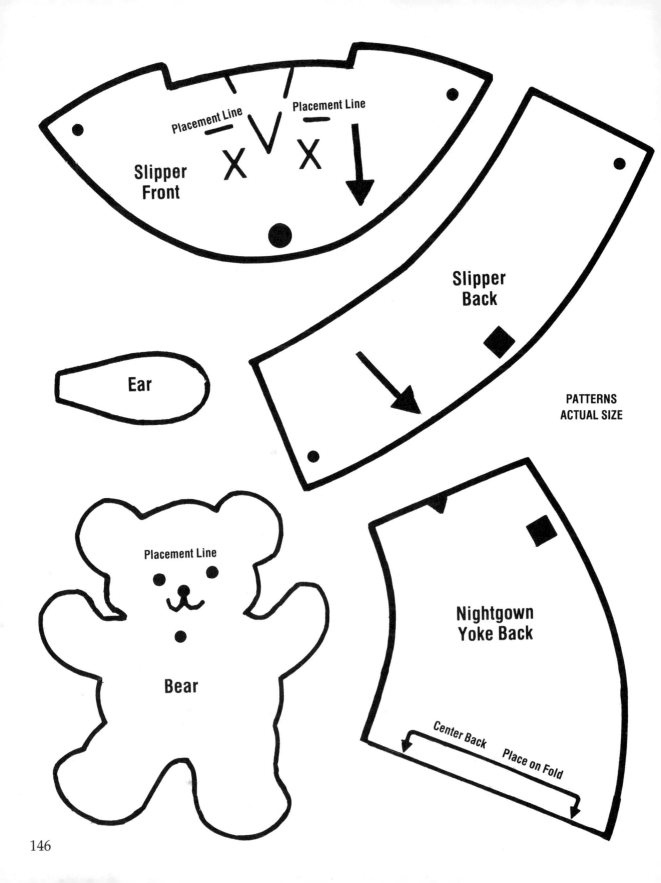

Slipper
Front

Placement Line   Placement Line

Slipper
Back

Ear

PATTERNS
ACTUAL SIZE

Placement Line

Bear

Nightgown
Yoke Back

Center Back   Place on Fold

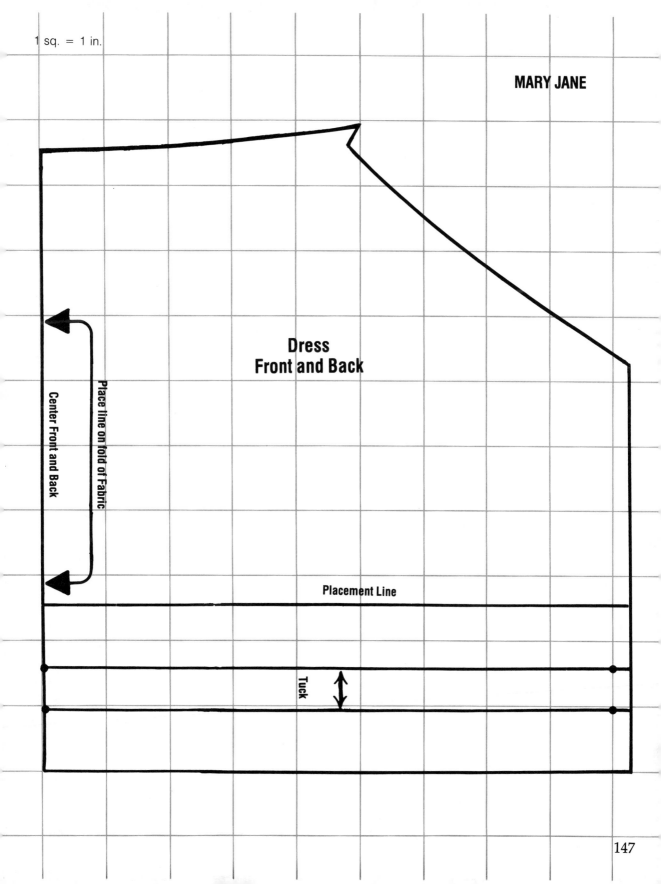

1 sq. = 1 in.

MARY JANE

**Dress
Front and Back**

Center Front and Back

Place line on fold of Fabric

Placement Line

Tuck

147

1 sq. = 1 in.

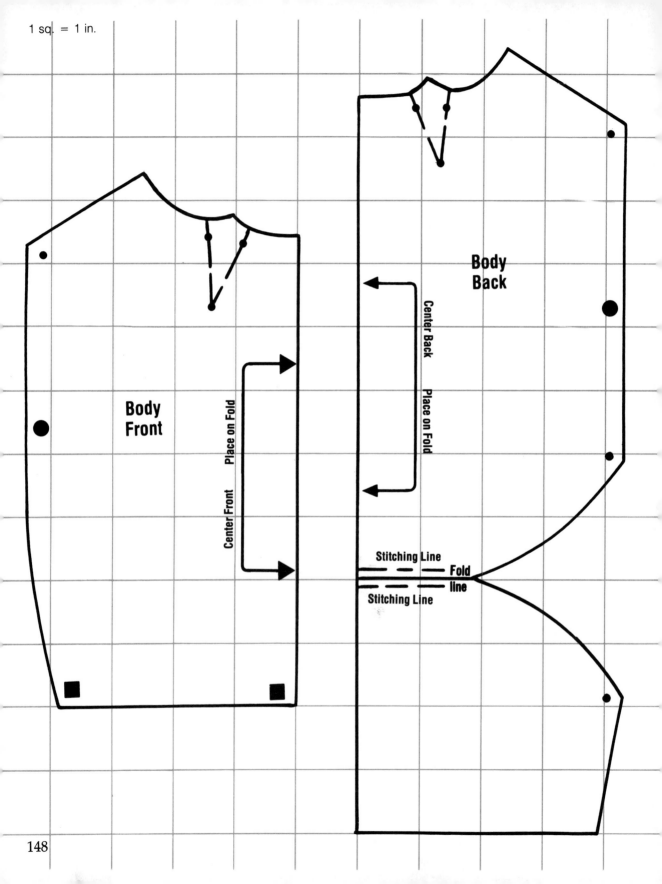

Body
Back

Center Back

Place on Fold

Body
Front

Place on Fold

Center Front

Stitching Line

Fold
line

Stitching Line

148

**PATTERNS
ACTUAL SIZE**

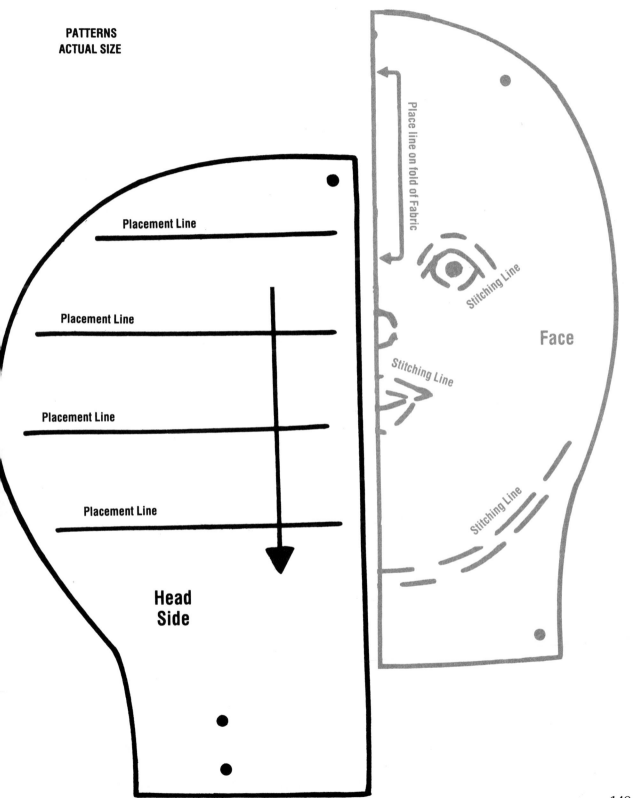

Placement Line

Placement Line

Placement Line

Placement Line

**Head
Side**

Place line on fold of Fabric

Stitching Line

Stitching Line

Stitching Line

Face

149

1 sq. = 1 in.

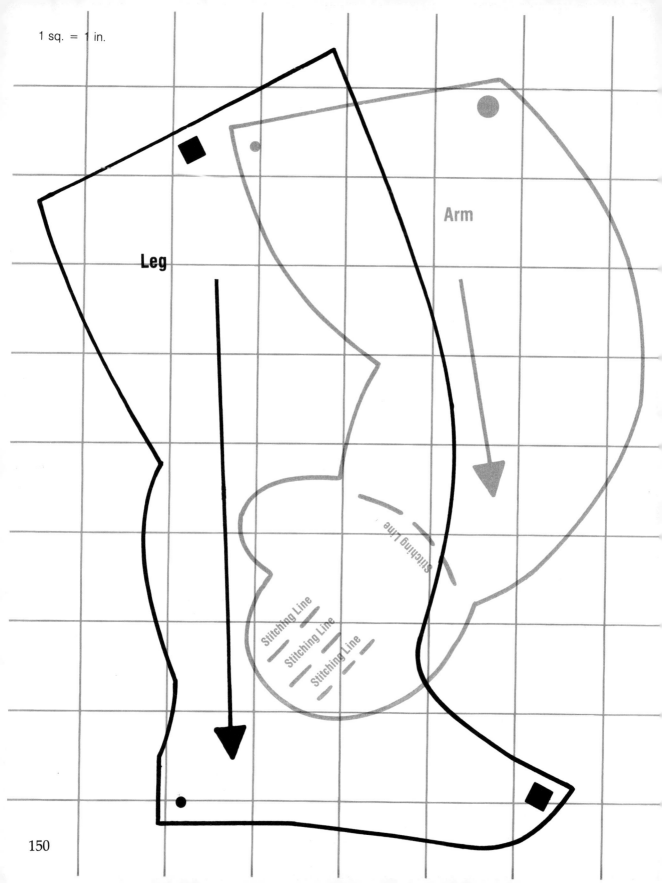

Leg

Arm

Stitching Line

Stitching Line
Stitching Line
Stitching Line

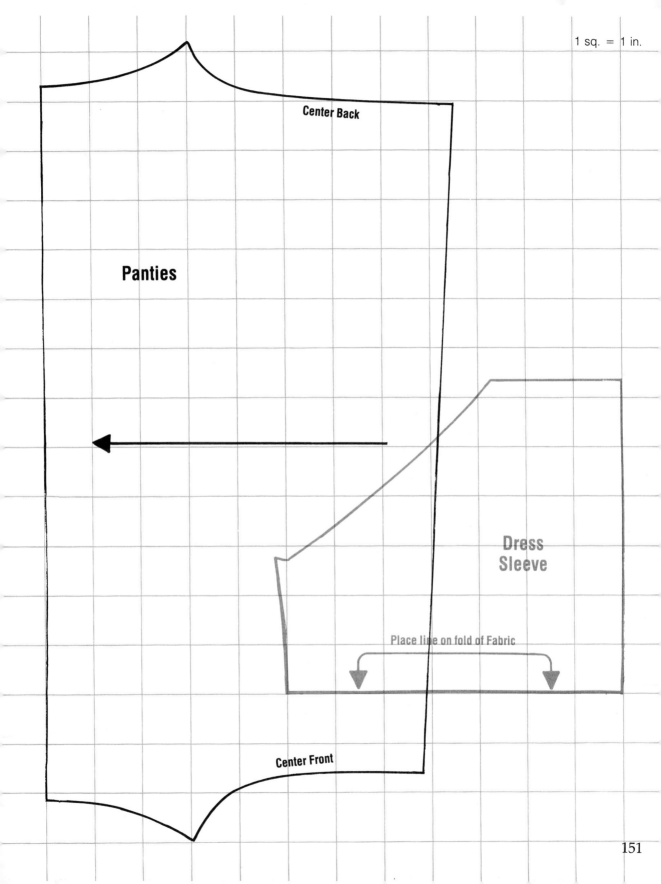

Panties

Center Back

Center Front

Dress Sleeve

Place line on fold of Fabric

1 sq. = 1 in.

151

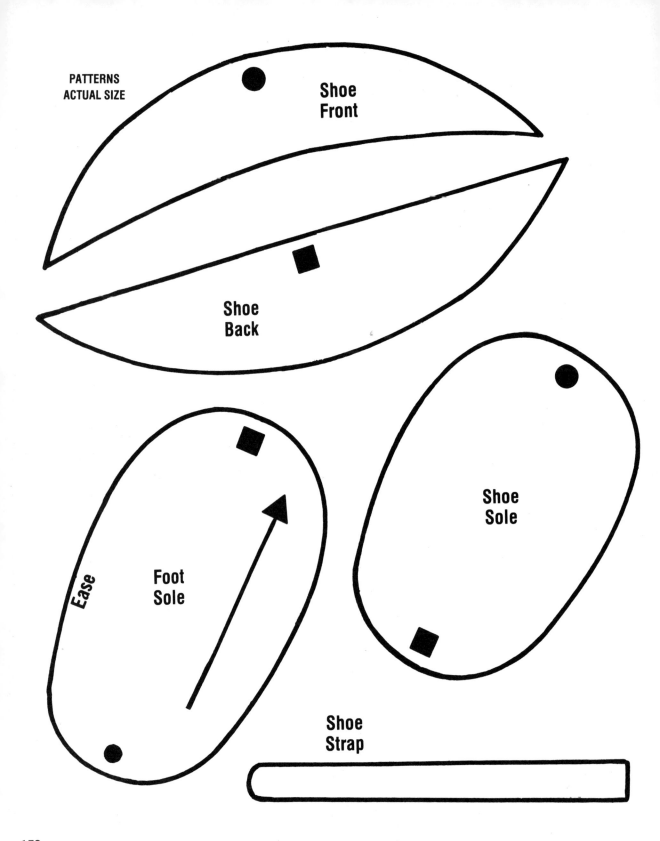

PATTERNS
ACTUAL SIZE

Shoe
Front

Shoe
Back

Shoe
Sole

Ease

Foot
Sole

Shoe
Strap

152

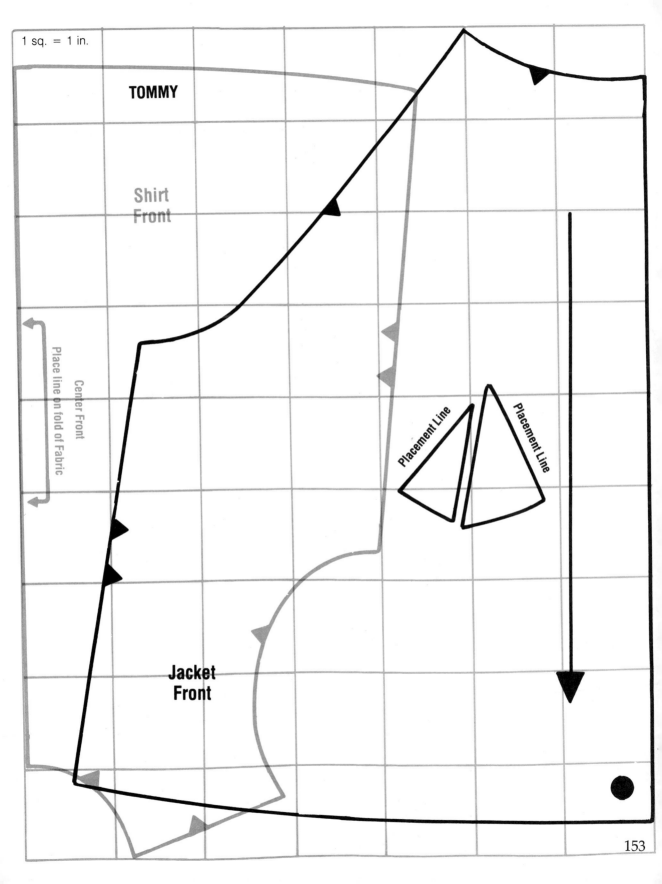

1 sq. = 1 in.

TOMMY

Shirt
Front

Center Front
Place line on fold of Fabric

Jacket
Front

Placement Line

Placement Line

153

1 sq. = 1 in.

Arm

Place line on fold of Fabric

**Jacket
Front Facing**

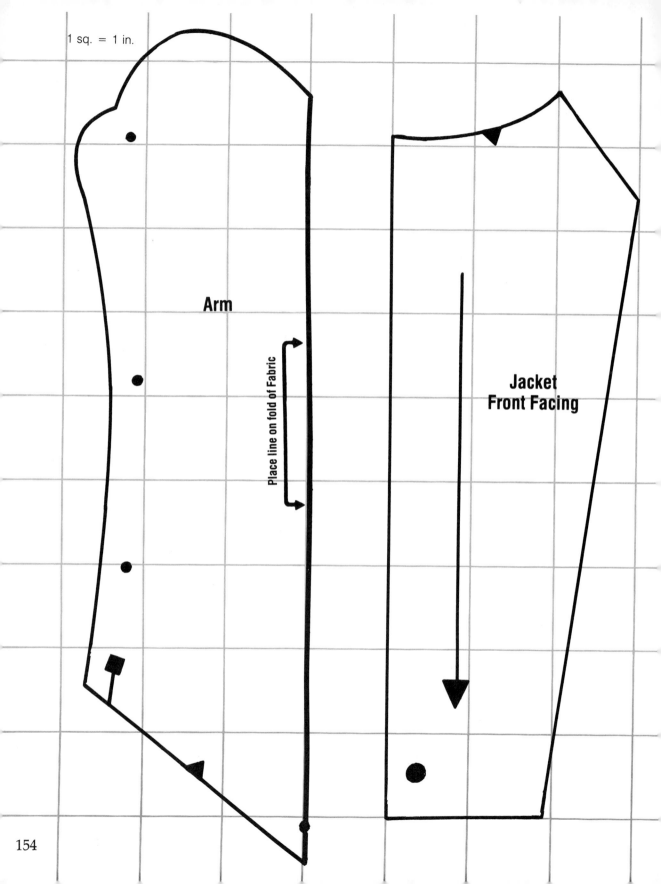

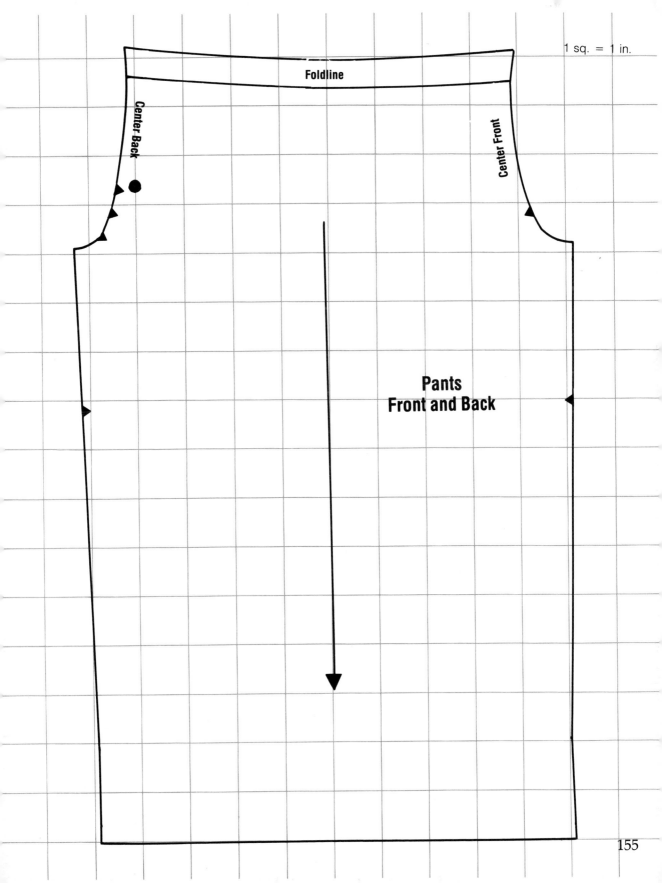

1 sq. = 1 in.

Foldline

Center Back

Center Front

Pants
Front and Back

155

1 sq. = 1 in.

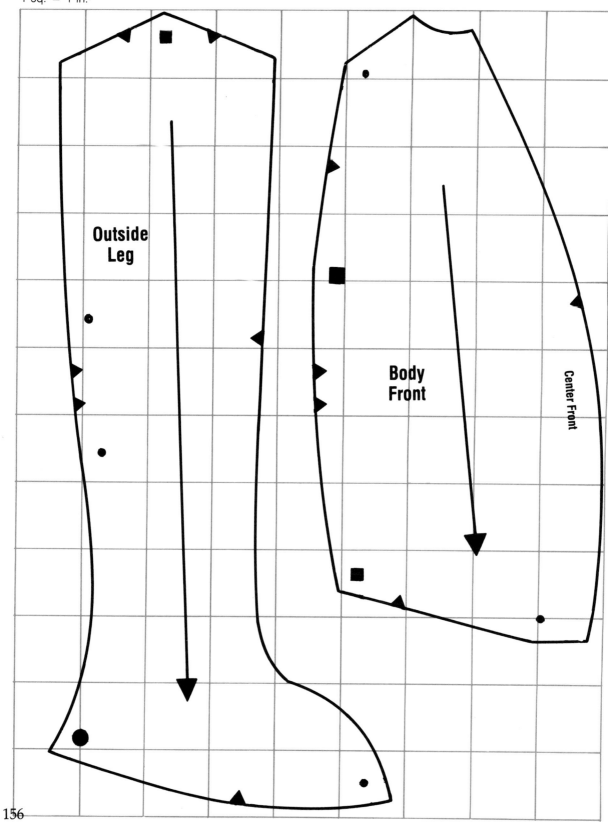

Outside Leg

Body Front

Center Front

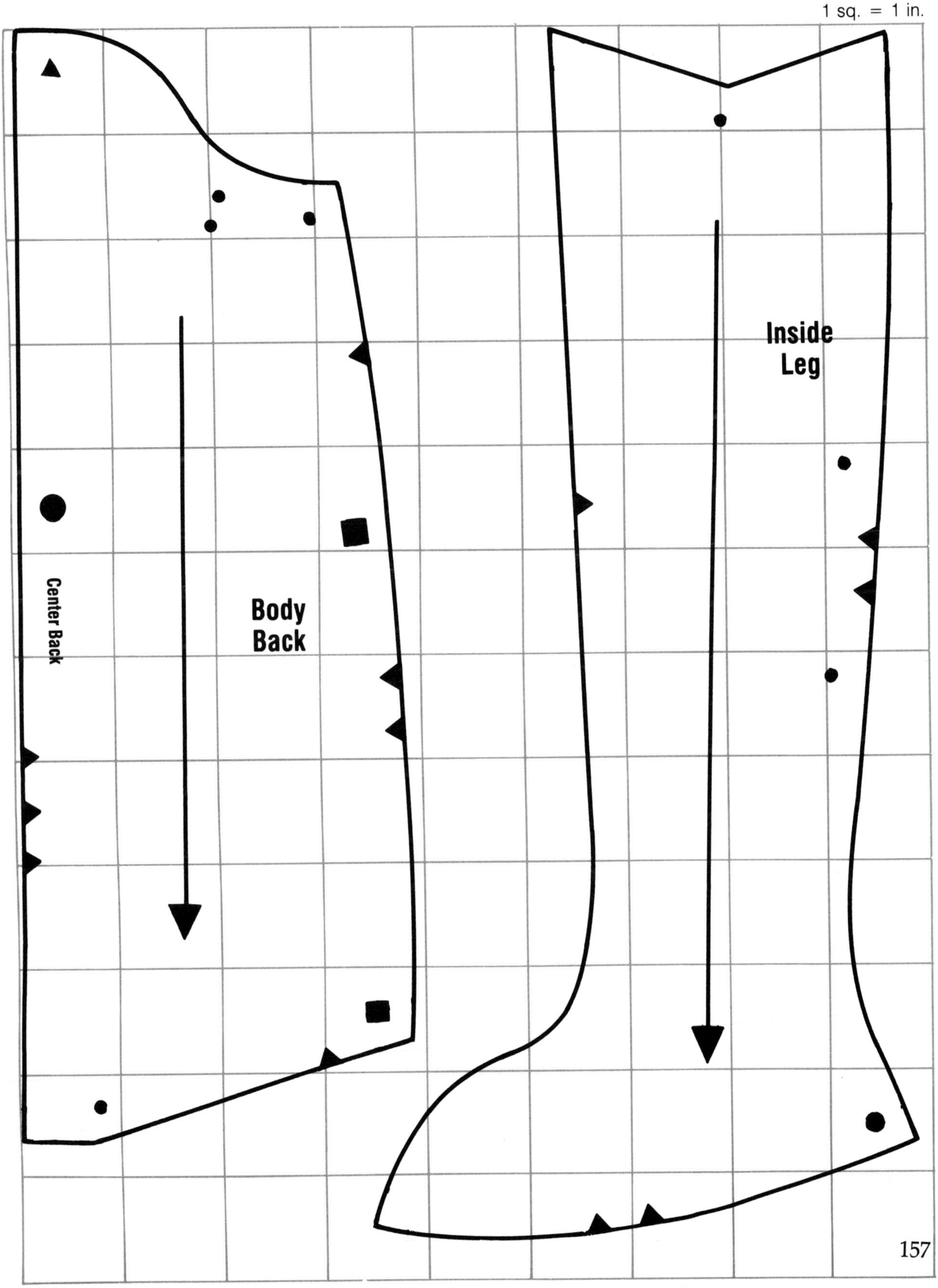
1 sq. = 1 in.
Center Back
Body Back
Inside Leg

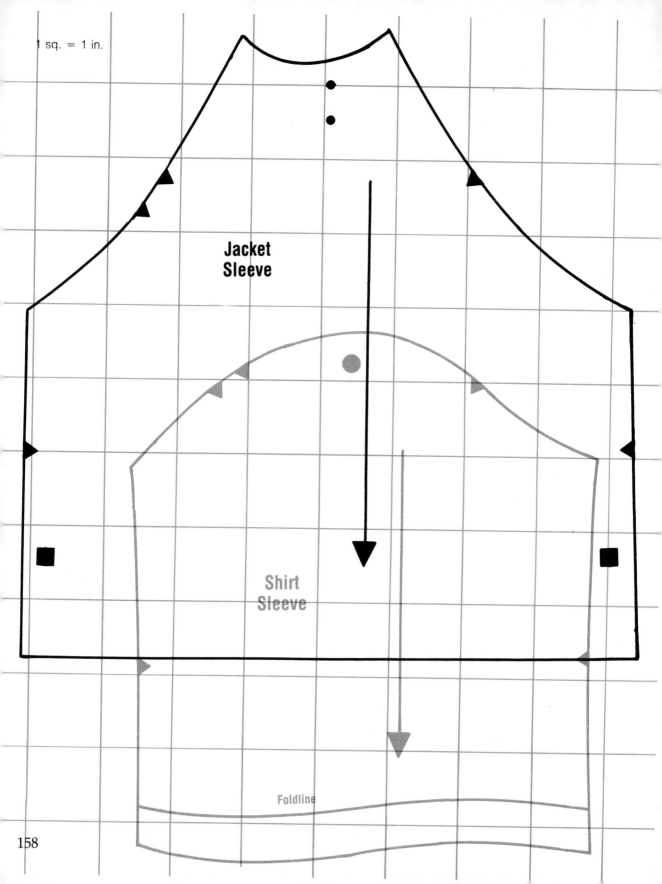

1 sq. = 1 in.

**Jacket
Sleeve**

Shirt
Sleeve

Foldline

158

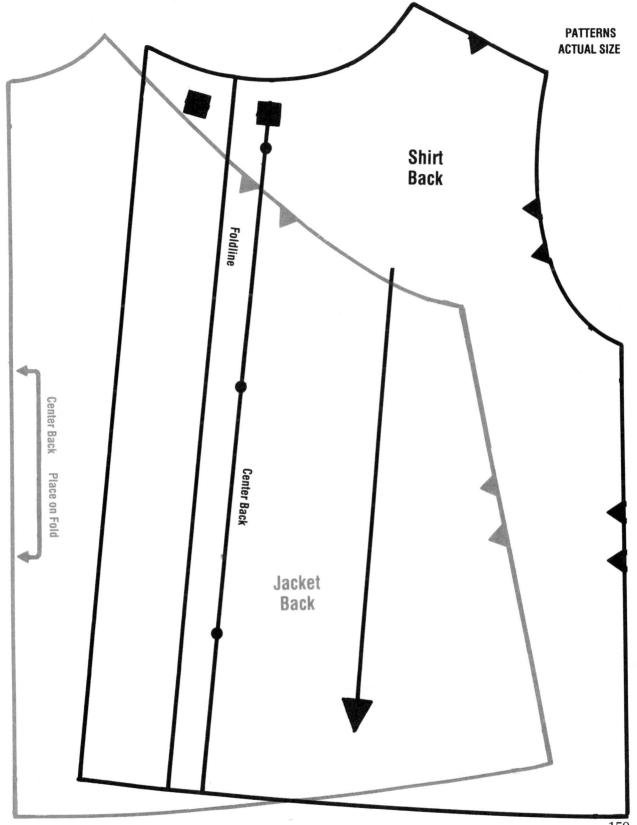

Shirt
Back

Foldline

Center Back

Center Back

Place on Fold

Jacket
Back

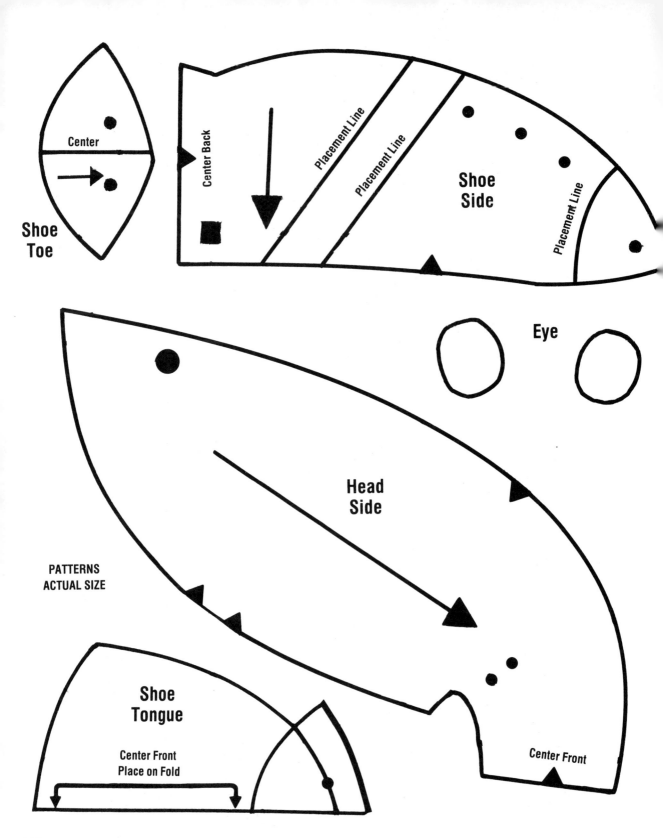

Shoe
Toe

Center

Center Back

Placement Line

Placement Line

Shoe
Side

Placement Line

Eye

Head
Side

PATTERNS
ACTUAL SIZE

Shoe
Tongue

Center Front
Place on Fold

Center Front

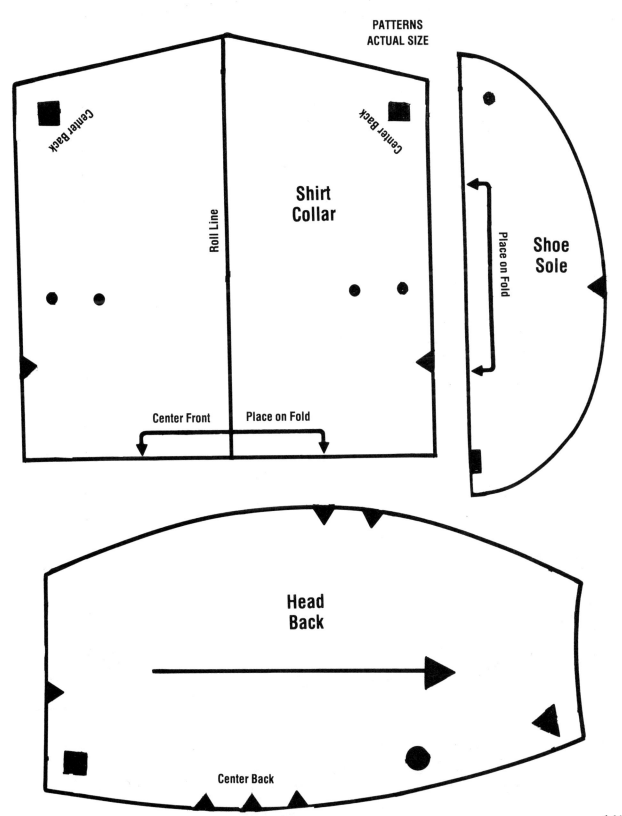

PATTERNS
ACTUAL SIZE

Center Back

Center Back

Roll Line

Shirt
Collar

Center Front

Place on Fold

Place on Fold

Shoe
Sole

Head
Back

Center Back

161

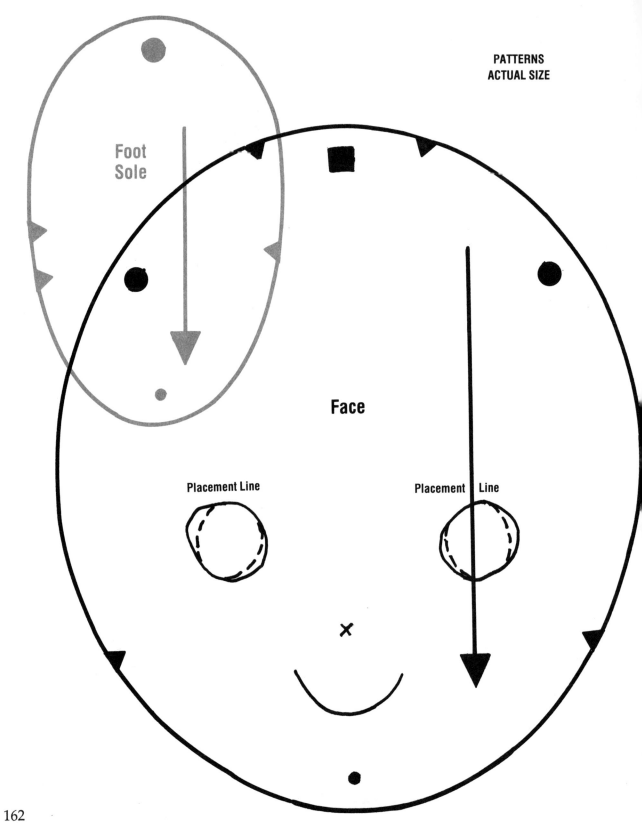

PATTERNS
ACTUAL SIZE

Foot
Sole

Face

Placement Line

Placement Line

162

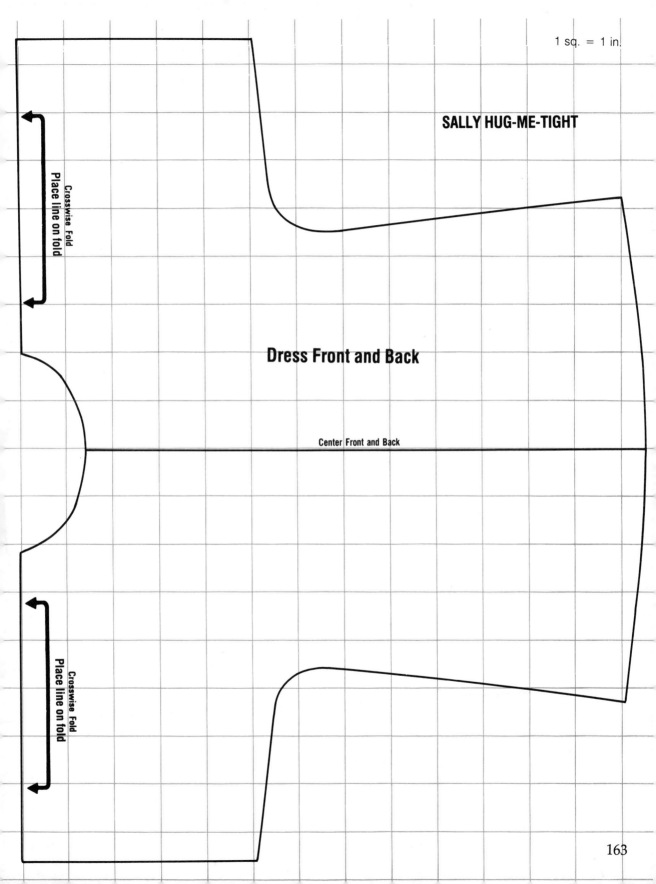

1 sq. = 1 in.

SALLY HUG-ME-TIGHT

Crosswise Fold
Place line on fold

Dress Front and Back

Center Front and Back

Crosswise Fold
Place line on fold

163

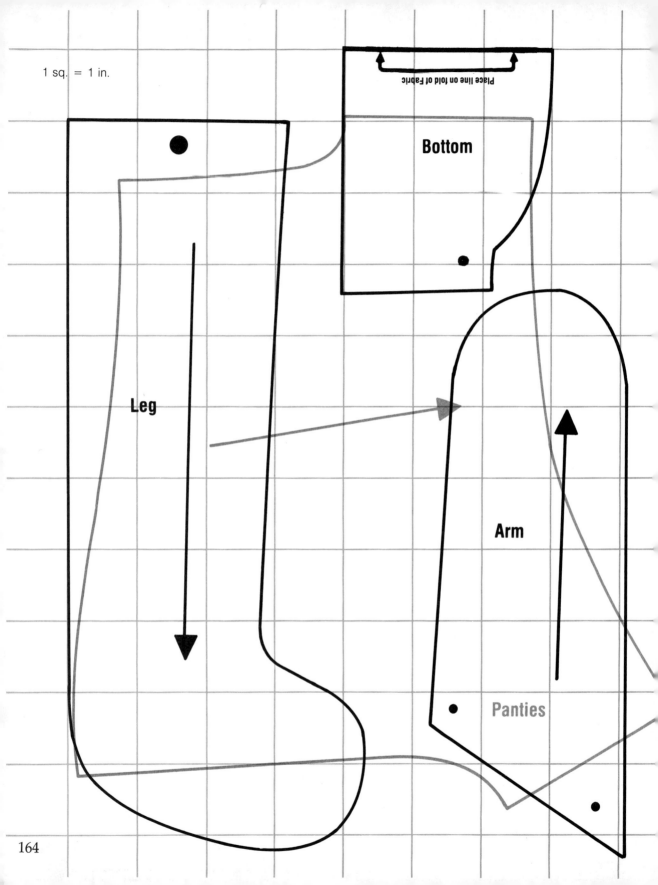

1 sq. = 1 in.

Bottom

Place line on fold of Fabric

Leg

Arm

Panties

164

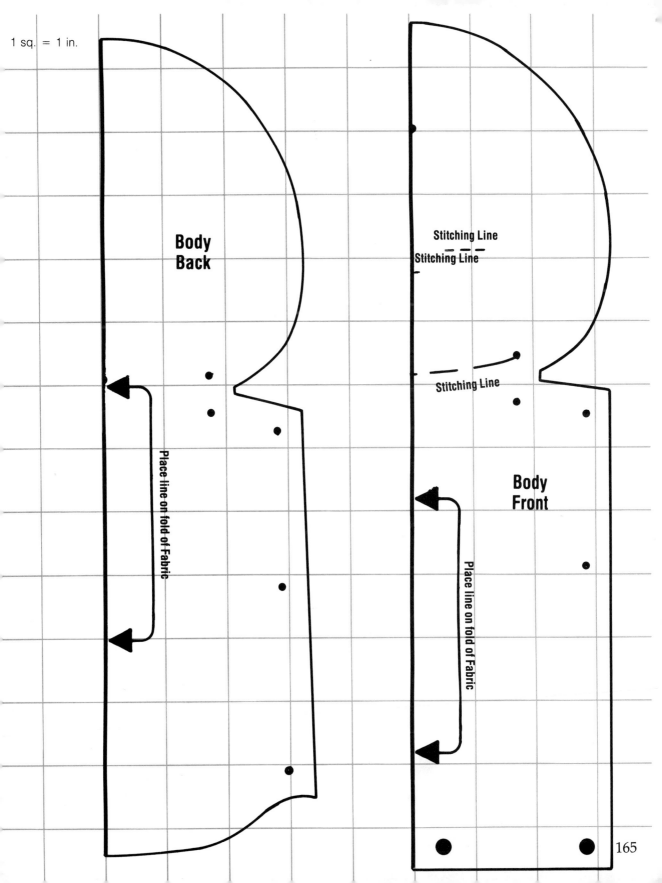

1 sq. = 1 in.

**Body
Back**

Place line on fold of Fabric

Stitching Line
Stitching Line

Stitching Line

**Body
Front**

Place line on fold of Fabric

165

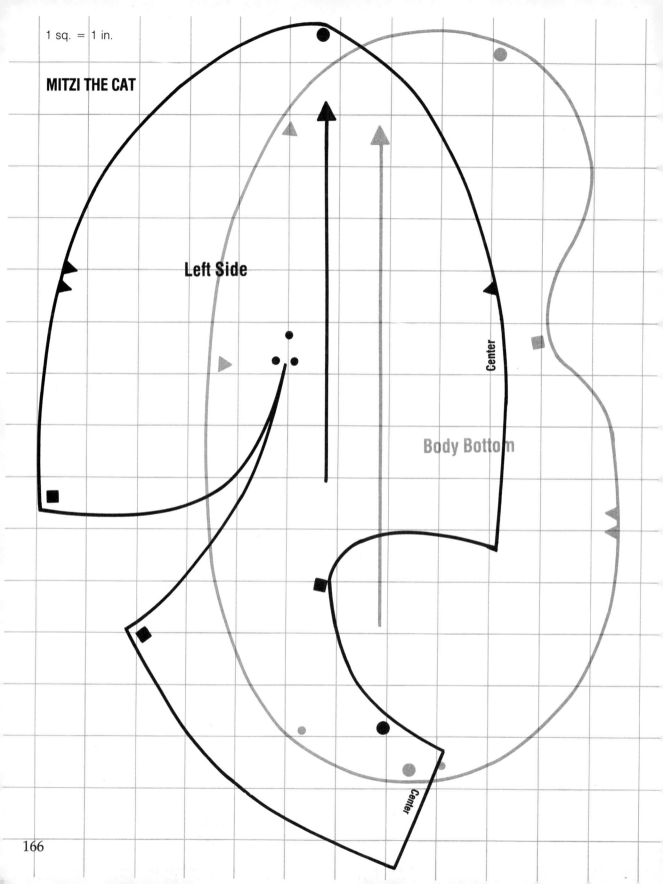

1 sq. = 1 in.

MITZI THE CAT

Left Side

Center

Body Bottom

Center

166

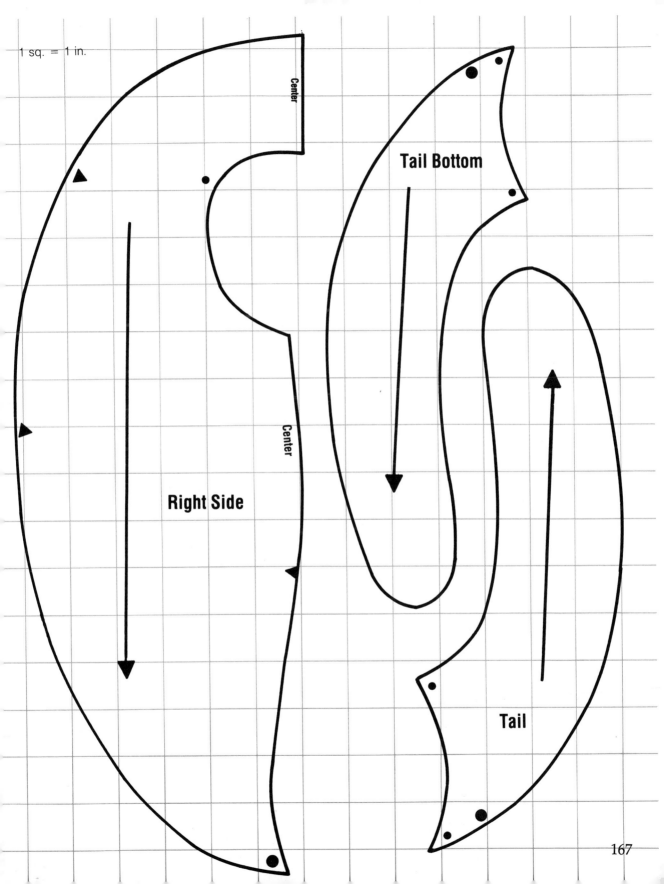

1 sq. = 1 in.

Center

Tail Bottom

Center

Right Side

Tail

167

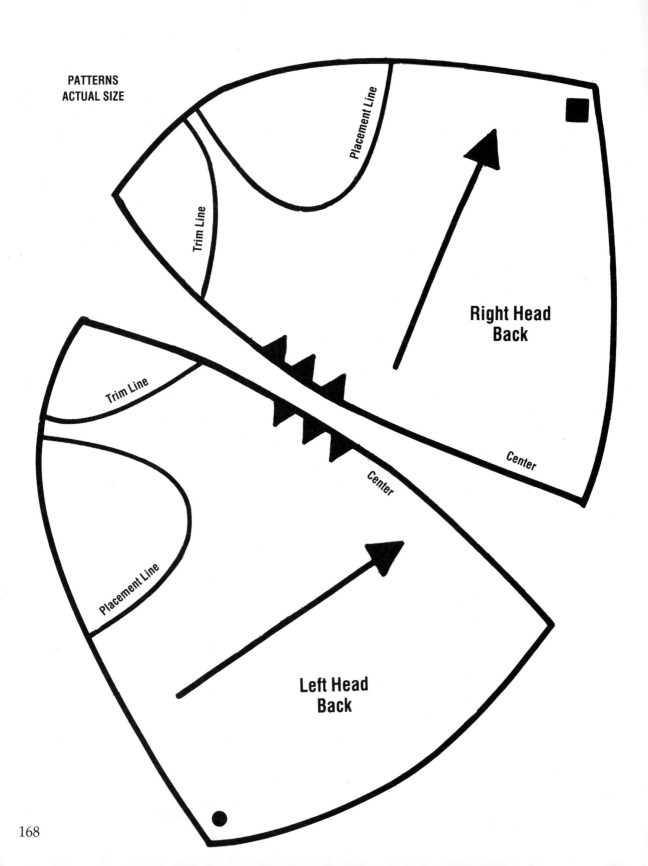

PATTERNS
ACTUAL SIZE

Placement Line

Trim Line

Right Head
Back

Center

Trim Line

Center

Placement Line

Left Head
Back

168

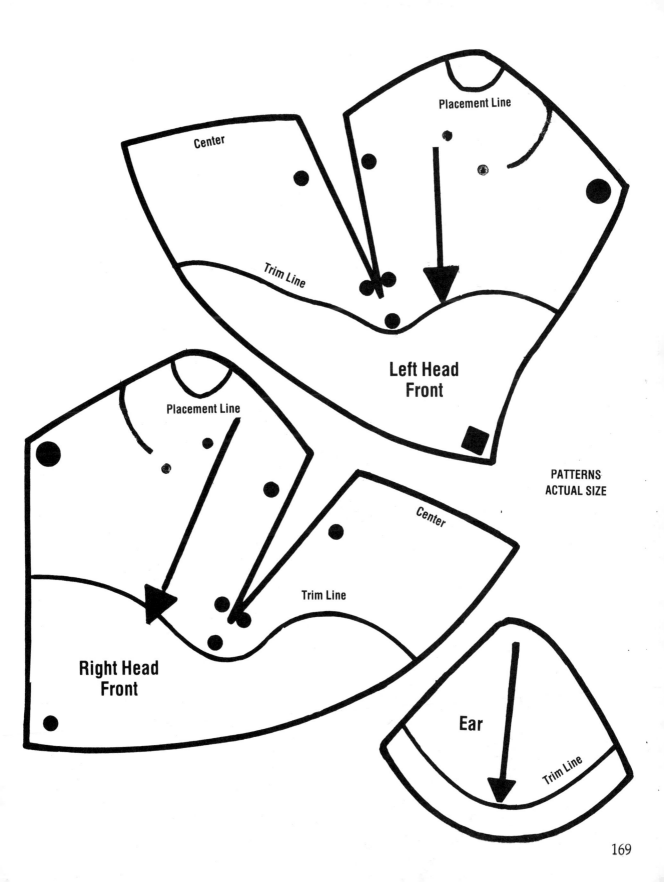

Center

Placement Line

Trim Line

**Left Head
Front**

PATTERNS
ACTUAL SIZE

Placement Line

Center

Trim Line

**Right Head
Front**

Ear

Trim Line

MR. AND MRS. MOUSE

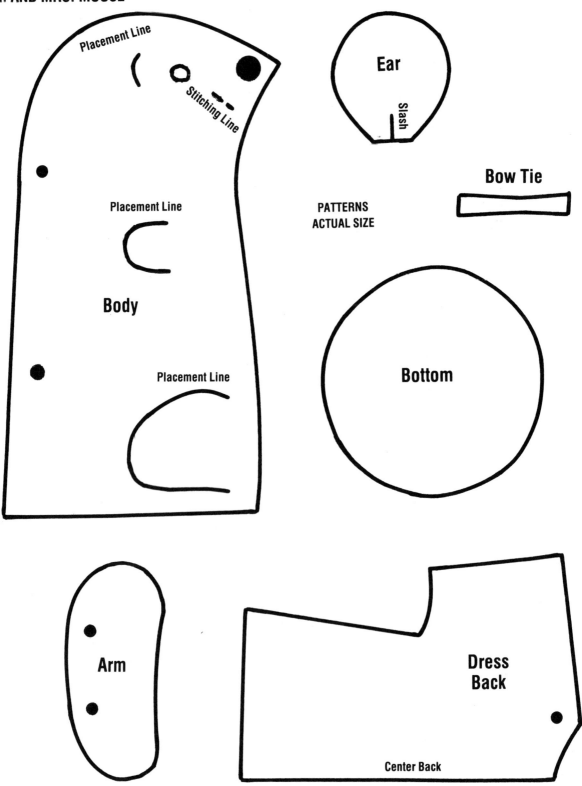

Placement Line

Stitching Line

Placement Line

Body

Placement Line

Ear

Slash

Bow Tie

PATTERNS
ACTUAL SIZE

Bottom

Arm

Dress
Back

Center Back

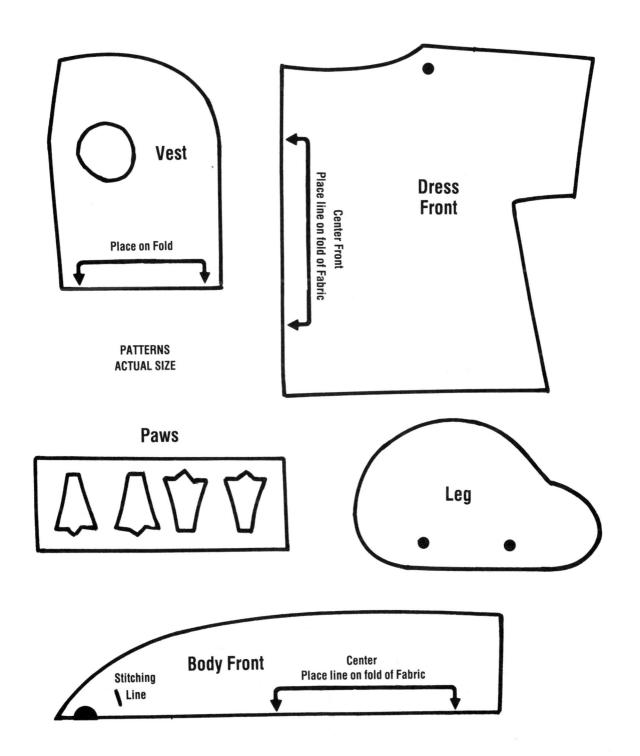

Vest

Place on Fold

PATTERNS
ACTUAL SIZE

Dress
Front

Center Front
Place line on fold of Fabric

Paws

Leg

Body Front

Stitching
Line

Center
Place line on fold of Fabric

171

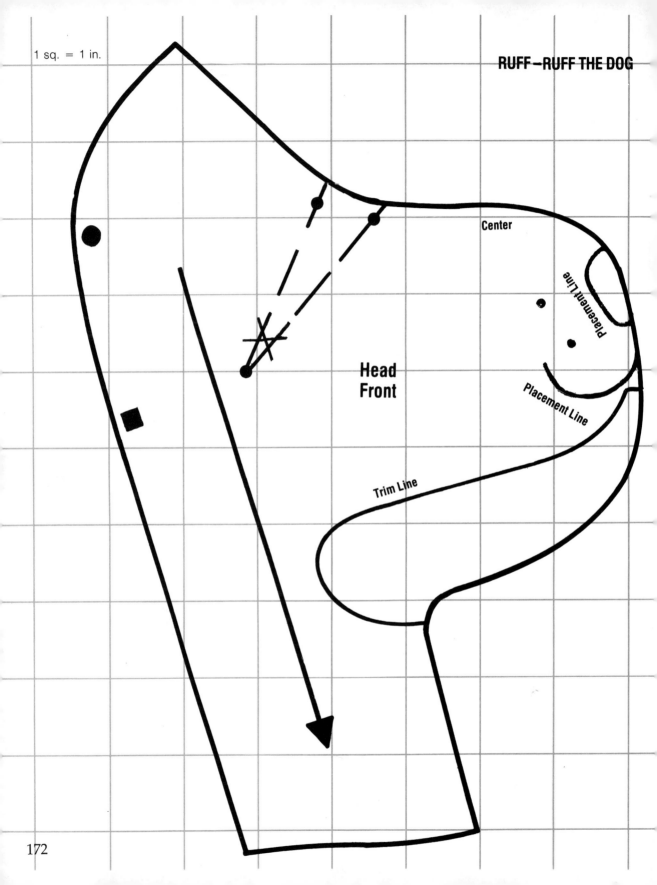

1 sq. = 1 in.

RUFF—RUFF THE DOG

Center

Placement Line

Head
Front

Placement Line

Trim Line

172

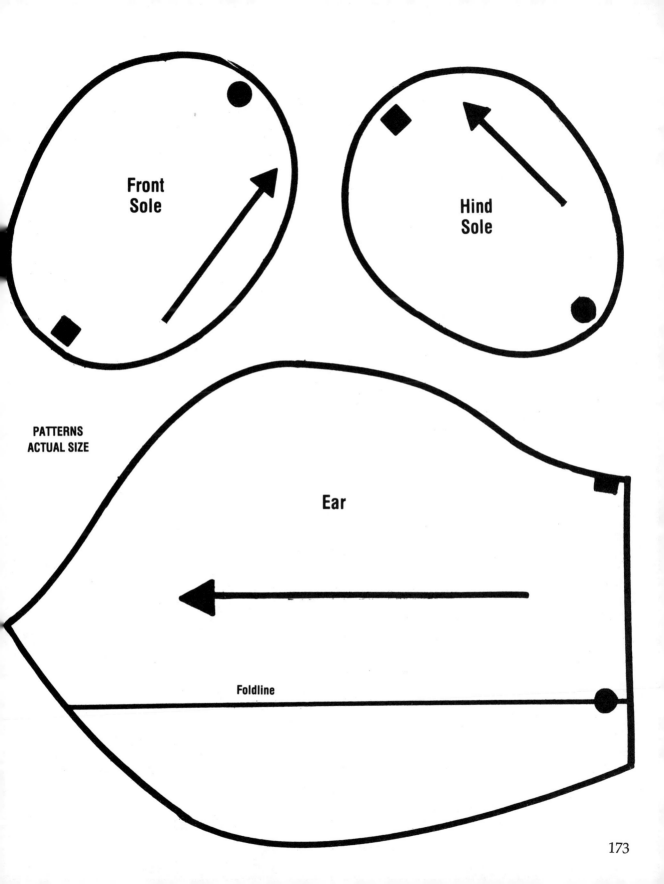

Front Sole

Hind Sole

PATTERNS ACTUAL SIZE

Ear

Foldline

173

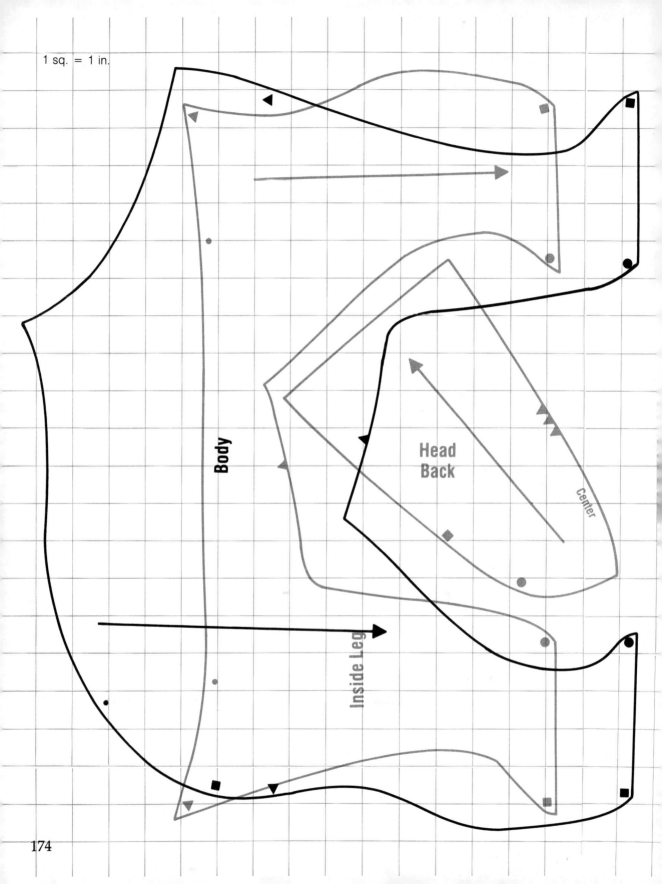

1 sq. = 1 in.

Body

Head
Back

Center

Inside Leg

174

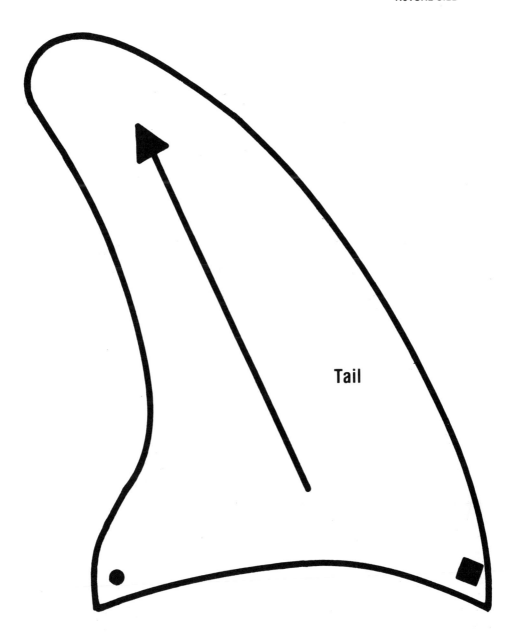

Tail

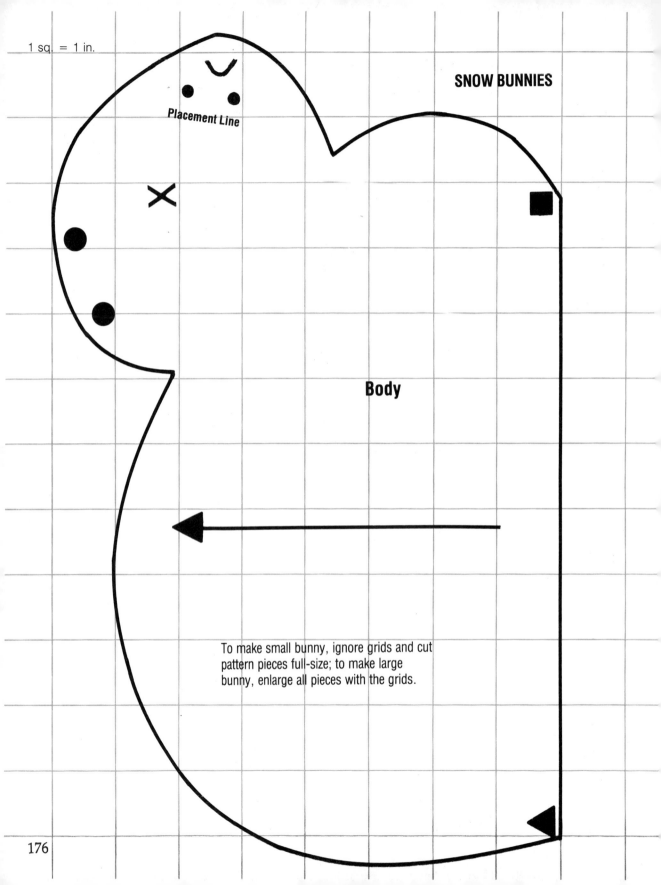

1 sq. = 1 in.

Placement Line

SNOW BUNNIES

Body

To make small bunny, ignore grids and cut
pattern pieces full-size; to make large
bunny, enlarge all pieces with the grids.

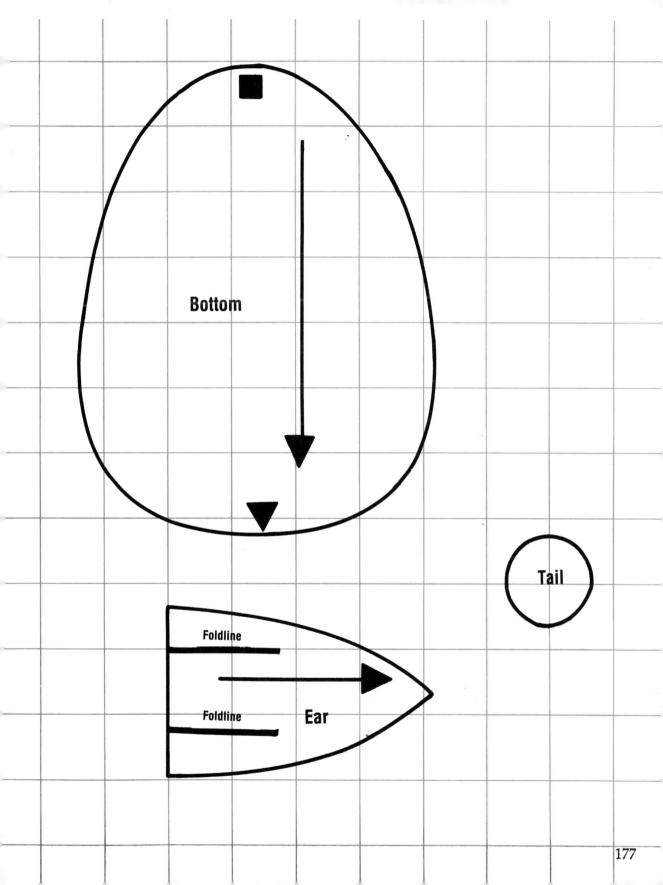

Bottom

Tail

Foldline

Foldline

Ear

1 sq. = 1 in.

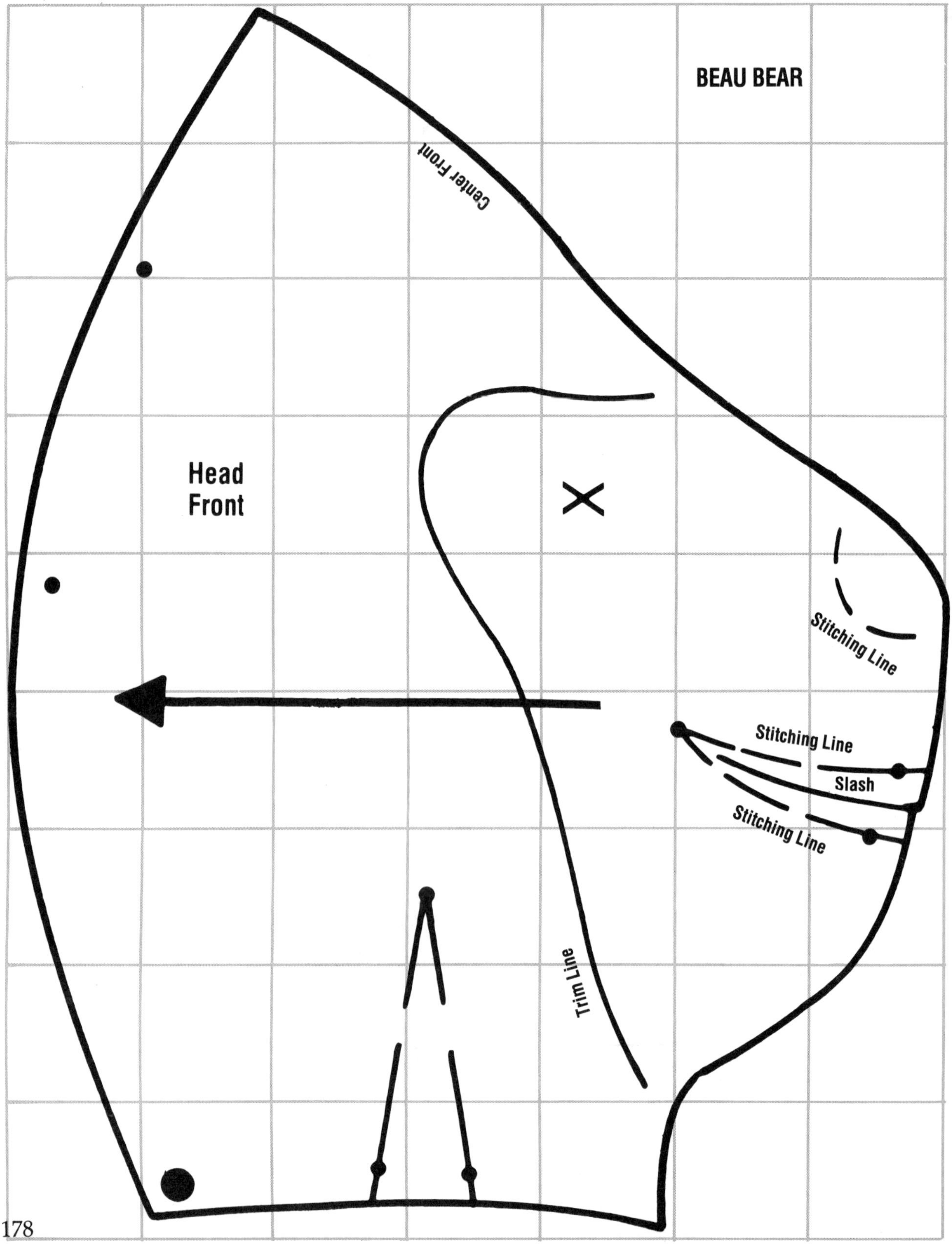

BEAU BEAR

Center Front

Head
Front

X

Stitching Line

Stitching Line

Slash

Stitching Line

Trim Line

178

1 sq. = 1 in.

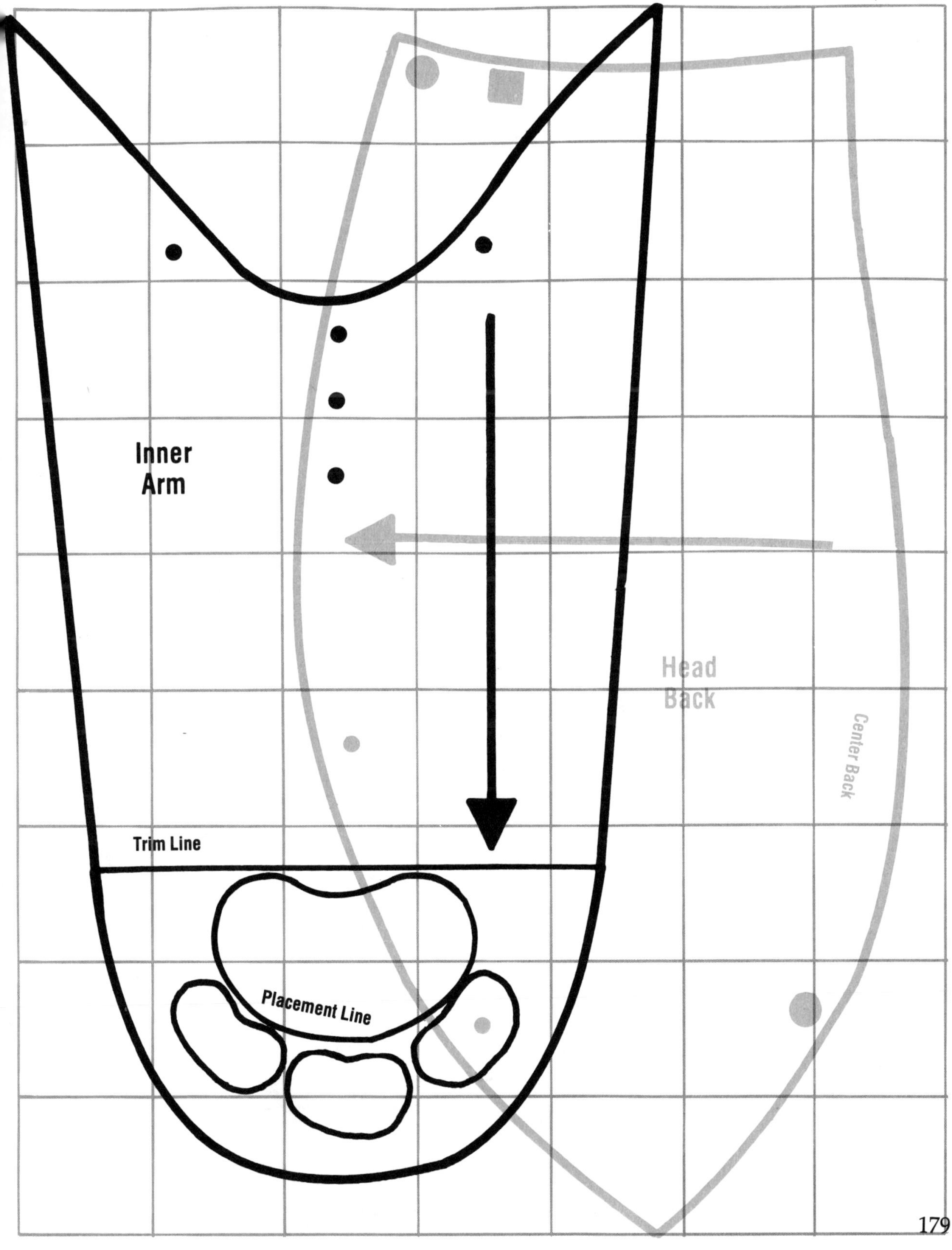

Inner Arm

Head Back

Center Back

Trim Line

Placement Line

179

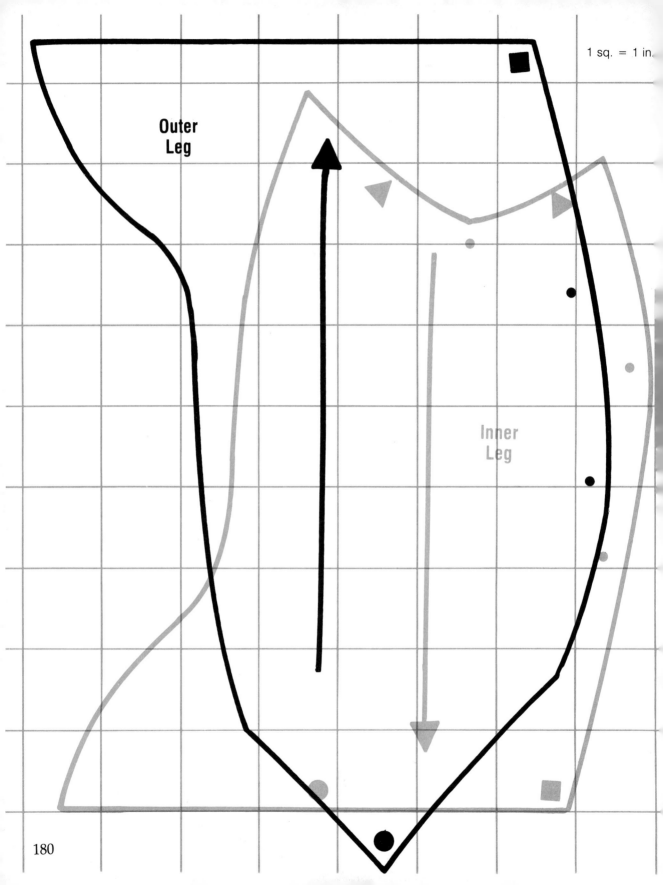

Outer
Leg

Inner
Leg

1 sq. = 1 in.

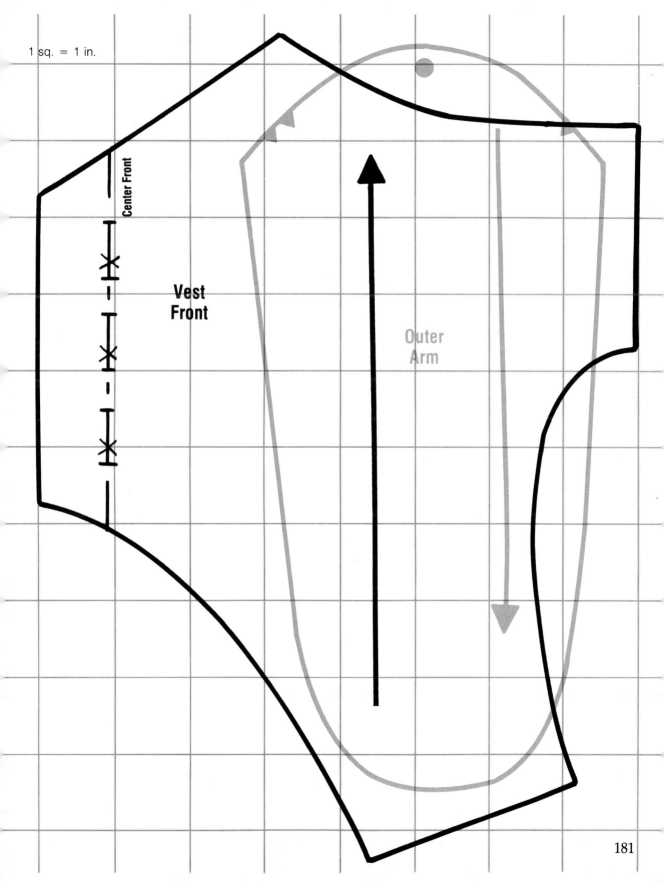

1 sq. = 1 in.

Center Front

Vest
Front

Outer
Arm

181

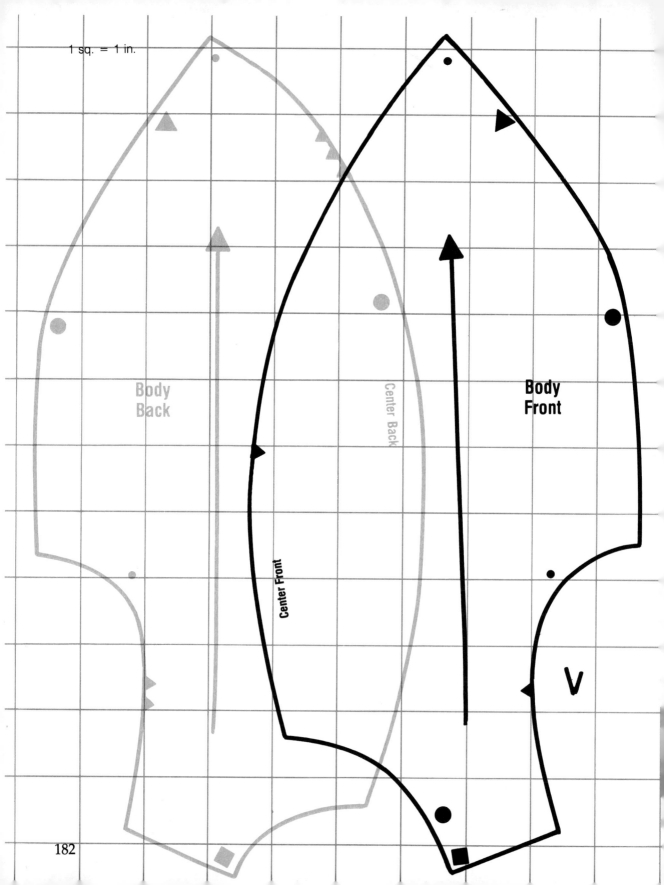

1 sq. = 1 in.

Body
Back

Center Back

Body
Front

Center Front

V

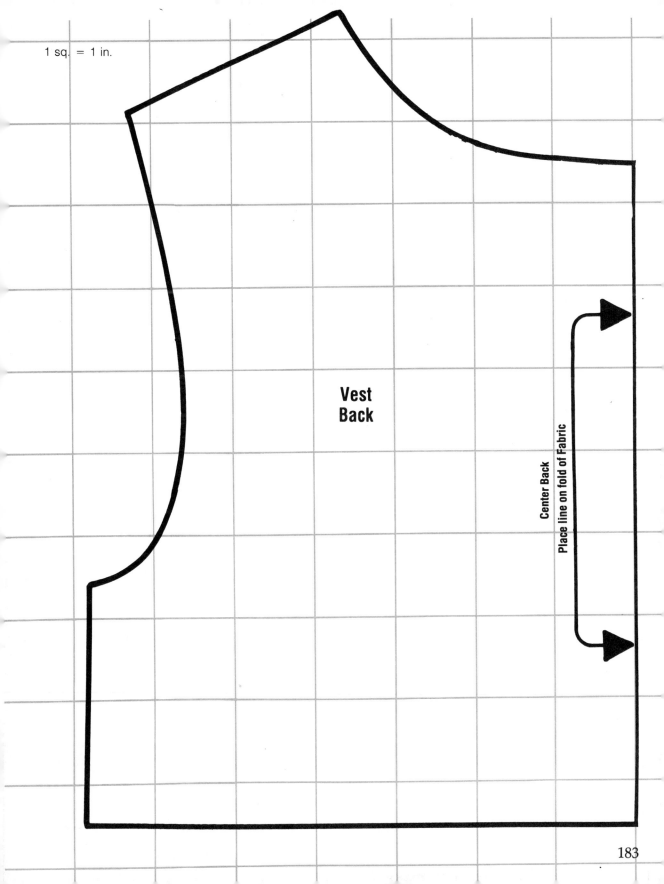

1 sq. = 1 in.

Vest Back

Center Back

Place line on fold of Fabric

183

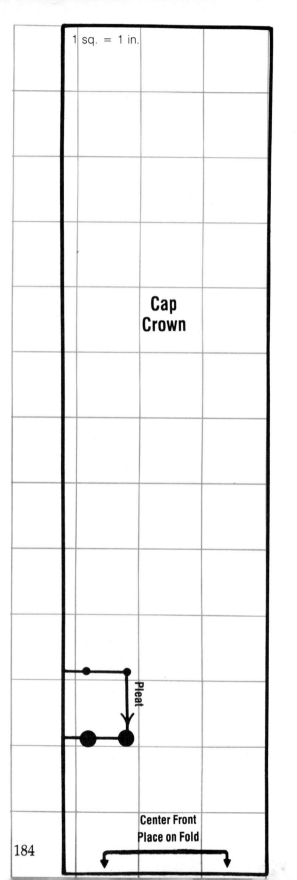

1 sq. = 1 in.

Cap
Crown

Pleat

Center Front
Place on Fold

Front
Paw

PATTERNS
ACTUAL SIZE

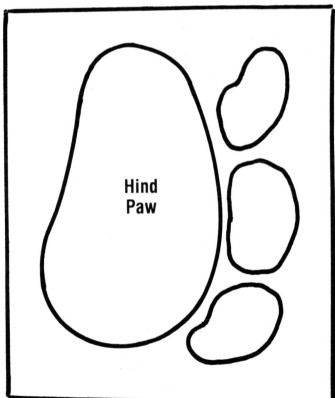

Hind
Paw

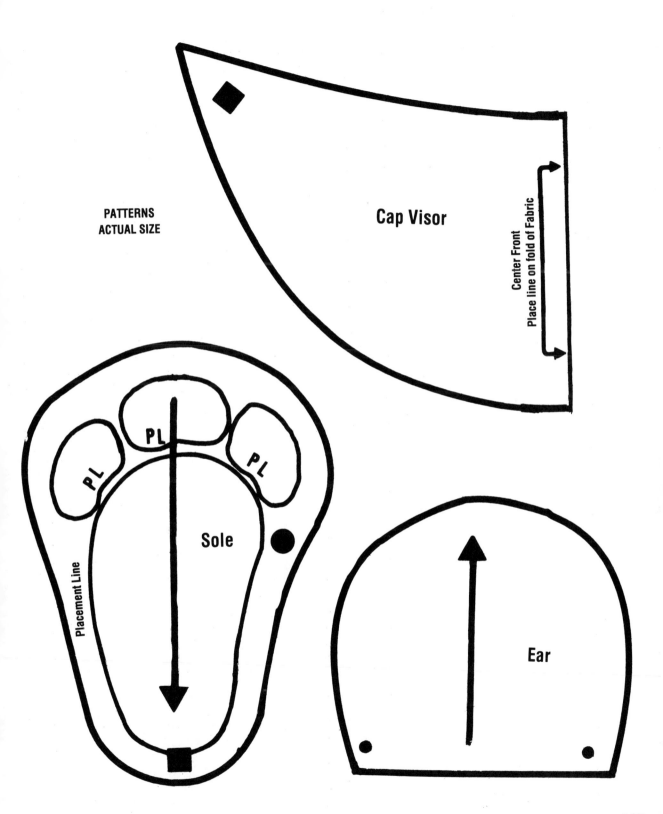

PATTERNS
ACTUAL SIZE

Cap Visor

Center Front
Place line on fold of Fabric

PL

PL

PL

Sole

Placement Line

Ear

185

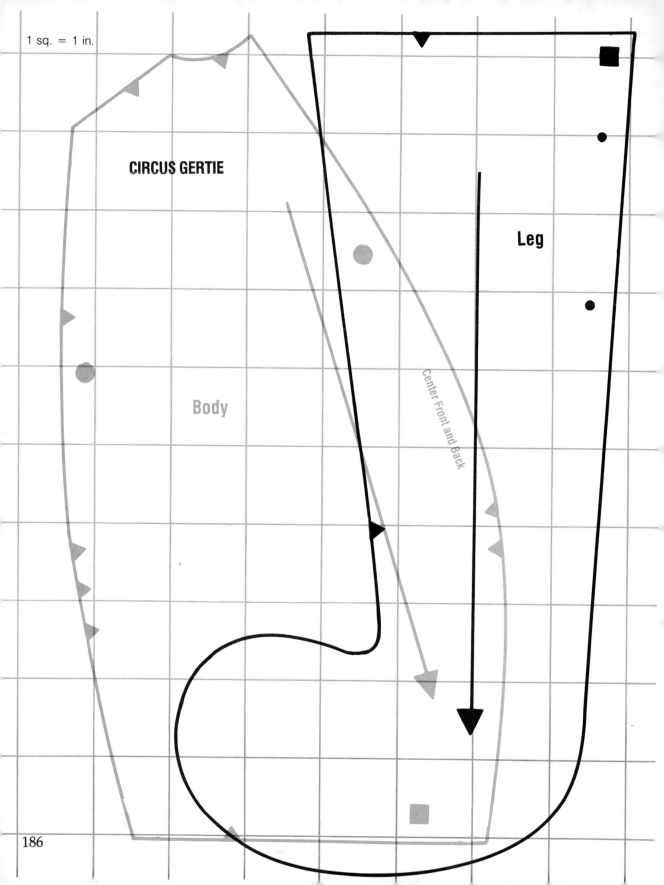

1 sq. = 1 in.

CIRCUS GERTIE

Leg

Body

Center Front and Back

186

1 sq. = 1 in.

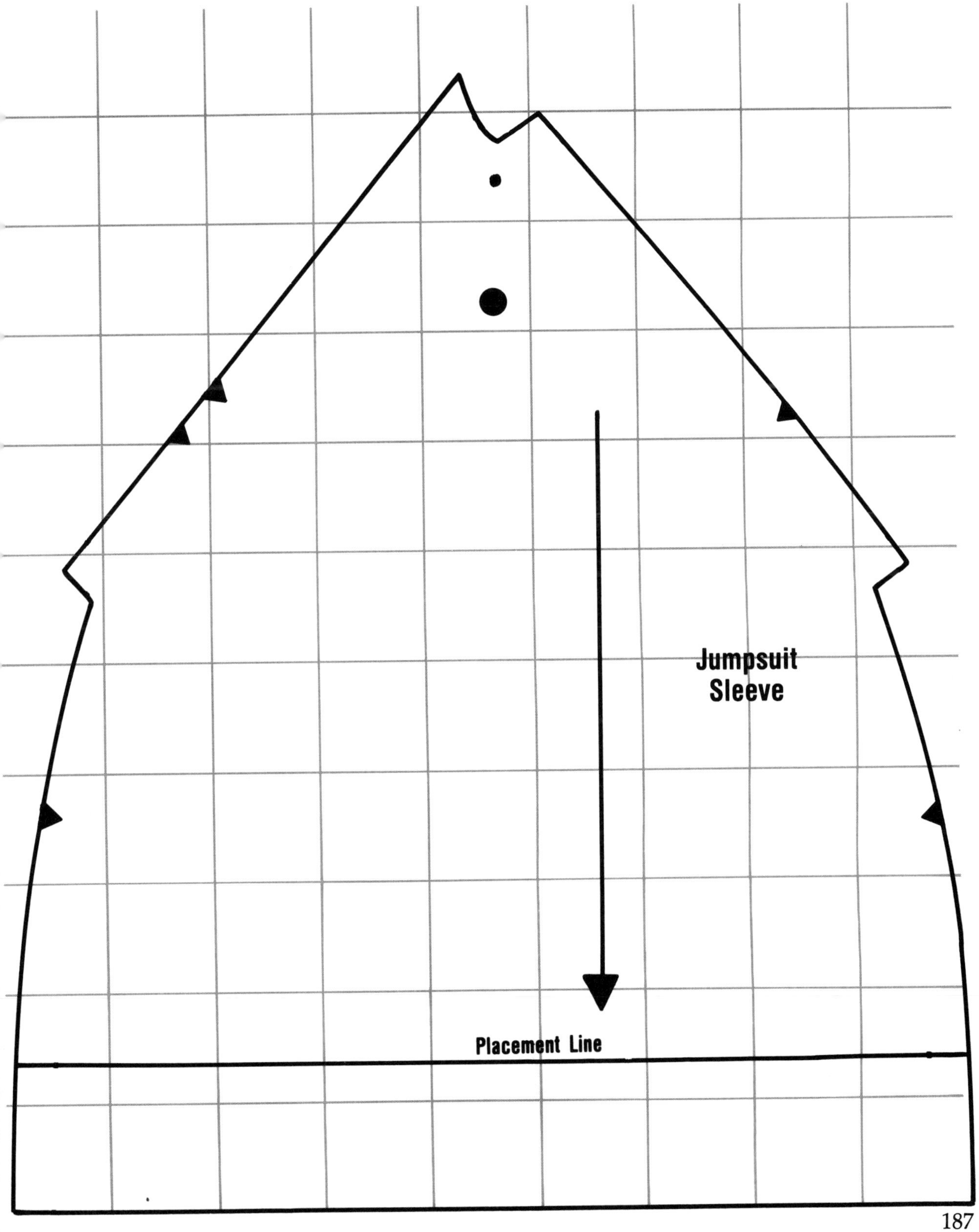

Jumpsuit
Sleeve
Placement Line

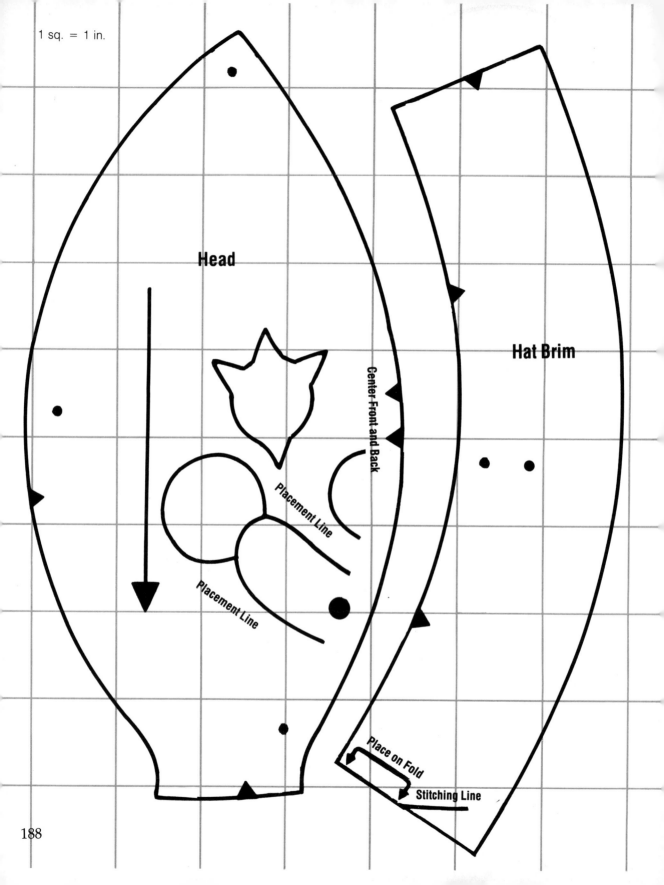

1 sq. = 1 in.

Head

Center-Front and Back

Hat Brim

Placement Line

Placement Line

Place on Fold

Stitching Line

188

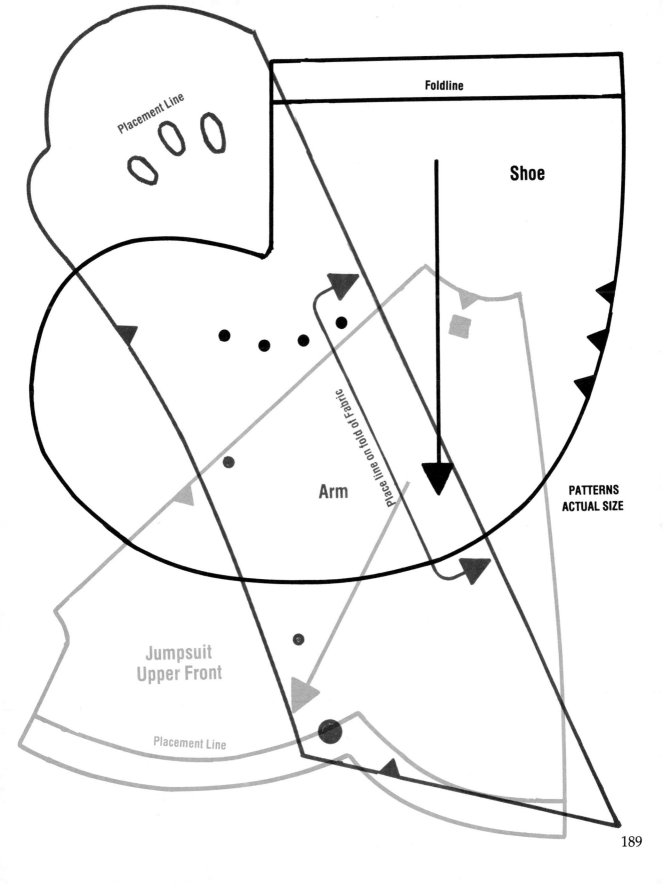

Placement Line

Foldline

Shoe

Arm

Place line on fold of Fabric

PATTERNS
ACTUAL SIZE

Jumpsuit
Upper Front

Placement Line

189

1 sq. = 1 in.

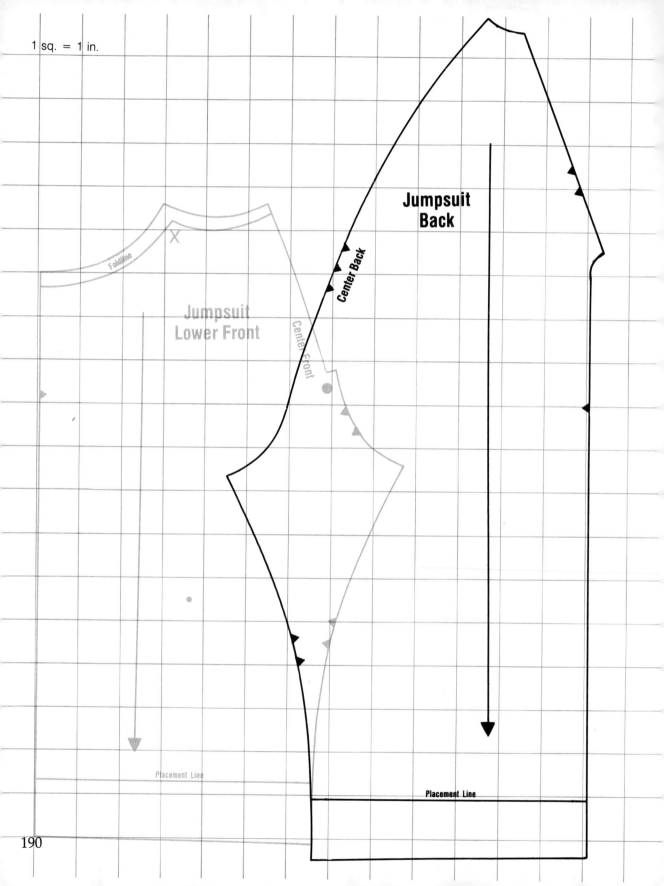

Foldline

X

Jumpsuit
Lower Front

Center Front

Center Back

Jumpsuit
Back

Placement Line

Placement Line

190

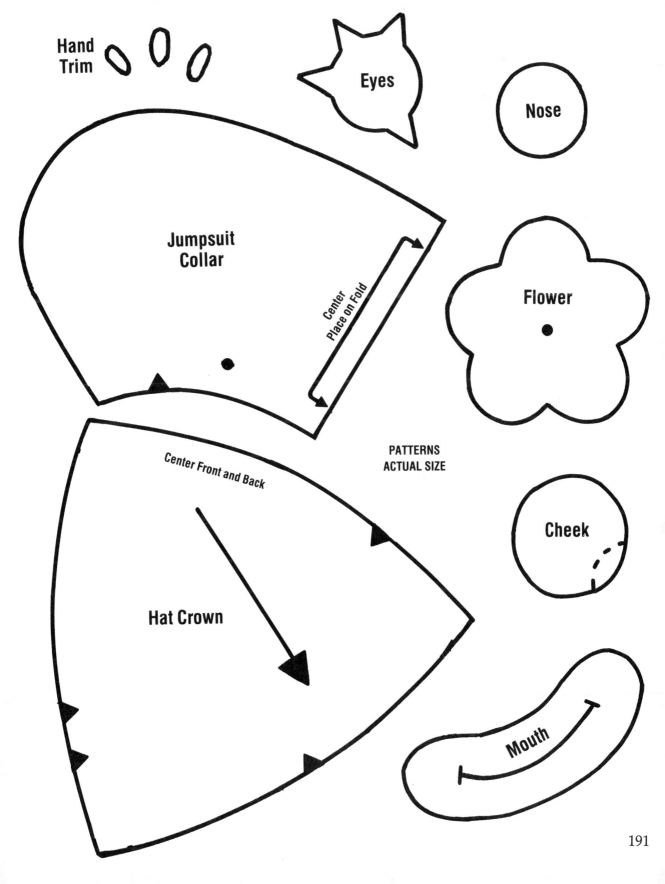

Hand Trim

Eyes

Nose

Jumpsuit Collar

Center
Place on Fold

Flower

Center Front and Back

PATTERNS
ACTUAL SIZE

Hat Crown

Cheek

Mouth

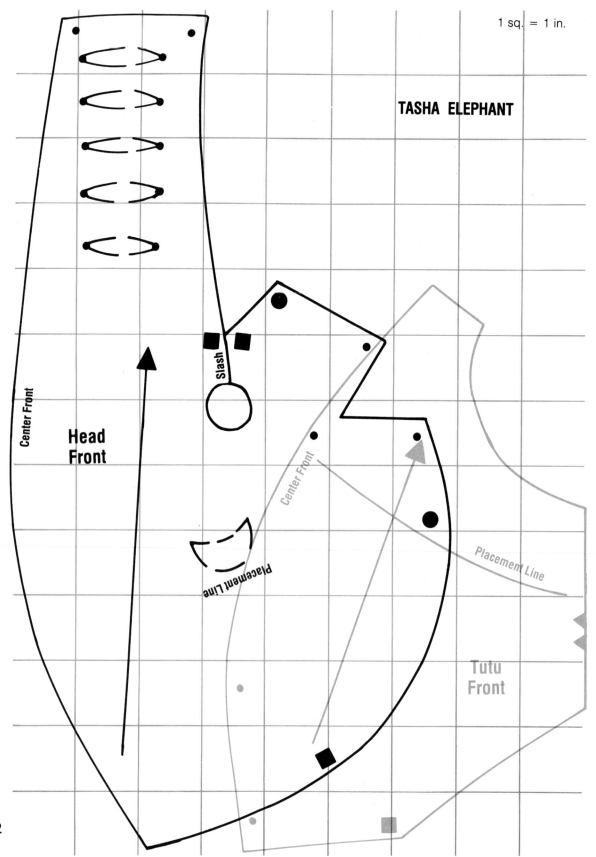

1 sq. = 1 in.

TASHA ELEPHANT

Center Front

Head
Front

Slash

Center Front

Placement Line

Placement Line

Tutu
Front

192

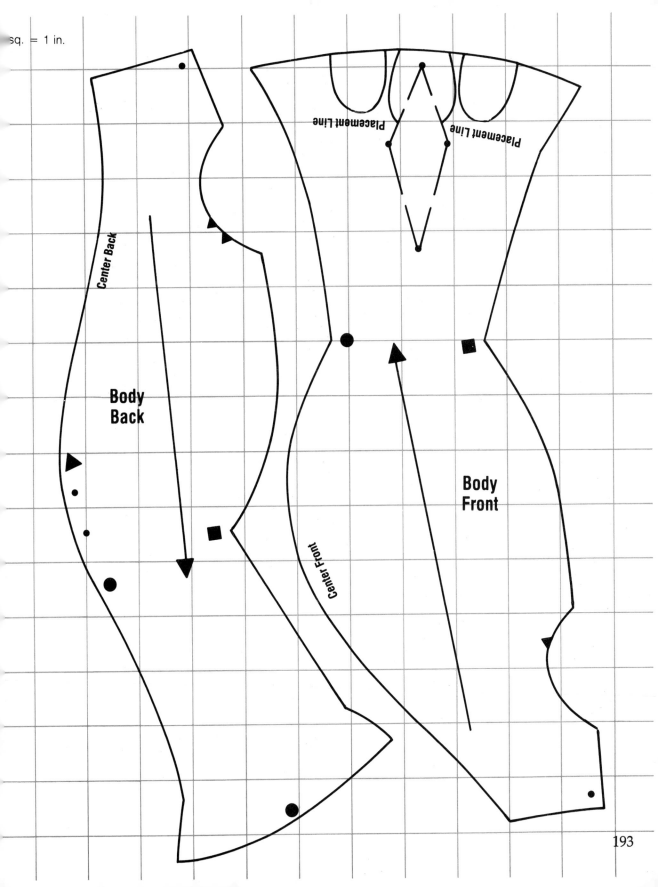

sq. = 1 in.

Center Back

Body
Back

Placement Line

Placement Line

Body
Front

Center Front

193

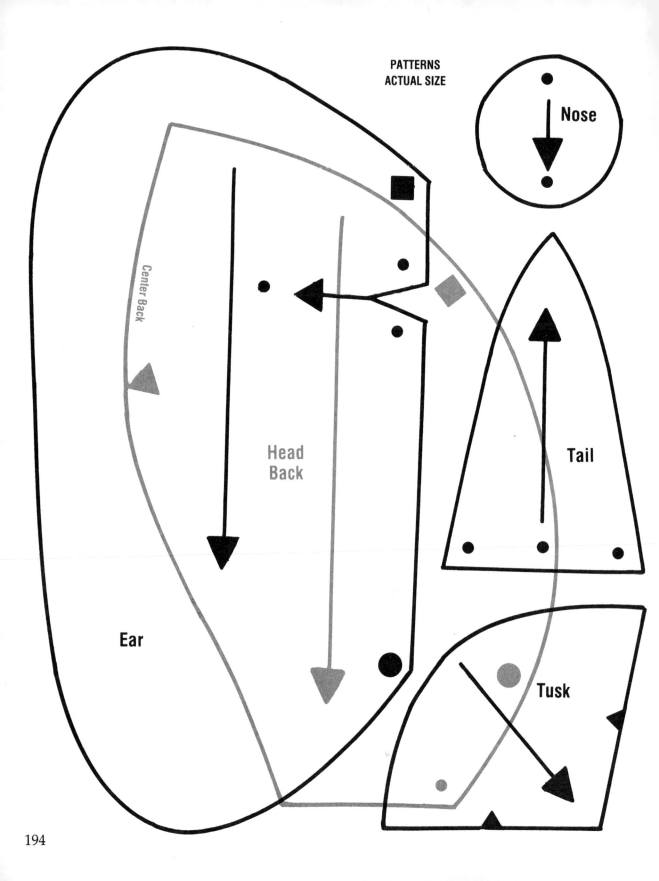

PATTERNS
ACTUAL SIZE

Nose

Center Back

Head
Back

Ear

Tail

Tusk

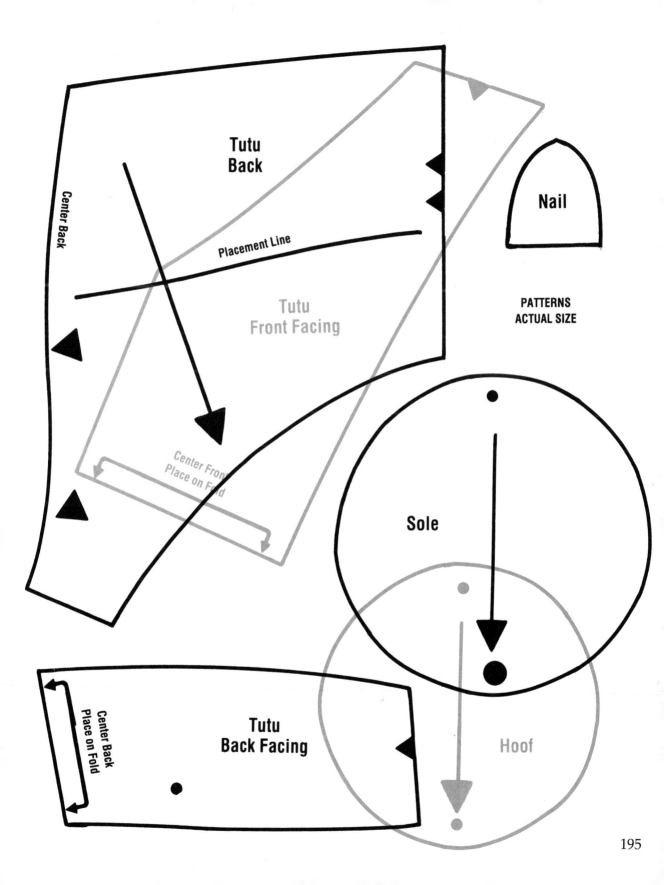

Tutu
Back

Center Back

Placement Line

Tutu
Front Facing

Center Front
Place on Fold

Nail

PATTERNS
ACTUAL SIZE

Sole

Hoof

Tutu
Back Facing

Center Back
Place on Fold

195

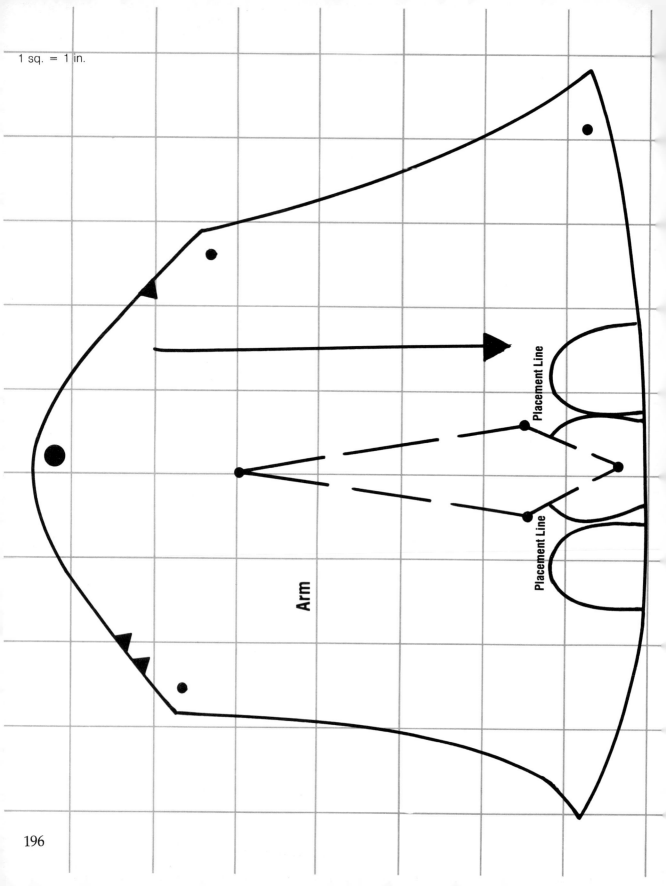

1 sq. = 1 in.

Placement Line

Placement Line

Arm

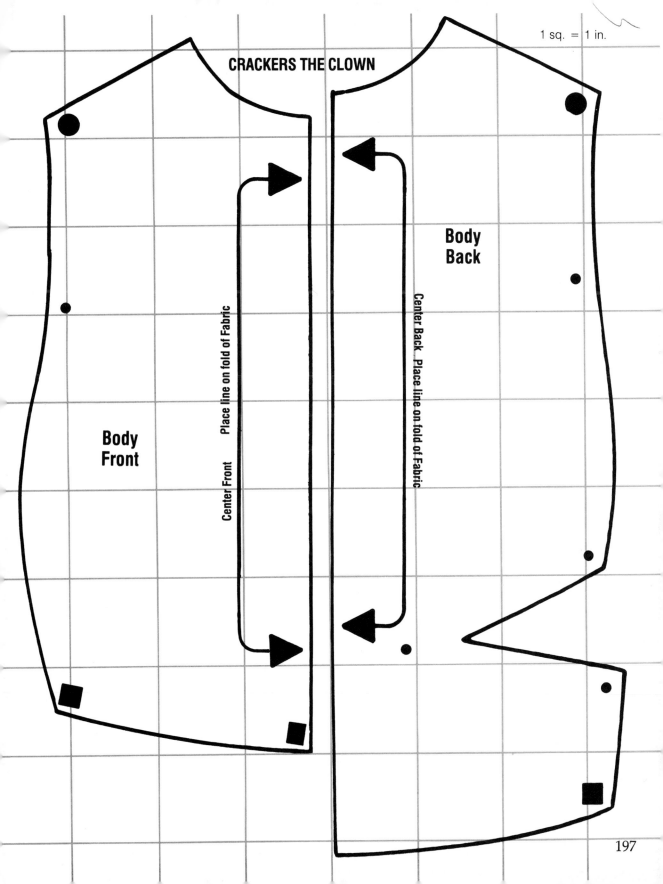

CRACKERS THE CLOWN

Body Front

Body Back

Center Front   Place line on fold of Fabric

Center Back   Place line on fold of Fabric

1 sq. = 1 in.

197

1 sq. = 1 in.

Arm

Leg

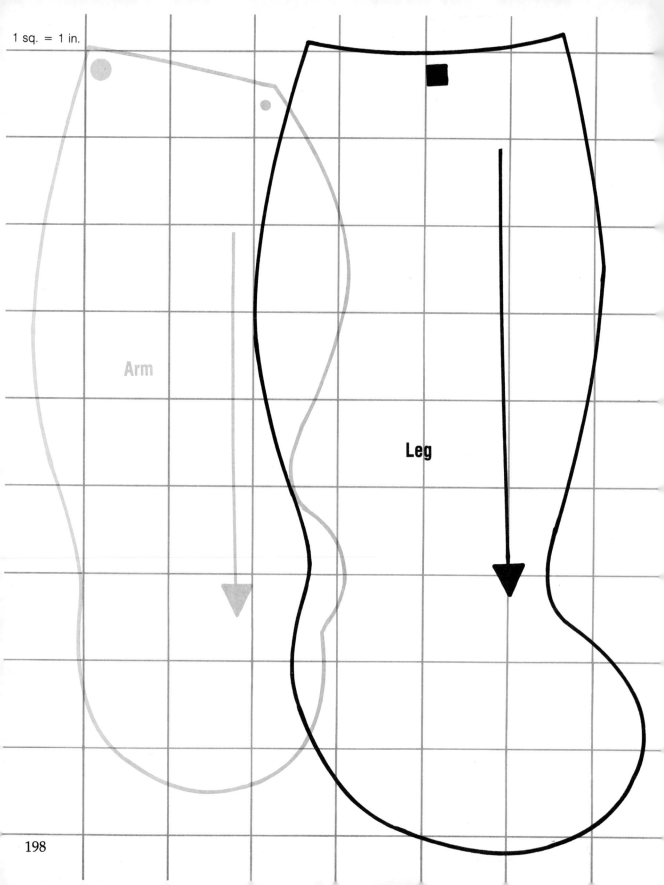

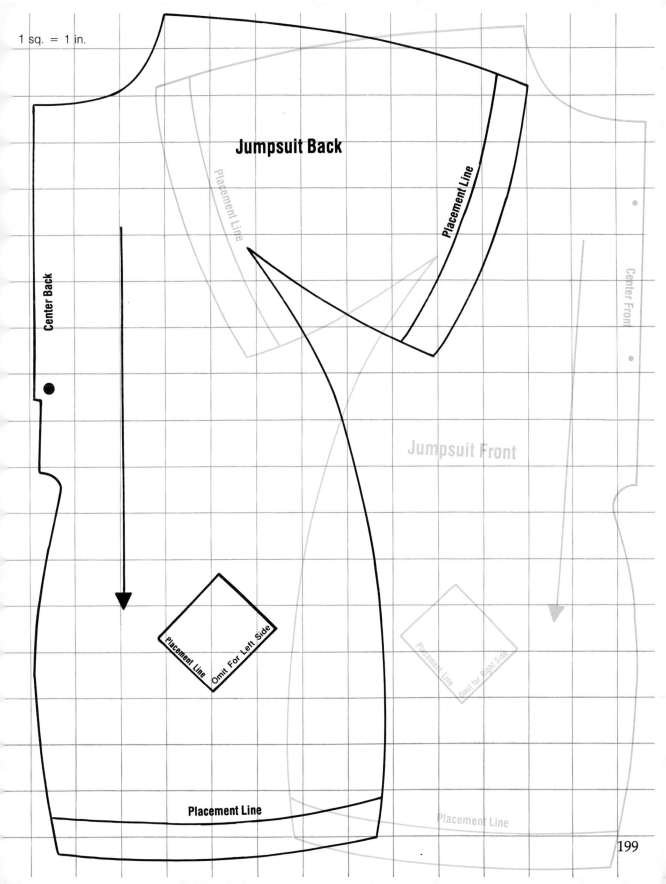

1 sq. = 1 in.

Jumpsuit Back

Placement Line

Placement Line

Center Back

Center Front

Jumpsuit Front

Placement Line   Omit For Left Side

Placement Line   Omit for Right Side

Placement Line

Placement Line

199

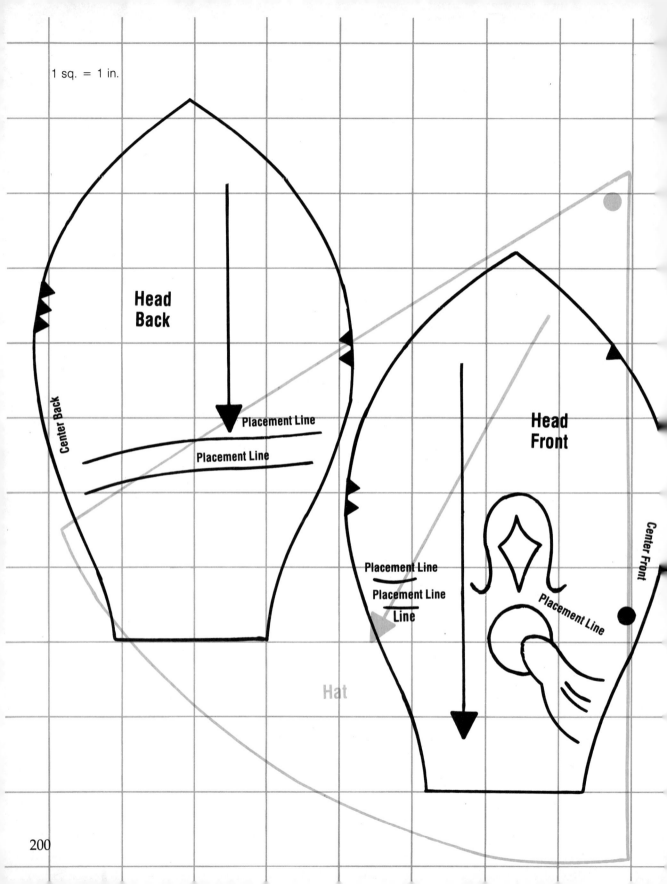

1 sq. = 1 in.

Head Back

Center Back

Placement Line

Placement Line

Head Front

Center Front

Placement Line

Placement Line

Placement Line

Line

Hat

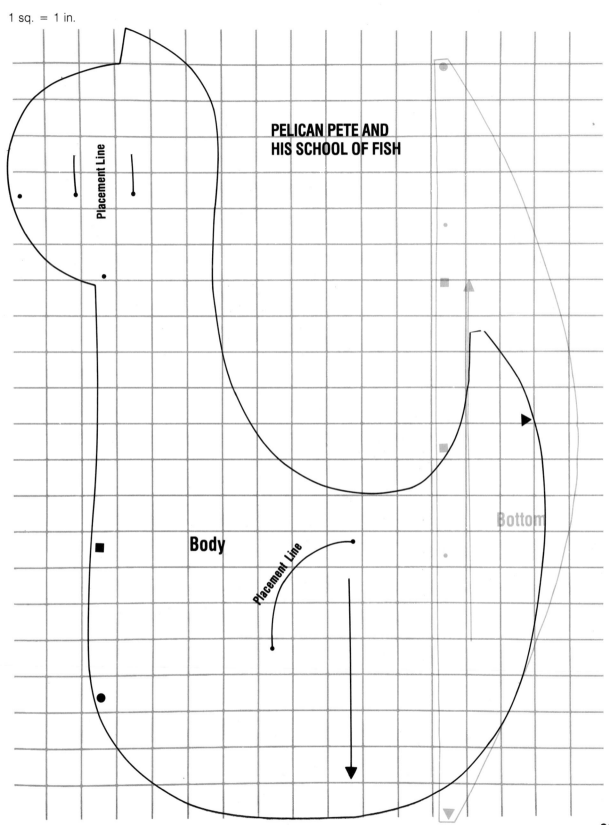

1 sq. = 1 in.

PELICAN PETE AND
HIS SCHOOL OF FISH

Placement Line

Placement Line

Body

Placement Line

Bottom

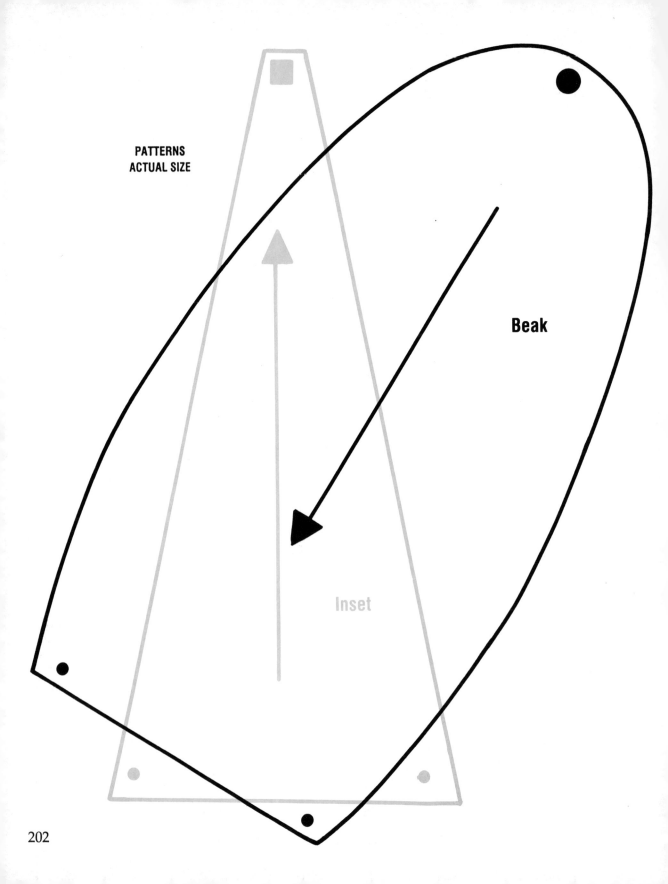

PATTERNS
ACTUAL SIZE

Beak

Inset

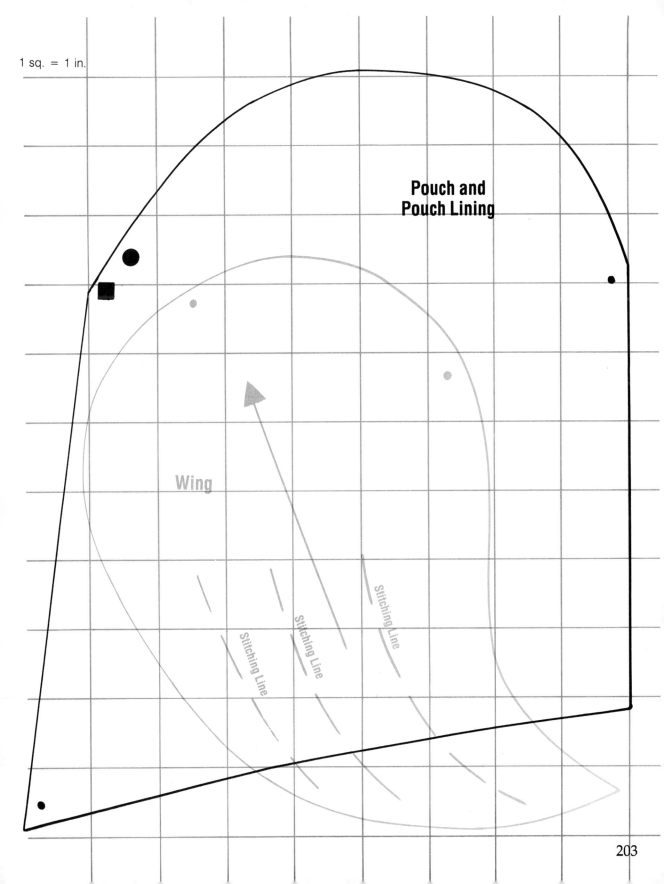

1 sq. = 1 in.

Pouch and Pouch Lining

Wing

Stitching Line

Stitching Line

Stitching Line

Stitching Line

1 sq. = 1 in.

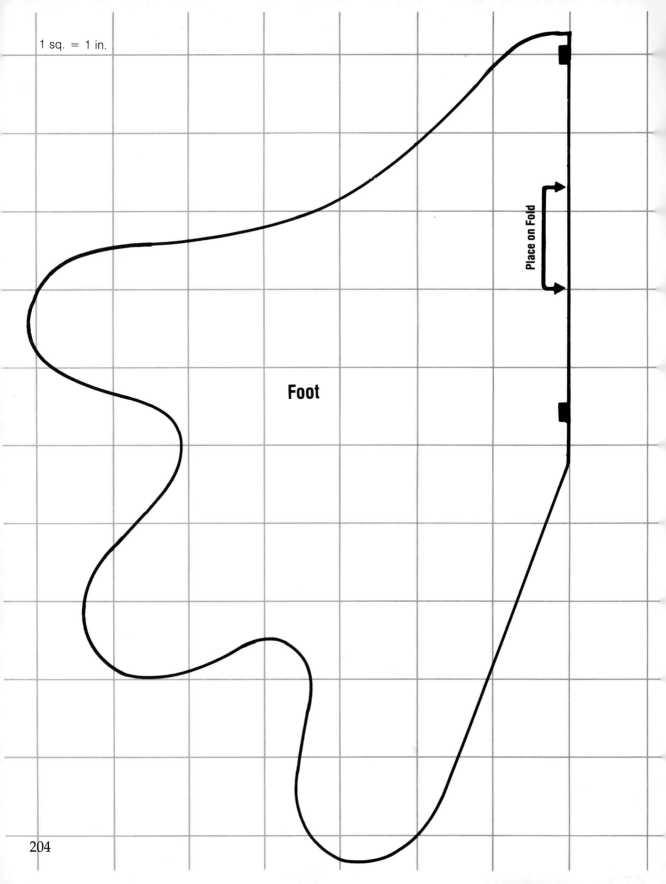

Place on Fold

Foot

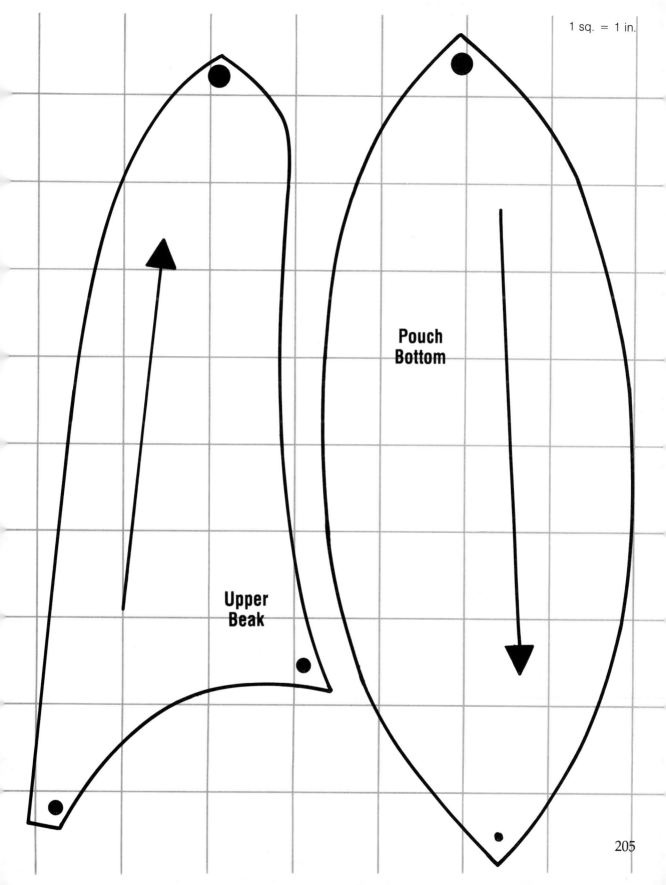

1 sq. = 1 in.

Pouch
Bottom

Upper
Beak

205

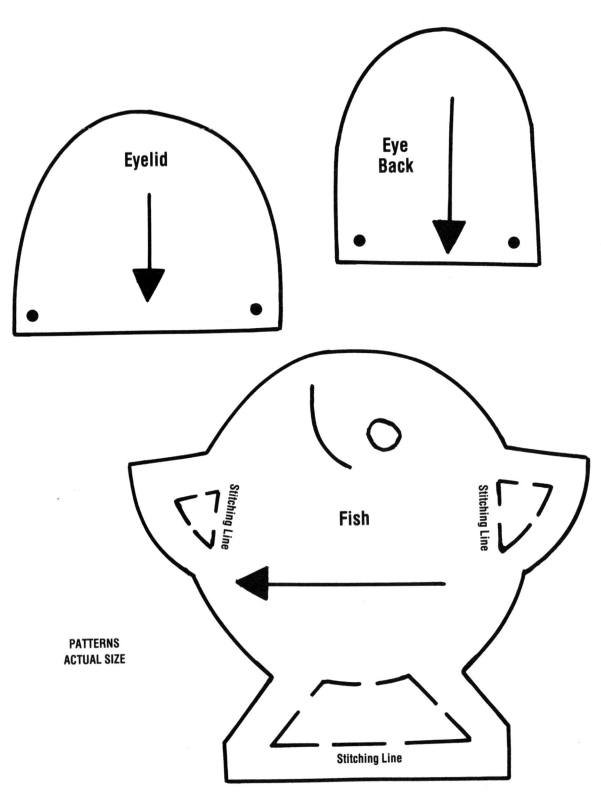

Eyelid

Eye
Back

Fish

Stitching Line

Stitching Line

Stitching Line

**PATTERNS
ACTUAL SIZE**

**Numbers
for Fish**

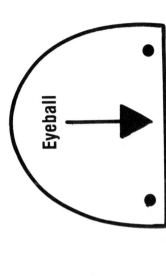

Eyeball

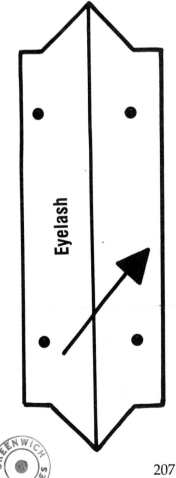

Eyelash

Index